Cecil Jenkins was educated at Trinity College, Dublin, before becoming a French government research scholar at the École Normale Supérieure de Paris. He has taught modern French literature and society at the universities of Exeter, British Columbia and Sussex, where he also served as Dean of the School of European Studies. While he has published in other fields, his writings on France include books on the Nobel Prize-winning novelist François Mauriac and the novelist, art historian and Charles de Gaulle's Minister for Culture, André Malraux, as well as *A Brief History of France*.

A BRIEF HISTORY OF

Paris

....

CECIL JENKINS

ROBINSON

ROBINSON

First published in Great Britain in 2022 by Robinson

13 5 7 9 10 8 6 4 2

Copyright © Cecil Jenkins, 2022

A CIP catalogue record for this book
is available from the British Library.

ISBN: 978-1-47214-615-1

Typeset in Scala by Hewer Text UK Ltd, Edinburgh
Printed and bound in Great Britain by Clays Ltd, Elcograf S.p.A.

Papers used by Robinson are from well-managed
forests and other responsible sources.

Robinson
An imprint of
Little, Brown Book Group
Carmelite House
50 Victoria Embankment
London EC4Y 0DZ

An Hachette UK Company
www.hachette.co.uk

www.littlebrown.co.uk

For Carol
Flower of the 14th arrondissement

Contents

....

Introduction

....

Nothing could have demonstrated more clearly the continuing significance of Paris than the worldwide reaction to the disastrous fire at Notre-Dame in 2019. The more dramatic since the flames could be seen on television lighting up the night sky, it brought forth immediate messages of sympathy from religious and political leaders across the world, along with pledges of contributions towards the reconstruction, which President Macron intended to see completed within five years. For the shocked Parisians, believers or non-believers, seen staring or weeping on the riverbank, this was a central icon of their identity, the guarantee of the continuity of their city since the Middle Ages. This was where Louis IX entered barefoot with his sacred relics, where Henri IV converted to the Catholic faith in order to unite the country, where Napoleon and Joséphine were crowned, where General de Gaulle ended his triumphal march down the Champs-Élysées after the Liberation of Paris. For the world at large, this was not only an internationally significant example of Gothic architecture, but a symbol of the central role that France has played in the political and cultural life of Western civilisation.

And the components of that historic role are on view on both sides of the river that has occupied a mythical place in the Parisian imagination, as captured in 'La Seine', the old song associated with Josephine Baker among others, which sees the river as feminine and Paris as the male lover: *car la Seine est une amante, et Paris dort dans son lit.* For there is indeed a remarkable concentration of significant sites on each bank of the Seine in central Paris. Take a ride on one of the river boats and on the Left Bank you find the once maligned Eiffel Tower, the Invalides with its handsome

Dome beneath which lies the tomb of Napoleon, the Musée d'Orsay with its rich collection of Impressionist and Post-Impressionist paintings, Notre-Dame with its façade at least spared the scaffolding, the Jardin des Plantes containing the important National Museum of Natural History, and the enormous ultra-modern national library the Bibliothèque François Mitterrand, also originally maligned but being gradually accepted. On the Right Bank, returning westward, you find the Conciergerie, where aristocrats spent their last days before execution, the Louvre, once the royal palace and now the most visited museum in the world, the Place de la Concorde, where once 'Madame Guillotine' awaited the tumbrils from the Conciergerie, the Grand Palais built for the Universal Exhibition of 1900 and the Palais du Trocadéro, with the esplanade on which Hitler did a delighted little jig following the fall of Paris in 1940.

This concentration of places of interest also makes Paris a manageable city for the walker. It should take little more than half an hour to walk, say, from the Luxembourg Gardens to the Place de l'Odéon, continue down the Rue Mazarine to the Institut de France, where the Académie Française holds its sessions, and along the quays past the *bouquinistes* selling their old books and parchments to cross the river and stroll through the Place du Carrousel between the Louvre on the right and the Tuileries Gardens on the left, to arrive at the Palais-Royal and then, if you are not too distracted, continue up to the Opéra. At every stage, as you notice some detail of an old building, or look along the Triumphal Way through the Tuileries Gardens to the distant Arc de Triomphe, you are walking in history. And you may be following in distinguished footsteps, for there has long been a Parisian myth of the *flâneur*, or stroller. The novelist Honoré de Balzac was a notable *flâneur*, even if he was often evading debt collectors, as was the poet Charles Baudelaire, even if it was a way of confirming his feeling of alienation from modern life, and of course another was the Surrealist André Breton, who had a magical view of Paris and saw it as the mysterious mirror in which to find the self.

And this concentration of places of interest, together with their architectural variety ranging from medieval to ultra-modern, is expressive of the fact that Paris historically has been more rounded than other Western capitals and has combined a wider range of areas of excellence. As one writer puts it, Paris was 'simultaneously a capital of the arts, politics, religion, finance, administration and science – especially medicine and physiology'.[1] This connects with the longstanding belief, which lingered into our own time with the idea of a 'cultural exception', that France had a universalist destiny. President Chirac stated it clearly enough in his last official address of 2007 when he declared: 'France is not like other countries. It has special responsibilities, inherited from its history and from the universal values which it has contributed to forging.' The belief goes back to the fusion of Church and state under Louis IX, or Saint Louis, in the thirteenth century. He had acquired what he took to be the original Crown of Thorns and fragments of the True Cross; he had built the magnificent Sainte-Chapelle to accommodate these precious relics; he had protected his independence from the Vatican, sanctified his own kingship and made France the equal of Rome or Byzantium. And since Paris was then the largest city in Europe, he had made it the cultural, spiritual and political capital of the continent.

For Louis XIV in his *Grand Siècle* of the seventeenth century, France was the modern equivalent of ancient Rome. It represented the summit of civilisation and as its God-anointed ruler he had the responsibility of creating the perfect society. At bottom, of course, he was rather unsure about Paris and he built his own glittering mini-capital at Versailles where he could exercise total control of the ballet-like formality of the autocratic society there – but he could rely on his formidable chancellor, Cardinal Richelieu, to bend the country to his vision of a completely ordered classical society and culture controlled by the state. So we have the new Académie Française regulating literature and language, along with an insistence on classical order in everything from architecture to garden design. In the great neoclassical tragedies, which represent the cultural highpoint of this period, we have the imposed unities of action, place and time. And it is striking that the desire of this society to see itself in terms of the eternal leads it – a century after Shakespeare had been presenting historical British figures on stage – to seek its self-image in plays about the ancient world.

In the eighteenth century, as society evolved and faith began to give way to belief in human reason, Paris became the international capital of the Enlightenment. It was all very civilised since the *philosophes* met regularly to engage in polite discourse in the elegant salons of aristocratic ladies such as Madame de Tencin in the Rue de Richelieu or Madame Geoffrin in the Rue Saint-Honoré. They were a varied group of thinkers, including the political philosopher Montesquieu, the scientist Fontenelle and the dramatist Marivaux, as well as those operating in several fields such as Voltaire or Diderot, not to forget foreign visitors such as David Hume, Edward Gibbon or Thomas Jefferson. The emerging ideas of evolutionary history and progress were then taken up rather less politely as the century wore on in the new cafés that were springing up, such as the Procope – which you can still visit today – or the Café du Parnasse. With the royal order failing perceptibly under the burden of debt and a succession of weak kings, and with the American War of Independence opening up a larger perspective, the discussion over the new craze for drinking coffee became excitable to the point that the historian Jules Michelet thought that this 'powerfully cerebral strong black coffee' might just have something to do with the French Revolution.

Black coffee apart, Paris has above all been the capital associated with the idea of revolutionary change. It was the stage on which the major social and political dramas of the Western world have been played out, even beyond the Glorious Revolution of

1789 – which Lenin was using as a template and almost a timetable for the Red Terror in Russia as late as 1918. It raised great questions. Was the Revolution inevitable? If it led to the Terror and the guillotining of its own leaders, was that inherent or because of opposition from the rest of Europe? Was Napoleon the saviour or the betrayer of the Revolution? The lack of a clear resolution led to aftershocks, starting with the 1830 Revolution, which brought a switch to constitutional monarchy but provoked the failed working-class Paris Uprising of 1832, described by Victor Hugo in *Les Misérables*. It was followed by the 1848 Revolution, which broke out simultaneously in several parts of Europe, but succeeded only in France with the setting up of a republic, a success ironically negated by the fact that the introduction of universal suffrage merely brought in another emperor, in the form of Napoleon III. The revolutionary story came to an end with the tragic episode of the Commune, when Parisians tried to establish self-government following the humiliating defeat in the Franco-Prussian War of 1870–1 and were ruthlessly put down in a sad start to the Third Republic.

None of this turbulent history prevented Paris from emerging as the world capital of fashion and luxury goods, which had originated with Louis XIV himself. In his fabulous ermine-lined robes and the red high-heeled shoes, which he designed himself – and which conveniently concealed his shortness – he was not only exerting social control, but deliberating promoting French fabrics, jewellery and fine furniture. The fashion trade then moved steadily from royalty to the aristocracy, from the personal designer – such as Marie Antoinette's Rose Bertin, who made a fortune – to the group designer and eventually, when the department stores opened up in the nineteenth century, to the upper bourgeoisie and the international market. As the trade expanded, so did the variety and increasing eccentricity of costume and hair styles. To a degree, this reflected the situation of higher-level women at a time when they had no real legal rights and when marriage was a contract between families rather than between individuals, so that men had mistresses and women competed by being decorative and fashionable, even at the cost of uncompromising corseting. As the market broadened socially, it spread through an army of designers such as Poiret, Lanvin and Schiaparelli until it arrived at Coco Chanel's 'little black dress', although there was a return to tight-waisted luxury following the Second World War with Christian Dior's New Look.

Yet fashion was only one aspect of Paris as it became the international capital of the high life and pleasure in the late eighteenth and the nineteenth centuries. Another that came down from royalty was fine cuisine – Louis XVI had his own personal cook in the Conciergerie and was well fed when he mounted the guillotine – and many of the highlights of modern gastronomy, from *sauce Mornay* to *crêpes Suzette*, were created in Paris in the nineteenth century. Another highlight for the *beau monde* was the Opéra, where it was important to be seen and where you studied the other boxes through your opera glasses to see who was with whom and be suitably shocked – or not – by the disreputable goings-on that sometimes occurred there. And that was not even the more popular *Opéra Comique* or the many *cafés-concerts* or the cabarets that would spring up in Montmartre. For at the heart of this fusion of entertainments, in a world where an actress could routinely be a courtesan, or a waitress a prostitute, was the quest for sexual pleasure, so that from the late eighteenth century through the *Belle Époque* to the 1920s, Paris was an international centre of self-indulgence. This is where the overweight Edward VII, when Prince of Wales, came to have his needs met on his specially designed 'love seat' – an elegant but slightly mystifying two-level contraption, and where many of the 'lost generation' of American writers of the 1920s – also drawn by the cheapness of the post-war franc – came to enjoy sexual freedom.

This heady mixture of revolutionary change, fashion and pleasure fed directly into the art of the period. Painters and writers were involved in the Commune or the Dreyfus Affair, as in the parallel and important theoretical battles over realism or naturalism in painting and literature. And just as the monarchy had always supported French art with commissions, so subsequent imperial and republican administrations supported it as a national resource. The Académie des Beaux-Arts, founded in 1795, provided professional training for local and foreign artists, there were regular salons or exhibitions and, of course, the various Expositions Universelles, notably those of 1878, 1889 and 1900, provided a window for French art. Moreover, just as governments from the Revolution to the Republic centralised political, administrative and educational structures in Paris, so the city became the essential home of French art and indeed the capital of world art in the nineteenth and early twentieth centuries, until the market moved to New York after the fall of France in 1940. So many of the terms used in art come from French, such as Naturalism, Impressionism, Symbolism, Cubism or Surrealism, just as our image of Paris itself is still conditioned by the paintings of Manet, Renoir, Degas, Toulouse-Lautrec or Caillebotte.

Yet this blend of art, fashion and pleasure against the background of revolutionary change is not all that Paris signifies. If you walk back down from the Opéra – assuming you have not just lingered in the arcades of the Palais-Royal – and stroll through the Tuileries Gardens, noting the golden statue of Joan of Arc on horseback as you go, you might cross back over the river by the elegant iron footbridge named after the former Senegal president Léopold Senghor. There you will find a man selling padlocks, for the use of lovers wishing to symbolise their union by attaching this 'love lock' to the many already covering the sides of the bridge. It started on the Pont des Arts, moved in 2015 when the weight of so many padlocks threatened the bridge, and testifies to the mythical belief that this historic city is also the capital of romance. And indeed, especially on a balmy night, with the reflections of its bridges and its illuminated ancient buildings shimmering in the river, it provides a compelling setting for so many love songs such as 'Sous les Ponts de Paris' and a whole range of films from *Les Amants du Pont-Neuf* to Woody Allen's *Midnight in Paris*. But if the Seine, as one writer testifies, 'is ideal for seduction', its power goes beyond that.[2] In fastening their 'love locks' to the bridge and throwing away the key into the water flowing below, those couples are seeking to lock symbolically into their union not just the beauty of this ancient city but its durability over time. Paris, for many generations now, has also been the capital of love.

The Emergence of Paris

So what's in a name? What associations does it carry? And where did the Parisii, as the first Parisians were known, come from?

Were they, as the fifteenth-century monk Regard argued, survivors of the siege of Troy who settled around some islands of the Seine and named their new capital after Paris, the lover of Helen? Or was it not rather, as an early sixteenth-century scholar maintained, that they were descended from the Parrhasians of Arcadia in ancient Greece and might have sought to emulate the mythical Heracles, known to the Romans as Hercules? More simply, as another authority maintained, did not 'the noble and triumphant city of Paris' derive its name from a temple to the Egyptian goddess Isis, giving Par Isis and thus Paris? And these are only some of the attempts to give a proper legendary status to what was increasingly seen as a city now rivalling ancient Rome in its grandeur and importance.

However, there was also the little problem that this settlement of the Celtic tribe known as the Parisii only became known as Paris in the course of the fourth century AD, having previously been known variously as Lucotocia or Leucotecia – rendered in French as Lutèce or as Laetitia to the Romans. This again was conscientiously confronted by the authors of two rival works that appeared in the same year of 1575 with the same resounding title of *Cosmographie universelle*. While François de Belleforest maintained that Lutèce took its name from an early king named Luce, André Thevet argued that it was drawn rather from the Greek word *leukos* meaning white and referring to the limestone used on Paris buildings – although the great satirical writer Rabelais suggested wickedly that the reference was to the whiteness of the thighs of the city's women. And if neither of these explanations worked, might it not just be that the reference was to a cult of Leucothea, the Greek 'goddess of the foam' who saved Odysseus from drowning in Homer's *Odyssey*? In short, there was some reluctance to contemplate the mundane probability that Paris derived its name from the Gaulish word *par*, meaning boat, and that the notoriously boggy Lutèce derived its name from the Celtic word *luco*, meaning marshland. You could hardly tell proud Parisians that their name was mud.[1]

Yet this muddy site on the Seine was the making of Paris, even if the only lingering echo of marshland today is the name of the formerly derelict but now fashionable district of Le Marais. Wider and flowing faster than today, the river at this point had a scattering of marshy islands, which have over time been consolidated into the two that we know today: the Île de la Cité, on which stand such signature buildings as the Sainte-Chapelle and the Cathedral of Notre-Dame, and the smaller Île Saint-Louis. Apart from the obvious advantages, that it made it easier to cross, that it offered a plentiful supply of fish, and that it made it possible to set up a more easily defended fortified settlement on the main island, this would enable the site to become an important crossing point for both north–south land traffic and east–west river traffic.

At a time when there was no developed road system and when the land was heavily forested, the river was important for moving both people and goods. Among the traces of settlements discovered in 1991, apart from a range of tools and ceramic objects, is a long pirogue, or dugout oak canoe, dating from around 4500 BC, which is now on display in the museum of Paris, the Musée Carnavalet. By 750 BC, in the Bronze Age, the Seine had become the essential conduit for the shipping of tin, a necessary ingredient in the production of bronze, from Cornwall to the copper-rich regions in south and central Europe. And by the time the Parisii had settled into the area around 250 BC, the tolls for crossing the wooden bridge and for passage along the river would enrich the settlement to the point that it was minting its own gold coins.

The Celts were a loose collection of tribes, originating in central Europe, that shared a similar language and similar religious and cultural traditions. The Senones tribe, of which the Parisii were a sub-group, had sacked Rome itself in 390 BC and only with difficulty been driven out. By the third century BC they controlled much of north-west Europe and had moved into the British Isles. Since the Romans called them the 'Galli', or barbarians, and since they also referred to them as the 'hairy Gauls' because they wore their hair long, it is ironical that our knowledge of the Gauls, since they left no written records, should be so dependent on the picture presented by their enemy Julius Caesar in his *Gallic Wars*. Caesar, of course, had his own political agenda, and a more nuanced and sympathetic treatment may be found in some recent studies.[2]

Nevertheless, Caesar's analysis of their society is clear and systematic. He observes two privileged classes exercising control: the Druids and the Knights. The Druids are normally the more powerful in that they control the worship of gods such as Mercury, Apollo or Jupiter, conduct public and private sacrifices and arbitrate on all disputes. The Knights are professional warriors, entitled to the spoils of their battles and, like the Druids, exempt from any tax or obligation. All other members of the tribe have no say and may be treated as vassals, while men exercise absolute control over wives and children. The general weakness of Celtic society in Caesar's view was that there was a lack of central control both within the constellation of different tribes and within the individual tribe itself, which rendered them vulnerable. And what followed would prove him right.

Campaigning with his army in Gaul between 58 and 53 BC, the ambitious Caesar's mission was at least ostensibly to protect the area from incursions by the Germanic tribes. He convoked a gathering of delegates from the various tribes at Lutèce in the summer of 53 BC and asked them to contribute money and troops towards his campaign. Suspicious of his motives as they were, they made a formal offer of some cavalry units but then conspired with other tribes to join in a general uprising against the Romans led by Vercingétorix in the following year. When Caesar dispatched his lieutenant Labienus to deal with them, the Parisii not only burnt the bridges but their whole fortified island township and regrouped on the opposite bank. However, Labienus misled them cleverly by apparently leaving the scene and by taking advantage of a passing storm to get most of his troops across by boat at night. In the ensuing battle, the Parisii lost their leader Camulogène and were heavily defeated by their more professional opponents, although some eight thousand of them would escape to join Vercingétorix in what would prove to be the decisive campaign against the Romans.

This would again bear out Caesar's insight concerning the ultimate inability of the loose federation of Gallic tribes to withstand a more organised opponent. For although Vercingétorix, pursuing a successful scorched earth policy, asked the Bituriges to sacrifice their capital, the present-day Bourges, they refused and suffered the massacre of forty thousand inhabitants. And when the Gauls were finally cornered in the fortified town of Alésia near the present-day Dijon, they fought bravely but suffered a catastrophic defeat, saw many thousands killed or enslaved and Vercingétorix dragged off in chains to Rome. Which was the end of the dream of an independent Gaul – and the beginning of a new phase in the chequered history of Lutèce.

The city suffered a prolonged slump following that defeat and, despite its strategic and commercial potential, it would take a long time to recover. It was rather sidelined in relation to other Gallo-Roman towns such as Lugdunum (Lyon) or Agedincum (Sens), each of which had a considerably larger population than the estimated six to eight thousand people in Lutèce. It was therefore only gradually over the next three centuries that the new Gallo-Roman Lutetia emerged and, since the right bank was marshy and subject to flooding, it developed essentially on the higher and largely unoccupied ground of the left bank. It was built on the standard Roman grid with a dominant north–south axis and a lesser east–west one. The north–south axis traversed the Île de la Cité by a new wooden bridge on either side and continued up the left bank along the present-day Rue Saint-Jacques. The island had a harbour on this southern side, and it may well have had some administrative buildings or a temple, but the emphasis was on taking advantage of the higher ground leading up to what would later be called the Montagne Sainte-Geneviève – where the Panthéon now stands in the present-day 5th arrondissement. This area was in effect the city centre, with a large rectangular walled forum containing a temple, a courthouse and a public assembly hall, as well as enclosed warehouses and shops whose offerings would doubtless have included staples of Roman cuisine such as Italian wine, olive oil, shellfish and artichokes.

There were three characteristically large Roman bath houses open to the public at different points, served with fresh water by an elaborate aqueduct. These included the Thermes de Cluny, the ruins of which have been incorporated into the adjacent Musée de Cluny, the highly informative museum of the Middle Ages – although a section of the ruins is still visible from the Boulevard Saint-Michel. On view are the *cardarium*, or hot pool room, and the *tepidarium*, or tepid pool room, but the most interesting and best-preserved room is the *frigidarium*, or cold pool room, which has intact architectural features such as vaults and consoles as well as fragments of wall painting and mosaics. The fact that the consoles, or supports on which the barrel ribs rest, were carved to resemble ships' prows lends support to the view that the bath house was probably built around the beginning of the third century by the influential guild of boatmen, the so-called Nautes, or *nautae* in Latin. For although little is known of the activities of other groups, it is clear that the boatmen continued to flourish through income from the ongoing traffic on the river.

The other notable Roman ruins, discovered to innocent general surprise late in the nineteenth century, are the Arènes de Lutèce. There is by contrast no trace today of the modest-sized theatre that is known to have existed on the opposite side of the Boulevard Saint-Michel from the Cluny ruins – off the street named after the great French classical dramatist Jean Racine, appropriately enough – where matinee performances of a tragedy by Seneca or a comedy by Terence would have been performed. The theatre could not have competed with the vast Arènes, an amphitheatre providing a more popular audience with gladiatorial combats, acrobats and doubtless the occasional execution by feeding the victim to the lions. This was an enormous structure seating some fifteen thousand spectators, or about twice the population, though there would also have been visitors coming in from nearby plantations. It is rather hidden away off the Rue Monge and, although there has been some restoration, little remains of its tall, tiered stand for spectators so that it requires some effort to imagine the original roars of excitement. Today it is a free public park frequented by the more dedicated tourist, older people enjoying the open space or the garden behind the stage, and teenagers displaying their acrobatic cycling or soccer skills.

In fact, the oldest historical monument in Paris, also to be seen in the Musée de Cluny, is the Pilier des Nautes, or the Boatmen's Pillar, an elaborately carved monumental stone column offered to the Emperor Tiberius in the first century AD by the Guild of Boatmen. Discovered in 1711 during excavations under the chancel of Notre-Dame, this is significant since it invokes both Celtic and Roman deities, suggesting that a high degree of fusion of Roman and Gallic cultures was gradually taking place. Of course, they had parallel polytheistic systems, with each having scores of gods, demi-gods and local gods

– providing, as you might say, a god for every occasion – so that the addition of another god or two did not fundamentally threaten the structure of the Roman belief system. But the rising threat from monotheistic Christianity was a quite different matter. Not only did it challenge the existence of the gods but, by conferring upon individuals a one-to-one relationship with a new single god, it altered their whole sense of the meaning of life and threatened the social order – slaves or vassals promised a heavenly time in the next life might no longer see the necessity of accepting a hellish time in this one. And although the persecution of Christians had already begun, the rising threat was dramatised by the martyrdom – and its subsequent mythification – of Saint Denis.

Although he was for long confused with another figure of the same name, Denis, or Dionysius, was possibly a Greek who was sent from Rome as a missionary. Since Christianity was formally forbidden, he delivered his message on the outskirts of the city. Although he did not directly advocate political or social revolution, his message resonated not only with slaves and many young people but with others feeling resentful at the Roman presence. It was not long before the simple masses he conducted drew the attention of the authorities and, along with his two acolytes Rusticus and Eleutherius, he was imprisoned, interrogated and condemned to be executed. And from that point onwards his legend is written into the streets of Paris. Taken up to Mons Mercurii, or Mount Mercury, by the Roman road now known as the Rue des Martyrs, he was pressed three times to recant and escape death, but he refused and was beheaded in front of the Temple on Mons Mercurii, which then became Mons Martyrum – now Montmartre. At which point the legend takes over to declare that, at the age of ninety, he picked up his head and walked six hundred paces northwards to the burial place which would soon become a shrine and eventually the site of the basilica of Saint-Denis, designed to house the remains of the kings and queens of France – but which perhaps sits a little oddly today not far from the Stade de France in an area once known as a communist stronghold which now houses a large Muslim population.

This helped to establish the new religion in the popular mind at a time when Rome itself was moving towards treating Christianity as the dominant religion of the empire. A significant shift was brought about by the Emperor Constantine the Great, who issued an edict putting an end to the persecution of Christians in 313. He also supported the first ecumenical council, the Council of Nicaea of 325, which brought together different strands of the Church in an attempt to resolve the Arian controversy, a dispute in which the orthodox trinitarian view that the Father, Son and Holy Spirit were equal was challenged by the unitarian view that, since Christ was begotten by God, he could not be equal to God. There has inevitably been a debate about whether Constantine, if only because he killed his wife and one of his sons, was genuinely converted to Christianity or whether he calculated in hard political terms that worship of a single god fitted in better with a cult of the emperor – with the empire under pressure there might have been an element of both. And although the Council marked a notable change of direction, the Arian controversy would linger on damagingly while, if any proof was needed that paganism was far from dead, it was provided by the arrival in Lutèce in 358 of Constantine's own nephew, the freethinking young general soon to be acclaimed as the Emperor Julian.

For by that time there had developed a major long-term threat to Roman Gaul in the form of the great westward migration of people that would straggle on from the end of the third century to the seventh century. Due to a cooling of the more continental climate in the east, leading to poor harvests and the need to find more nourishing homelands, this would combine with the fall of Rome in the fifth century to change the composition and the face of Europe. The incursions had begun in the year 275 when Franks, Alamans and others rampaged through some sixty towns in Gaul, wrecking, burning and killing as they went. This had led the survivors in Lutèce to protect the forum with a walled surround, using stones from the wrecked buildings for the purpose, and to defend the bridges of the Île de la Cité with fortresses. Yet this very retrenchment gave the city, although it was smaller than some other centres in Gaul, an enhanced strategic importance as a secure rearguard base from which to resist the invaders. By providing winter quarters for several Roman emperors, Lutèce would gain in status as a temporary imperial capital.

The first and most notable of these was Julian, who enjoyed wintering and philosophising for several years in his 'dear Lutetia', which he describes as follows:

It is a small island lying in the river; a wall entirely surrounds it, and wooden bridges lead to it on both sides. The river seldom rises and falls but is usually the same depth in the winter as in the summer season, and it provides water which is very clear to the eye and very pleasant for one who wishes to drink. For since the inhabitants live on an island, they have to draw their water from the river. The winter too is rather mild there, perhaps from the warmth of the ocean ... and it may be that a slight breeze from the sea is wafted thus far ... A good type of vine grows thereabouts, and some individuals have even managed to make fig-trees grow.[3]

It was in fact here in the year 360 that Julian was declared emperor by his troops, although in the event it was an offer he could not safely refuse. Partly because of rivalries in Rome, he was ordered to give up half of his army so that it could be redirected to the east. The news not only caused panic in the population, afraid of losing its protection, but brought an angry reaction from the troops themselves, including Alamans and Franks who had joined on the understanding that they would not have to cross the Alps. They confronted their popular young commander, demanded that he disobey the order and finally proposed that he solve the problem by declaring himself emperor. Julian failed to talk them down, took a day to weigh the odds – including the probability, it is suggested, that they would have killed him if he had refused – and was finally acclaimed emperor.[4] After which they happily followed him to Rome to enforce his claim officially.

Two further emperors – Valentinian I and his son Gratian – would winter in Lutèce during the long struggle to prevent the incursions of the barbarians. These were not quite as barbarous as the Romans made them out to be since they had organised societies and some of their members were integrated to the point of serving in the Roman legions. However, they were quite diverse and in conflict with one another, so that the situation was becoming increasingly chaotic, with the Alamans settling in Alsace, the Burgundians in Burgundy and Savoy, the Visigoths in the south-west and the Saxons in the North Sea coastal area, while the Franks, a federation of Germanic peoples, would go on to dominate the area of present-day northern France, Belgium and western Germany. Under pressure themselves from the Huns in the east, they would go on to attack successive Roman commanders and besiege Paris in the process. The end of Roman Gaul and the Pax Romana was in sight and the era of the Franks, who would give their name to France, had begun.

Yet the Christian Church was also expanding into the void, alongside (if initially in competition with) the Franks, and Paris was about to acquire its patron saint in the form of Sainte Geneviève, whose enormously tall statue now stands on the Pont de la Tournelle, leading on to the Île Saint-Louis. Born around the year 422, she was consecrated a virgin by the bishop at the age of fifteen, led an extremely austere life and engaged in charitable activities.[5] When Attila, the fearsome leader of the Huns, advanced on Paris in 451 and the terrified population was bent on flight, she insisted that prayer would deter him and set about organising resistance, so that when Attila bypassed the city and advanced instead on Orléans her reputation was made. While it is probable that Attila did so for his own strategic reasons, there is no doubt about the reality of her contribution ten years later, for when the city was subjected to a prolonged siege by the Salian Franks led by Childeric, she broke the blockade by using barges to bring in wheat from the countryside. Even when Childeric's son, Clovis I, became ruler of northern Gaul in 486 to found the Merovingian dynasty, she attempted to influence him and worked in conjunction with his Christian wife Clotilde to encourage him to convert – which Clotilde would not find easy.

The Merovingians, who would rule over the Frankish lands for the next two centuries, were named after Clovis's grandfather Merowech, a semi-legendary figure who may or may not have been fathered by Neptune the sea god and whose strength may or may not have resided in the exceptionally long hair that became an essential attribute for his descendants. Clovis, who clearly had a lot to live up to, was as ambitious as he was brutal and appears to have modelled himself on the Emperor Constantine the Great. Succeeding his father as king of the Salian Franks at the age of sixteen in 481, he proceeded to free Gaul from the remnants of the Western Roman Empire by defeating its final commander Syagrius at the Battle of Soissons in 486. Syagrius sought refuge with the Visigoths, but under the threat of attack they handed him over to be executed, while an ally of Clovis who had failed to take part in the battle was also eliminated.

Clovis's next step was to set about enlarging his kingdom by systematically getting rid of competition from other tribes. Over the next twenty years, after neutralising the Ostrogoths by marrying off his sister to their king Theodoric, he defeated the Alamans at the Battle of Tolbiac, routed the Burgundians near Dijon and decimated the Visigoths at the Battle of Vouillé, by which time he had enlarged his Frankish kingdom and established it as a major force in western Europe. He also wrapped things up by murdering every potential competitor in sight, including his own relatives, the king of Cambrai along with his two brothers – 'and many other kings and blood relations' according to Saint Gregory of Tours, the sixth-century bishop and historian. Gregory goes on to say that, if Clovis then began to complain that he did not have a single relative in the world to help him in a crisis, 'he said this not because he grieved for their deaths, but because in his cunning way he hoped to find some relative still in the land of the living whom he could kill'.[6] Clovis was good on detail.

Despite Clotilde's entreaties, Clovis took his time about converting. This was partly for personal reasons, since despite her prayers their first son, whom she had secretly got baptised, died immediately, while their second son fell gravely ill and almost died in the same fashion. He eventually tried conversion as a last resort at the Battle of Tolbiac when, under severe pressure from the Alamans, he gambled that if he won, he would agree to be baptised – which he finally was after the victory. However, he was always acutely aware of the problem presented by religion at the political level. For although Christianity had expanded considerably in Gaul, with many churches being built, the old Arian controversy, more than a century after being declared a heresy at the Council of Nicaea in 325, had not gone away and had left the Church divided. Not only that, but orthodox Catholicism as opposed to the Arian version was actually in a minority among the Frankish tribes – Clotilde herself had been an isolated figure when a princess at the Burgundian court. On the other hand, the Franks were becoming increasingly Romanised, Latin was becoming the official language for the state as for the Church, and the Gallo-Roman governmental and legal structures remained largely in place. To the extent that he would have seen Rome as the prestigious model for an ambitious growing state, and insofar as he may have been understudying Constantine, he would need to unify the kingdom he had conquered in relation to its fundamental beliefs – and he would need to play it cannily.

He had already been approached after the Battle of Soissons by a bold, but in its way flattering, letter from the Bishop of Reims, who advised him always 'to defer to the bishops and always respect their advice. If you are on good terms with them your province will be better able to stand firm.'[7] Clovis saw this as a good deal so long as he could bend the partnership to his own political ends, using the Church both to legitimise his victories and to create support for him among the population. So, he consulted with the bishops, built churches – if not quite 'one after each murder' as has been suggested[8] – and before his death convened a council of bishops in Orléans, which passed many decrees on the duties and privileges of the clergy, the right of sanctuary and the obligations of citizens.

Clovis's adoption of the more orthodox Catholic form of Christianity, as opposed to the Arian strain of most other Germanic tribes, led to widespread conversion among the population and eventually to religious unification across the Frankish domains. To crown his success, his pursuit of the Roman model of greatness was recognised by the Byzantine emperor Anastasius, who granted him the title of consul so that, having chosen Paris with its imperial echoes as his capital, he could enter the city in glory, after which he proceeded to issue the Lex Salica, a code of law for the new dispensation. And although Paris had been rather marginal to his pursuit of power so far, it also gained in prestige from the fact that he chose to be buried in Paris at the abbey dedicated to Sainte Geneviève, though his remains were later transferred to lie alongside those of other royal figures in the basilica of Saint-Denis.

There is no doubt that Clovis, even by the standards of the time, was an unusually brutal operator. There is also no doubt that he is a highly significant figure in the political and religious history of his country. For many French people, especially those who believe in the 'true France' or *la France profonde*, the history of France begins only with Clovis – whose name, incidentally, would evolve into the very royal Louis, a common name for French kings up to the nineteenth century. As President de Gaulle put it: 'the decisive factor for me is that Clovis was the first king to be baptised. My country is a Christian country and I count the history of France as starting with the accession of a Christian king bearing the name of the Franks.'[9] Certainly, Catholicism would gain greatly over the next two centuries of Merovingian rule from this new partnership between Church and state. Paris alone would gain around a dozen churches over the period, including a basilica on the Montagne Sainte-Geneviève, later rebuilt to become the very secular Panthéon of today, and of course the future necropolis of French royalty, the basilica of Saint-Denis. Many miracles would be recorded, and many saints created, to the point that the characteristic literature of the period became *Lives of the Saints*, such as that of Gregory of Tours. Significantly also, the increased importance of the Church would combine with the Roman imperial posture to ensure that Latin would become the basis of the French language in the future.

However, Clovis, after unifying the Franks and getting rid so ruthlessly of possible competitors, seemed – from our modern perspective at least – to have thrown it all away. His kingdom was divided on his death between his four sons, thus creating four provincial kinglets and inaugurating a pattern of concentration and fragmentation that would plague the area for several centuries. Power would be dispersed to the point that it could effectively be taken over by local or regional aristocratic figures as by the so-called 'mayors of the palace', while kings would often be reduced to token rulers or be dubbed, as some of them were, the *rois fainéants* or 'do-nothing kings'. In this chaotic situation Paris retained its symbolic value as capital, a trophy to be squabbled over at times and the place where the church councils were traditionally held, but it had been reduced, as one study puts it, to 'a sort of common capital of a fictitious Merovingian state'.[10]

The blockage was eventually resolved to a large extent by two significant mayors of the palace, a giant of a man called Charles Martel or Charles the Hammer, and his short, younger son duly dubbed Pépin le Bref. Charles not only re-established central control over the squabbling provinces, but is widely considered to have saved European civilisation by his victory over an invading Muslim army at the Battle of Tours in 732. Pépin, ambitious to rule as a proper king rather than as a mayor of the palace and to be legitimised by the Church, had the nominal claimant to the Merovingian throne despatched to a monastery, had himself anointed by Archbishop Boniface in 751 and then had himself approved by the Pope in 754. This was significant as a deal whereby he had the monarchy sanctified by the Pope in exchange for undertaking to reform his own church, which was in some disarray with clerics getting secretly married or bishops building up their own personal estates. And it was with this pact that he initiated the Carolingian dynasty.

Yet, if Pépin had himself anointed in Paris, he paid little attention to the city, while his son Charlemagne, who increased the connection with Rome by being crowned by the Pope in 800 as emperor of what would be known as the Holy Roman Empire, chose Aix-la-Chapelle as his capital, leaving Paris even more sidelined. Moreover, the fragmentation continued when Charlemagne's successor Louis the Pious died and the empire was fought over and divided into three, with West Francia including Paris falling to Charles the Bald, who did not choose to live in Paris at a time when it was under severe pressure from Norman raids.

It should be appreciated that, while all these monarchical manoeuvres and broad historical changes would obviously determine the framework within which Paris would develop, the living conditions in the city had been harsh. The streets were unsafe at night for want of lighting. People lived in often crowded wooden houses, which, since they also used firewood for heating, were all too subject to fire, as in the great fire of 585. The houses were also dark inside, since glass was still a novelty associated only with kings and cathedrals, making it necessary to use waxed cloth or some such substitute. For food, they were heavily dependent on bread and there had been frequent famines, as in 588, 640 and 651. The Roman aqueduct having fallen out of use following the sacking of Lutèce in 275, the water was polluted, and the muddy streets served as a channel for rubbish and excrement. People were therefore subject to a range of diseases for which there was no medical provision even after the creation of the first hospital, really a charity refuge: the Hôtel Dieu, founded by the Bishop of Paris in 651. The situation of women would have been particularly difficult, with no independence and their existence legitimised only as virgins or mothers. Above all, with no education and with information coming to them in the form of myth or rumour, people knew little or nothing of the world beyond. It was a time when you needed to believe in miracles.

However, no miracle was forthcoming from Charles the Bald when the Vikings came calling in their tall ships in 845 and started pillaging the town. He bought them off, which obviously only encouraged them to come back for more so that there were regular damaging raids over the next forty years. Eventually, in 870, Charles was driven to replace the Grand Pont with a much stronger stone-based bridge that could be closed to enemy ships, while the two bridges were reinforced by fortresses called *châtelets* – the larger one of which has left its name on the Place du Châtelet of today. Fortunately also, the old Gallo-Roman wall surrounding the Île de la Cité was strengthened in 885 – just in time for the Parisians to crowd in with their worldly wealth and their saintly relics to resist a fresh onslaught by the Vikings. The monk Abbon describes in a heroic poem how they held out against attacks by catapult, ram and flaming longboat, showering the Vikings and their painted shields with arrows, stones, hot water, pitch or what-ever they could find until the Vikings contented themselves for a whole year with ravaging the town outside and the surrounding countryside while waiting to be bought off again, this time by Charles the Fat.[11] The price of all this heroism for the population, whether in lives lost through an epidemic if not through the fighting itself or through the wreckage of their homes, was high.

Meanwhile the gradual fragmentation of power continued – through another serious epidemic that hit the city in 945 – until succession to the throne became a matter of dispute to be resolved by election. Significantly, it was the Archbishop of Reims who manoeuvred cleverly to have Hugues Capet elected king of the Franks at Noyon some 60 miles from Paris in 987, while Hugues returned the compliment by then having himself ceremonially crowned by the archbishop in Reims. So far so good, but he was surrounded by competing regional rulers and he controlled in practice only the Île de France and the Orléanais. He then took a strong precautionary step towards guaranteeing the future of his line by having his son crowned as his successor. Although he paid no particular attention to Paris, his eccentric son Robert the Pious, who succeeded him in 996 – and who got himself excommunicated at one point – began to restore the royal palace on the Île de la Cité and built a church on the site of the present Sainte-Chapelle.

So, at the end of this first millennium, what could a rather exhausted, dilapidated and marginalised Paris expect from this Capetian dynasty – which, after this shaky start, would nevertheless endure and largely shape France over the next three centuries?

Medieval Paris: Cultural
Capital of Europe

....

It was not until the twelfth and thirteenth centuries that Paris
ceased to be a 'mere crossroads', as Jean Favier puts it, to become
a proper capital city.[1] For in practice that could not happen until
the Capetian kings established a stable kingdom from a jigsaw of
different areas. The royal domain itself consisted of the Île de
France and the Orléanais, with the addition – temporarily, as it
would soon turn out – of the duchy of Burgundy. There were the
apanages, or domains resulting from the practice of dividing
estates among the sons, which were hereditary but could revert to
the throne if the incumbent had no issue. There were large
provincial fiefdoms such as Flanders or Guyenne, which were
formally part of the kingdom but were virtually independent, and
then there were the increasingly large domains owned by the
Church. Since all this led to local private wars and widespread
dissension, it was not an easy task for kings to strike a balance
between these disparate elements, make the right marriages,
choose the right alliances, raise enough money and fight whatever battles were required to enlarge and unify the kingdom. The
need for a fixed capital, indeed the very idea of one, would depend
on their success. Meanwhile, they were the 'itinerant kings',
moving from place to place and trailing the royal archives in the
baggage train behind them – at least until these were seized by
Richard the Lionheart in 1194 after the Battle of Fréteval.

This complex situation would not make life easy for the two
kings who followed Robert the Pious. Indeed, the reign of Henri
I, who ruled for almost thirty years from 1031 to 1060, itself came

out of a typical territorial dispute. He had combined with his younger brother Robert, with the support of their mother, in an abortive revolt against their father five years earlier but, on the king's death, his mother supported Robert. Which left Henri to buy off his brother with the duchy of Burgundy – which their father had fought so long to acquire. Although he neutralised a threat from the Count of Flanders by marrying his daughter, his two attempts to invade Normandy ended in failure and although he did acquire the county of Sens, this could not compensate for the loss of Burgundy. Since he also became involved in unhelpful disputes with the Holy Roman Emperor and with the papal legate, who objected to the selling off of bishoprics, it is fair to say that his most notable contribution to Paris was to have his remains interred nearby in the basilica of Saint-Denis.

This at least was more than his successor Philippe I would do, apparently feeling that he was not deserving of the honour since he had conducted an extended quarrel with Pope Urban II and did not respond positively to his call in 1095 to join the First Crusade. His reign was indeed complicated by the fact that he repudiated his wife Bertha, on the grounds that she was too fat, and married Bertrade de Montfort, which led to him being excommunicated – more than once, since he could not keep away from her – and hardly helped his relations with the Church, especially since he too was raising money by selling off Church domains and offices. He was frequently involved in trying to clamp down on over-mighty regional barons and suffered a serious loss of prestige when he was defeated by his own vassals in 1079. He did, however, have some successes. He had long been seeking to contain the ambitions of his vassal the Duke of Normandy – William the Conqueror, who became king of England in 1066 – and he now defeated him in battle and came to an agreement whereby William stopped trying to conquer Brittany. He also gained the small but strategically important county of Vexin and bought the domain of Bourges, but what his reign mostly illustrates is the extraordinary difficulty of kingship amid the chaos and violence of the time.

Paris was about to endure this yet again, just three years into the reign of Philippe's successor, Louis VI (r. 1108–37), when the Comte de Meulan took advantage of the king's absence in Orléans to invade the Île de la Cité, pillage the royal palace and smash the bridges to block a counterattack, leaving the inhabitants to take on the aggressors by themselves. The fact that they did so quite heroically did not entirely compensate for the damage done to an already damaged city. So how, given the disturbance of the time, did Louis VI, known both as Louis le Gros (the Fat) and Louis le Batailleur (the Warrior) – although he became too fat in his forties to lead from the front in battle as the warrior – begin the process that would lead to the extraordinary transformation of the fortunes of both Paris and the kingdom over the next two centuries? He did it both by understanding the basic problem and by working closely with the Church in the form of the Abbé Suger of Saint-Denis.

The Holy Roman Empire – 'neither holy, nor Roman, nor an empire', as Voltaire famously quipped – was a concept or an aspiration rather than a developed reality and the whole of western Europe at this time displayed a hotchpotch of competing entities: kings, dukes, counts and bishops of various degrees of size and importance. This was reflected in the kingdom of Louis le Gros, where the lack of any authoritative hierarchical order between these entities inevitably led to almost bewildering confusion.[2] Louis exemplified this situation himself since he was now also Comte de Vexin and therefore notionally the vassal of the Abbé de Saint-Denis, his own chief counsellor. Such confusion was a recipe for ongoing conflict, with these dukes and knights sallying forth from their new, initially wooden, castles to assert or enlarge their rights in this uneasy, squabbling free-for-all. The Church had long been concerned about this and had tried, firstly, to introduce a 'Truce of God' – which would forbid fighting on certain days of the week, thereby accepting fighting on other days of the week – and, secondly, to deflect the violence towards the world outside Christendom. And both feature in the passionate call of Pope Urban II at the Council of Clermont in 1095 for Christians to join the Crusade to liberate from the Muslims the holy city of Jerusalem:

Oh, race of the Franks, we learn that in some of your provinces no-one can venture on the road by day or by night without injury or attack by highwaymen, and no-one is secure even at home. Let us then re-enact the law of our ancestors known as the Truce of God. And now that you have promised to maintain the peace among yourselves, you are obligated to succour your brethren in the East, menaced by an accursed race, utterly alienated from God. The Holy Sepulchre of our Lord is polluted by the filthiness of an unclean nation. O most valiant soldiers, descendants of invisible ancestors, be not degenerate. Let all hatred depart from among you, all quarrels end, all wars cease. Start upon the road to the Holy Sepulchre to wrest the land from that wicked race and subject it to yourselves.[3]

While the Pope's plea would have some general effect and while the kingdom would gain prestige from the fact that the call to arms had been made at Clermont, Louis le Gros was still faced with the task of putting down the robber barons of various degrees who were imposing tolls upon merchants and pilgrims, terrorising the peasantry or pillaging churches and monasteries. He confronted in battle such offenders and pretenders as Hugues de Puiset, Hugues de Crécy and his own half-brother Philippe, as well as the so-called 'raging wolf' Thomas de Coucy, a notorious torturer. He dealt with nobles who had allied themselves with Henry I of England, gathered a coalition to counter a threatened invasion by the Holy Roman Emperor, responded to appeals for help and largely established not just the unchallengeable authority of the king but his role as protector. He also gained the important duchy of Aquitaine by marrying off his heir, the future Louis VII, to Eleanor of Aquitaine – who would have her own major role in history.

Louis le Gros also, unlike his two immediate predecessors, grasped the necessity in this situation of working closely with the Church and especially with the Abbé Suger of Saint-Denis. Nor was it simply that this could glorify and give a religious status to the monarchy, thereby constituting it as the ultimate authority in a scattered and violent kingdom. It made sense at the simple practical level, if only because with churches, monasteries and other religious institutions sprouting all over the city, the Church had become the largest landowner in Paris. These institutions often possessed large plots for the growing of food or keeping of animals, and even owned subsidiary properties. For example, the abbey of Saint-Germain-des-Prés enjoyed an area as large as the present-day 6th and 7th arrondissements combined, as well as a scattering of properties in the surrounding countryside – it even ended up with its own prison when the Pope freed it from the bishop's jurisdiction. Again, as the only source at that time of organised education, the Church could provide monks to staff offices of the state, as it could also provide work for serfs, servants, builders and craftsmen in such fields as jewellery or tapestry. Louis recognised that it was an essential part of the fabric of the society, as Suger recognised that the throne was essential to the security and advancement of the Church.

Although he also served as adviser in other areas, Suger's main contribution was the reconstitution of Saint-Denis as the holy place of the monarchy. The abbey had been immensely rich but had suffered from the Norman invasions and the behaviour of the monks had become notably loose, so in addition to freeing the serfs he re-established the rule of abstinence and the practice of silence. He then set about the gradual reconstruction of the basilica, designing the façade to echo the Roman arch of Constantine with three wide portals, before going on to take a significant step towards what would become known as the Gothic style with a new chancel. The novel features now involved – the pointed arch, the ribbed vault, the ambulatory with radiating chapels or the flying buttresses making possible the insertion of large clerestory windows – all pointed to the aim of the Gothic style to flood what had traditionally been dark buildings with light. And when the nave was rebuilt in the Gothic style a century later with two magnificent rose windows, the picture would be complete. Saint-Denis with its new basilica would provide a fitting resting place for past kings and for the royal symbols, would draw pilgrims to view relics and bathe in its inevitably mythologised history, and would help Paris to become not only the home of the hitherto itinerant kings, but the greatest city in the kingdom.

For this to be achieved, however, the two long-serving kings who followed would need to establish the strong and stable national framework that would enable the city to develop. Louis VII (r. 1137–80) hardly achieved that, although the compensatory factor was that he appointed the competent Suger as regent when he went off on the Second Crusade and Paris now became the effective capital for the conduct of national business. It is hard not to feel a little sorry for Louis, for circumstances were initially against him. Deeply pious and bent on becoming a monk, he became king by accident when his brother died. He had been married off to Aliénor (Eleanor) d'Aquitaine by his father, whose interest lay in acquiring wealthy Aquitaine rather than in the fifteen-year-old Aliénor, so the question of compatibility did not arise. The pious Louis was married to this beautiful, feisty, impressive young woman, who was used to the more relaxed ways of the court of Aquitaine and who complained that she had thought she was marrying a king but had only married a monk. She shocked the court with her independent, extravagant ways and it was probably to keep an eye on her that he foolishly took her with him in 1247 – along with a bevy of her ladies – on the Second Crusade. However, the crusade turned out to be a disaster and he suspected her also of having had an affair with her uncle. On their return, Aliénor tried and failed to get an annulment but eventually, on the grounds that she had not yet produced a male heir, Louis divorced her.[4]

This turned out to be a strategic blunder, since she retained her title to the duchy of Aquitaine and took it with her when she married Henry Plantagenet, who within two years would become King Henry II of England. For although Henry was supposed to be Louis's vassal, he now ruled not only England, but also Normandy and the whole coastal area right down to the Pyrenees – a major threat, which Louis would have to leave for his wilier and more determined son Philippe Auguste (r. 1180–1223) to confront. And confront it Philippe Auguste certainly did, for he fought for over thirty years against the armies of three successive Angevin kings: Henry II, Richard the Lionheart and King John. By the end he had gained Normandy, Brittany, Anjou, Maine, Poitou and Touraine, conquests that he consolidated at the Battle of Bouvines in 1214 by defeating an Anglo-Flemish-German coalition led by the Holy Roman Emperor Otto IV – in effect establishing his kingdom as a leading European power. Having come home early from the Third Crusade, he now sensibly avoided involvement in the brutally murderous Albigensian Crusade proclaimed by Pope Innocent III against the heretical Cathars in Languedoc, which opened the way for the crown to absorb what was left of Languedoc and enabled him to devote more time to dealing with affairs in Paris.

Before going off with no great enthusiasm to the Third Crusade in 1190, Philippe Auguste had been so concerned at the thought of leaving the city vulnerable during his absence that he set in train the construction of a defensive wall around Paris. This turned out to be a monumental structure, 5 kilometres in circumference, with walls 9 metres high surmounted by turrets which incorporated, on the western side facing potential Norman attackers, a formidable fortress with walls up to 4 metres thick called the Louvre – deriving its name, a little surprisingly for art lovers perhaps, from *louveterie*, meaning the headquarters of the wolf hunt. The section on the Right Bank, now the larger and more developed area, was only completed in 1209 and the Left Bank section, where the university was expanding, in 1215. The security afforded by the wall encouraged the development of vacant plots of land, attracted newcomers and defined the boundary of Paris for several centuries to come. Since the wall was mostly financed by the city, it also illustrates Philippe Auguste's policy of collaborating with the middle class of the towns, giving them protection both from enemy attacks and from demands by the nobility, building them into the structure of municipal government and, in exchange, receiving their financial support and their loyalty.

While it is hard to grasp the gulf in living standards in this early period between royals and nobles on the one hand and the common people on the other, the situation was slowly starting to change. One reason was a certain loss of influence by the nobles who, if they had not been killed in the Crusades, had often been impoverished by the need to kit out and maintain a private army for such a lengthy campaign. The main reason, however, was that Paris, having been given a period of relative peace, was now able to develop economically with the support of the throne. And it will be no surprise that the increase in trade was intimately connected to the city's favourable position on the river, or that the centrally connecting guild, or *corporation*, would once again be that of the water merchants (as the boatmen were now termed) who controlled river trade in both directions. They were given space to build their own port, a monopoly of river trade and dispensation from various taxes until they became important to the point of playing a leading role in municipal affairs. Every other year, the merchants – so long as they were born in Paris

– elected a provost and four magistrates to represent them in the *parloir aux bourgeois*, or city hall, in order to maintain standards, deal with infractions and impose fines.

Another ancient trade connected to the river was that of the butchers, who operated in the engagingly named Rue Massacre-Moyenne on the Île de la Cité before moving in 1096 to larger premises with some twenty-three stalls. The animals brought by boat could be held on the Île Saint-Louis before being slaughtered, while the river provided both water for cleaning and a convenient repository for some of the blood and waste. The area was still left famously filthy and reeking not only of offal but of the smells produced by such dependent crafts as tanners or tallow candlemakers. Here again, the trade moved socially upward when a group of families came together in larger premises, achieved a monopoly with the tenancies passing strictly from father to son, and became another important financial and political force. Further trades were accommodated by the creation in 1137 of a market on the Right Bank for dealers in wheat, vegetables and fruit, as well as for haberdashers. This was followed in 1181 by the creation of two *halles*, or covered markets, initially for drapers and weavers but which developed over the years into a grand bazaar. These also gave their name eventually to the famous Halles, the central fresh-food market – which the novelist Émile Zola described as 'the belly of Paris' and which is where people went with their friends for a steaming bowl of onion soup at one o'clock in the morning after a good night out – until it was replaced in 1971 by a largely underground modern shopping mall.

In the *Livre des Métiers* produced in 1268, the provost of Paris Étienne Boileau listed 101 trades, ranging from florists and hosiers to saddlers and locksmiths. The approved practice was to set up a guild to control recruitment and regulate standards by requiring candidates to pay a fee, be examined for competence and have their test piece approved before being accepted to serve a fixed number of years as apprentices. The guild, with its elected representatives, would also aspire to play a part in municipal politics. As time went on, there tended in key trades to be the inevitable *embourgeoisement*, with entry being restricted on a father-to-son basis and producing a privileged closed club. By the fifteenth century this had inevitably produced a reaction from the would-be apprentices, who organised against the system, set up their own trades and – ironically but equally inevitably – became just as elitist and dynastic in their turn.

Bourgeois, from *bourg* meaning town, was originally a precise legal term before taking on the general social and even political connotations that it was later to acquire. The term *bourgeois de Paris*, as defined by royal order in 1287, meant a male individual who had lived in Paris for at least a year, who owned a house, as around a quarter did, who paid the residence tax and who in addition, by a further royal order of 1295, could produce a reference from a priest testifying to the fact that he regularly attended mass. In addition, by a procedure akin to the dynastic trend of the trades, it was possible for him to make his citizenship hereditary on payment of a large fee. With the gradual development of the economy, this would lead to the development of a distinction between *petits bourgeois* and *grands bourgeois*. The latter, often those who had enriched themselves through the luxury trades or through banking, would eventually become a closely knit and politically important group, supplanting the lesser nobility in the process.

Meanwhile, a glance at living conditions in the medieval city can be sobering. By 1328, the number of households officially listed in Paris had risen to sixty-one thousand, which suggests that the population had jumped from at most twenty-thousand in the year 1000 after the Viking invasions, to at least two hundred thousand – and which in fact made it the most highly populated city in the Europe of that time. Of these only a quarter were taxed, implying that the majority were deemed to be too poor to contribute. Just as the owners tended to be master artisans protected by their guilds, so the poor were essentially apprentices, servants, valets or day labourers, living very much from hand to mouth and ill able to confront illness or accident. Since many of these had come in from the countryside in search of work, they tended to be younger and often too poor to be able to marry and find a stable life. The density of the housing was such that, although the poor were largely clustered on the Left Bank or in the suburbs, rich and poor often lived side by side in the same street – or even in the same house, where the owner let out a garret or a master artisan provided a room in lieu of wages for a trainee. The houses, especially in areas where trades were clustered, were often narrow and glass for windows was rare up to the fifteenth century. With little municipal control of standards, it was only in 1374 that houses were officially required to have their own latrines, so houses often had an outside cesspit but, since this required regular emptying, the standard practice was to empty the chamber pot out of the window – with or without the standard cry of *Gare l'eau!* to the pedestrians passing below.

In matters of hygiene, indeed, it took Paris a good few centuries to catch up with the Romans, with their long-forgotten bath houses including public lavatories and their paved main streets. Public bathing in the river had long since been considered indecent and although some public bath houses were established in the thirteenth and fourteenth centuries, perhaps under the influence of the returning crusaders, they too were phased out, not only because of their dubious reputation but because medical opinion at the time took a poor view of the use of hot water. The irregular, unpaved streets were strewn with rubbish and excrement, both human and animal, since dogs and other animals wandered freely – it was a pig running into the legs of his horse that saw the heir of Louis VI thrown and killed in the street in 1137. So once again it was Philippe Auguste, repelled by the stench and the sight of people slithering through this nauseous muddy mixture, who started having the streets paved, although there would be no pavements in our present-day sense until the eighteenth century – to the benefit initially of fastidious patrons of the

Comédie-Française. Since chamber pots went on being emptied out of the windows, however, it was a good idea to hug the wall, or to *tenir le haut du pavé* – which by extension came to mean to lord it over others.

With due deference to the Emperor Julian, who had found water from the Seine pleasant to drink, the quality of drinking water in Paris was a serious problem not only in the Middle Ages but right up to the late nineteenth century. The specific reason was that the phreatic or underground water table, some 5 metres down, was continuous with that of the river, which was now heavily contaminated. This was due not only to the human waste and rubbish generated by such as butchers or tanners in Paris itself but to similar waste, including leakages from cemeteries, from further upstream. There was fresh water from the Bièvre river, a tributary of the Seine, and from wells, but the easiest source was the Seine. Indeed, there was a pervasive official view, understandable for the Middle Ages but less so after that period, that the water from the Seine not only tasted better but was purer. And it even took some courage for Baron Haussmann, then prefect of the Seine, to explode that myth by establishing in Paris a Compagnie Générale des Eaux in 1860 to control standards, and by setting up an elaborate system of aqueducts to bring in clean water from outside Paris.

Until the sixteenth century, medicine was taught in Paris as little other than a branch of theology. Although a faculty of medicine was established it 1274, it was recorded as having only thirteen books in its library in 1395 and it was only set up in dedicated premises in 1470.[5] Given the primitive state of medical knowledge at this time, hospitals were essentially refuges operated by the Church in line with the basic Christian value of charity. They were not for the better off, who could more comfortably and more safely be looked after at home, but rather for the dispossessed and the excluded: they were designed to provide food, shelter and comfort for such groups as abandoned children, orphans, lepers or the old and the infirm. Although they were often funded by the wealthier citizens by way of legacies and donations, they were run by the Church with religious personnel. Unfortunately, the human sympathy did not go hand in hand with knowledge about the spread of infection so that, although they did maintain minimal hygiene and wash the sheets, the habit of putting several people into the same bed – for reasons of space or companionship? – caused ravages. The oldest hospital in Paris was the Hôtel-Dieu, which expanded to the point of having five hundred beds whereas others, often established in houses given by donors, might have only a handful of places. As the number grew from the twelfth century onwards, some developed a particular specialism, like the Quinze-Vingts – so named because 15 multiplied by 20 equals 300, the number of patients – which was originally a refuge for the blind and is today the highly regarded national ophthalmology hospital.

If Paris gradually became famous as the centre for university education in Catholic Europe at this time, it is essentially because of its reputation for theology. The cathedral school of Notre-Dame led the way, with such teachers as Maurice de Sully and Pierre Lombard, but early in the twelfth century theologians such as Guillaume de Champeaux and Pierre Abelard began to set up their own independent schools outside the jurisdiction of the bishop. By the end of the century, as Franciscans, Dominicans and other orders obtained the right to teach, there were no fewer than ten such schools competing for space on the Left Bank – and the Latin Quarter, as it has been called since the nineteenth century, was born. The attraction was at once that there was increasing intellectual curiosity in the air, and that attendance at the schools could lead to well-rewarded jobs in the Church and ultimately, perhaps, in the service of the king.

However, the courses were exceptionally long, with six years of general arts followed by long years of canon law and then up to fifteen for the doctorate, so relatively few of the students went the full distance. Given the concentration of so many students in one area, plus tensions between different regional or national groups and the fact that some were as young as fourteen when they entered the system, it is not surprising that there were regular problems with drunkenness, fighting and licentious behaviour. This did not endear the students to the bishop or to the police, which intervened brutally in 1200 against the students when they were engaged in a running battle with the locals. When the colleges protested at the harsh punishment meted out, Louis-Philippe handed the problem neatly back to them by decreeing that such offences should be judged by an ecclesiastical rather than a civil court. This level of independence – and responsibility – was assumed when Robert de Sorbon founded his college in 1257 in the Rue Coupe-Gueule (Cutthroat Street), now the tamely named Rue de la Sorbonne. Placed directly under the aegis of the faculty of theology, the new college became known as a haven of moderation and religious orthodoxy, keeping a safe distance from the doctrinal battles of the period.

As for doctrinal battles, the most celebrated figure from this period is Pierre Abelard (1079–1142), although that is also because his love affair with Héloïse figures prominently in the Western pantheon of tragic lovers. One of those who broke away from the existing tradition to set up his own school, he was a charismatic teacher who confidently outshone his senior colleagues and drew far larger audiences. In his late thirties, when he was teaching liberal arts and Holy Scripture at Notre-Dame, he was entrusted by a canon named Fulbert with the education of his seventeen-year-old niece Héloïse. They fell in love, she became pregnant and had the child secretly in Brittany, where it was christened by the exotic name of Astrolabe – after a Persian astronomical instrument – and entrusted to Abelard's sister. However, Fulbert insisted that they get married, which they did – secretly, to avoid the ruination of Abelard's clerical career – but when Abelard tried to hide

Héloïse in a convent to quieten the rumours, Fulbert assumed that he was trying to abandon her permanently and sent men to castrate him. After which Abelard became a monk at Saint-Denis, taught there until his view of the Trinity was condemned and thereafter led a somewhat wandering life, while Héloïse became a nun and eventually a learned abbess. Their love seems to have been very real, but since neither could nor would challenge the clerical structure with its enforced celibacy enclosing them, the tragedy was inevitable. And tragedy is invested with such grandeur that it almost seems improper to wonder what happened to the baby Astrolabe – the date of whose death is unknown.

'Truly that man loves to question everything, wants to dispute everything, divine as well as secular', wrote Guillaume de Saint Thierry, an influential fellow theologian.[6] If Abelard was the idol of students but a thorn in the flesh of many of his established colleagues, it is because he was moving away from the contemplative or mystical approach and attempting to bring logic and rationalism to the study of theology. His method was dialectical in that he would present students with arguments both for and against some proposition, in the belief that the truth would emerge from exhaustive discussion. It is by this approach that he attempted to resolve apparent contradictions in the doctrine such as the relationship between God's omniscience and human freedom: if God knows in advance that I am going to commit a certain action, how can I avoid doing so, and so how can that act be free? If he solved this to his own satisfaction, he seemed to some senior colleagues to be sailing too close to the wind. As again, when he argued that it was not a harmful act in itself that constitutes a sin, but rather the intention to commit it, was he not denying the objective difference between good and evil? Eventually, his approach led him to be condemned by a council of bishops, after which he retired to a monastery and died in disgrace. This was the other tragedy, equally inevitable since once again he was operating within the closed system bounded by his own faith and was to that extent, in Roger Lloyd's phrase, 'the orthodox rebel'.[7]

It was in the reign of Louis IX, or Saint Louis (r. 1226–70), the only French king to be canonised by the Catholic Church, that the alliance of throne and Church approached its high point. With economic expansion and military successes, France was emerging as the most populated country in Europe, while Paris was by now not only the undisputed capital of France, but the largest city in Europe – some five times larger than London, which had no more than forty thousand inhabitants. Moreover, with its university attracting international students, Paris was emerging as the cultural capital of Europe. And Louis IX, for several reasons, came to be seen as the ideal Christian king for this golden time.

In the first place, not only did he keep the nobles in check, but he tidied up the feudal jigsaw by making an advantageous deal with Henry III of England, whereby he ceded Limoges, Cahors and Périgueux in return for Henry's renunciation of any claim to Normandy, Anjou, Maine, Poitou and Touraine. He also traded his claim to Barcelona and Roussillon for the King of Aragon's claim to Provence and Languedoc. Secondly, while his ascetic and absolutist piety led him to tolerate torture by the Inquisition or mutilation of the mouth for blasphemy, he nevertheless did much to reform the legal system, banning the brutal trial by ordeal, introducing the presumption of innocence and encouraging the use of Roman law. Again, his reputation was enhanced by his participation in the Seventh and Eighth Crusades, the first of which he financed by confiscating the property of the Jews. Both were disastrous failures, as it turned out, since he had to be ransomed after capture on the first and died of fever on the second, yet his participation added greatly to the prestige of a king who, however stark his religious zeal, was seen as brave and good and honourable. And he further burnished his reputation by patronising the arts, financing a large rose window for Notre-Dame cathedral and providing Paris with a Gothic marvel in the form of the Sainte-Chapelle.

The cathedral of Notre-Dame de Paris, so spectacularly situated on the Île de la Cité but so tragically burnt down in April 2019, was for many the heart and soul of the city, the symbol of historical continuity and the centre for national ceremonies, not to mention – from the spot where the bishop's penitential ladder once stood, as it happens – the starting point for measuring distances to and from the capital. Begun in 1160 and largely complete by 1260, it developed the Gothic techniques pioneered by Suger at Saint-Denis and it had magnificent rose windows, the one donated by Saint Louis being especially large and impressive. As with the Gothic style in general, the architecture operated on several levels. It impressed initially as much by the sheer size and majesty of the structure as by the extent and variety of the sculpted figures on its façade – which were originally painted and gilded. Beyond that, and unlike Islamic art, which allowed of no representation of the human figure – as Alistair Horne reminds us[8] – it operated as a picture book for the illiterate population, telling the Christian story both in sculpture and in scenes in the richly coloured stained glass that seemed miraculously animated by the changing light of day. Yet alongside saints or devils or gargoyles, it had images or sculptures of ordinary people doing ordinary things – a man bringing home a bale of corn, another killing a pig, or a husband and wife squabbling – in such a way as to merge the everyday with the miraculous and suggest that, even if people were not equal in life, they were equal at the higher level of legend. Finally, this was uniquely a large stone building that was open to everyone, where the homeless could go for sleep or the fugitive for sanctuary, where traders touted their wares, where there were regular fairs on the cathedral square and which, in effect, served as the town centre. It was compelling architecture.

In contrast to Notre-Dame, the Sainte-Chapelle was a private chapel built in only six years from 1242 to 1248. Attached to this grand residence, with its impressive entrance hall adorned with statues of kings going back to Clovis, its monumental staircase and its private royal quarters, there were two chapels: the 'low chapel' for the use of the staff and the 'high chapel' for the exclusive use of the Louis himself. This high chapel certainly lives up to its reputation as a masterpiece of the radiant Gothic style, for the walls themselves seem to be made of warmly coloured stained glass narrating the Old Testament story in scene after scene – interrupted only by two windows which tell the story of Louis's acquisition of the holy relics. Since it was to create a home for these that the chapel had in fact been built, they were prominently displayed beneath a canopy symbolising sovereignty and the people were allowed to enter once a year, on Good Friday, to marvel at them. He had bought from the emperor of Constantinople what was said to be the Crown of Thorns, as well as two pieces of the Cross, a fragment of the spear which pierced Christ's side and various other items. That he paid a colossal sum for these – they added up to about four times the cost of construction of the high chapel itself[9] – is indicative of the fundamental importance he attached to them. Kings before him had dreamt of making Paris the equal of Rome or Byzantium and Louis had already shown signs of protecting his independence from the Vatican, as though anticipating the later concept of the absolute monarch as deriving his authority directly from God. With these relics, which appeared to suggest a privileged line of descent from Christ himself, he was moving beyond the functional alliance of Church and state towards a fusion of royalty and religion, towards a sanctification of kingship itself.

Paris in Turmoil: Fourteenth and Fifteenth Centuries

....

Paris entered the fourteenth century – and what would begin to look like a different world – in the reign of Philippe IV (r. 1285–1314), otherwise known as Philippe Le Bel. Handsome though he was, he was seen as stiff, unable to be at ease with others or even with himself, and indeed was once said to be like an owl, in that he just stared silently at people. It may be that he was insecure, since he lost his mother at an early age and was not brought up in an emotionally secure environment, but his contemporaries do seem to have found him a cold and enigmatic figure. Historians have also tended to raise puzzled questions about him. If he was so pious, for example, did he have to be so ruthless? Or in his attempt to make considerable changes in the governance of the kingdom, was he in charge of his officials or was he to some extent being manipulated?

In fact, his broad aim seems clear; it was to translate his grandfather Saint Louis's dream of a fusion of throne and religion into hard political reality. His was an absolutist 'religion of monarchy' and, in practice, of the *French* monarchy. Not just because the French king was the most powerful in Christendom and the chief supporter of the Church, but because he had a quite direct relation with Christ himself through his ownership of the Crown of Thorns and other relics – which is why they had been bought for such a staggering sum. He had been anointed with holy oil, he had been blessed with the ability with a wave of his hand to cure the then current disease of scrofula – swollen neck glands – and, in short, he had been invested with the awesome and sacred duty of exercising absolute power in his Christian kingdom. It is doubtless true, as Strayer suggests, that 'he understood and practised this religion rather better than he did Christianity', but it explains the governing idea behind his actions.[1] He had to protect the sainted throne from any untoward opposition from the Vatican or other political structures of the Church – and he would indeed take on the Pope with a vengeance. He had to increase the kingdom whenever the opportunity arose and defend it from any manoeuvres by major vassals – and he fought ultimately successful battles with the Count of Flanders and the King of England. He also had to restructure the justice system, in order to establish clearly that he was the final arbiter.

Of course, the kingdom was still something of a patchwork of different entities – noble domains, *apanages*, bishoprics, duchies and so on – which while nominally subservient to the throne enjoyed a degree of organisational independence. In the case of justice, for example, different courts might have different practices and standards, although they do seem to have shown a similar severity – the penalty for theft in Paris, as detailed by Geremek, was mostly hanging, but could also be 'dragging and hanging, dragging and beheading, buried alive, banishment, or ears cut off plus flogging'.[2] However, to reorder all this to suit his major ambitions, Philippe needed to achieve central control of the machinery of government and in particular, since fighting battles was expensive and the royal domain itself could never produce enough funds for his needs, he needed to achieve control of the finances. So, he set up something approaching a modern national treasury in the Palais-Royal on the Île de la Cité, staffed by professionals rather than by representatives of the nobility or the high bourgeoisie. To support this, he set up a national consultative body within which his officers could argue the need for the series of taxes, which he proceeded to raise, and secondly seek to mollify the discontent of the nobles and bourgeois, who felt excluded from the process – although they did not object to his dispossession and expulsion of the Jews.

Initially, Paris gained from this new treasury since it brought in prosperous professionals to staff the offices as well as nobles who wanted a pied-à-terre near the seat of power. This brought in good business for various trades and increased the value of property. However, Philippe had not only been imposing various taxes and tariffs, he had been manipulating the currency, and when in 1306 he brought in a new 'hard currency', which rectified the situation but could double or even treble the rents, there was a riot. A crowd stormed and pillaged the house of the king's close adviser Étienne Barbette, who had demanded that they pay their rents in the new money, and then went to the Temple, where Philippe was staying. While it is possible that they wanted not to threaten but to explain their position to the king, that never emerged as a consideration and more than a score of them were executed. And this was only one of the episodes that darkened Philippe's reputation among his subjects.

A spectacular scandal occurred in 1314 when the wives of his two sons, the future kings Louis X and Charles IV, were accused of having adulterous relations with two young knights, who were also brothers, in the guard tower in the city wall known as the Tour de Nesle. Did Philippe feel that this was such a threat to the reputation of a hereditary and saintly monarchy that it must be seen to be punished severely – even at the cost of publicising the affair and damaging the reputation of his sons? Or is it simply that his ruthlessness was the mirror image of his absolutist faith and perhaps that he did not feel close to his sons? Whatever his motives, the two young knights were condemned, flayed publicly in the market square, castrated, with their genitals being thrown to the dogs, then disembowelled, beheaded and strung up by the armpits on the gibbet in the public square. Which left the honour of the saintly monarchy intact.

However, the most celebrated examples of Philippe's determination to assert the absolute primacy of his throne are doubtless his battle with the Pope and the affair of the Templars. When in

1302 Pope Boniface VIII tried to insist on his right to impose taxes on clerical institutions within the kingdom, Philippe called a council of French bishops and mustered support from nobles and bourgeois in order to condemn him. Boniface reacted by threatening to excommunicate him and issue a papal interdict upon the whole country, whereupon Philippe dispatched his counsellor Nogaret with an armed escort to arrest the Pope and have him condemned by a Vatican council. It is said that Nogaret, along with a Roman noble who was a personal enemy of Boniface, found the ageing Pope alone, abandoned and prepared to be killed in a summer palace at Anagni. They took him prisoner, but the locals soon reacted and freed him, which enabled him to return to Rome, where he declined and died a few weeks later. The affair caused a widespread scandal, but it certainly made Philippe's essential point; that there was no power, spiritual or temporal, that could challenge the legitimacy of a decision of the king of France. To make doubly sure, however, he manoeuvred to get himself a new pope, a proper French pope, in the form of the Archbishop of Bordeaux, who became Clement V and moved the papacy to Avignon. Which would provide Philippe with cover for his attack on the Templars.

The Knights Templar, famous for their white mantles adorned with a red cross, were members of a religious military order founded in 1119 that had played a famous part in the battles of the Crusades. They had since expanded to the point of having fortified centres throughout Europe and in the Near East, though the Grand Master Jacques de Molay now had his seat in Paris. Over the two centuries of its existence the order had become immensely rich, through legacies, donations and monies left in trust by knights leaving for the Crusades. With up to 90 per cent of its membership being in fact support staff, it had managed a complex international structure, become a lender to royalty and developed almost to the point, it has been suggested, of becoming the world's first multinational corporation.[3] Also it had privileges and exemptions granted by the Vatican, which gave it the right to operate freely across borders and therefore a status independent of the throne. To Philippe's eyes, however, the Crusades were over, the order no had longer any clear spiritual purpose, yet it was ensconced in a fortified enclave in the capital of his kingdom, assuming the privileges of a state-within-the-state and in a position to wield its wealth as a competing power. Also, the throne was in debt to it, and it would be helpful to get hold of its money.

He began to combine with Pope Clement V, who was often reluctant but finally compliant, to bring the Templars down. They first proposed a merger of the order with another order, the Knights Hospitaller, which would have enabled Philippe to exercise more control, but the Templars' leader innocently rejected that. This led to a very efficient simultaneous dawn raid on Friday 13 October 1307, which saw Jacques de Molay and scores of his knights arrested. The two principal charges, apart from others such as fraud or concealment of assets, were of heresy and homosexual practices. Although some of the accused admitted under torture that they engaged in dubious initiation ceremonies and the like, the charge of heresy and idol worship was always implausible. As for the charge of homosexual activity, although Philippe might well have been genuinely shocked by this, it is hardly surprising, as Strayer points out, to find this in single-sex clerical institutions and especially in a military order where it might actually have been encouraged in the interest of bonding.[4] However, Philippe's mind was made up, dozens of the Templars were tortured and burnt at the stake, while de Molay and a colleague, having retracted their confessions, were burnt separately at the western tip of the Île de la Cité. De Molay, the legend has it, prophesied ominously that he would soon see them again in the presence of God. Philippe duly died within the year from a hunting accident. As for Clement, who died almost at once, his tomb at Uzeste in the Gironde is rarely visited and his name only lingers on the label of a Bordeaux claret.

*   *   *

Philippe may well have set his country on the course to becoming a modern national state, but France and England were still tied together by the old intermingled feudal ties almost like conjoined twins. So, when the Capetian dynasty ran out of male heirs in 1328 and the king's closest relative turned out to be Edward III of England, who still had title to Gascony, the barons reacted and chose a native king in the person of Philippe, Comte de Valois. Of course, this was merely the latest phase of a competition between rising nations that went back to William the Conqueror and there were background economic drivers at play, especially since France was now the most successful country in Europe and Paris far outshone London. With tensions still persisting, Philippe tried to put an end to the whole story by taking back Gascony in 1337, but Edward reacted more strongly than expected by renewing his claim to the French throne, which precipitated a war.

This turned out to be a confused and intermittent affair, with the two sides circling around each other initially in the hope that a full-scale conflict might be avoided and that the issue might still be resolved by diplomacy. It was also complicated in that the Scots supported the French and the Flemish the English, while the action moved around on land and from land to sea. Indeed, the first significant victory was when Edward's navy defeated the French fleet in the Battle of Sluys in 1340, which enabled him to move troops and supplies more easily to the continent. After a truce negotiated by the Pope, the fighting moved to Gascony and, with the French tied up there, Edward took Caen and marched on Paris. Philippe caught up with him, but at the Battle of Crécy in 1346 the French knights suffered a crushing defeat at the hands of the English longbowmen. Even so, Edward contented himself with capturing Calais rather than advancing on a nervous Paris and at this point, even though another attempt by the Pope to mediate came to nothing, the cost of the war for both sides was enough to lead to another truce in September 1347. This, as it happened, was just in time for the arrival of the Black Death in the following month, though at least the Parisians could not guess that the costly fighting so far was merely the overture to what would be known as the Hundred Years War.

Needless to say, Paris was no stranger at this time to natural disasters. The Seine flooded at intervals, as in 1326, when the bridges were destroyed, causing food shortages. There were periodic famines due to ruined harvests, as in the Great Famine of 1315–17, which may have been due to prolonged volcanic activity in faraway New Zealand, but which affected most of Europe and announced the end of the increase in populations. In Paris itself, with food so scarce and the prices so high, the excluded poor could sometimes be seen lying dead or dying in the street. In addition, most people lived in crowded and insanitary conditions, there was little or no hygiene, and many were in straitened circumstance because of raised rents and taxes. And given that medicine had no relevant solutions to offer at this stage, it was inevitable, as Cazelles points out, that within living memory Paris should see an epidemic of one contagious disease or another – mostly of smallpox, flu or whooping cough – every five or six years, and particularly badly in the years 1317, 1323, 1328, 1334 and 1340–1.[5] So the arrival of another epidemic in sequence was not initially a surprise.

The pandemic known as the Black Death, which may have killed up to half of the population of Europe, is believed to have arisen in the East and to have come along the Silk Road, wreaking havoc on the way, before crossing the Mediterranean by way of black rats on ships and moving gradually northwards along the coastal areas. It arrived in Paris via Normandy in the summer of 1348 and disappeared in 1350, only to recur at regular intervals thereafter. Caused by the fleas on the black rats, although it passed on to fleas on humans, it came in two strains, the bubonic and the pulmonary. The bubonic was the more frightening, since it caused the flesh to blacken where the fleas had bitten and left buboes, or lumps in the groin, caused by swelling of the lymphatic glands, but it was only lethal in around 40 per cent of cases. The more deadly version was in fact the pulmonary one, which attacked the lungs and the mucous membranes and swept its victims away within three days.

The Parisians, being all too used to calamities, seemed initially to take this one in their stride. After all, it seemed to affect mainly the poor and their children, who were already weakened by famines and disease, or else limited categories such as carers, priests, notaries and gravediggers. The wealthy, living in better conditions and in a position to leave the city – as did the King's Council for a lengthy period – fared very much better. However, as the death toll moved steadily towards killing perhaps seventy thousand people, or around a third of the city's population, serious questions began to be asked, both at the practical and the philosophical level. At the king's request, the medical faculty of the university produced a report that asserted that the plague was caused by an unfortunate astral configuration in the form of a conjunction of three planets, which had produced 'a great pestilence in the air'. Since it also denied, in the face of the evidence, that there was person-to-person transmission, the doctors had no answer and their remedies, such as bleeding, could do more harm than good. Nor was there a plausible answer at the religious level. The Church organised solemn processions to chase away demons and the Bishop of Paris promoted the cult of Saint Sebastian – until he too died from the pandemic.

The Parisians would therefore have to live and die with this plague, which would return cyclically and have a long-term effect at both the economic and the philosophical level. If rents fell because of the death or flight of tenants, and if wages rose due to the shortage of manpower, the cost of food and other items seemed to rise even faster, creating social tensions. It was at the philosophical level, however, that the effect was most profound. For what did it mean, this unusual plague, and who was to blame?

Was it the Jews? Or was this God's punishment for our own sin, as believed by the Flagellants who lashed themselves ritually as they processed – innocently spreading the infection as they went? Yet this capricious epidemic seemed to make no distinctions, so was it God's judgement on Man himself? Or was it even God's judgement on the Church, which seemed mysteriously to suffer disproportionately even in its closed communities, with thirty-two deaths in a single nunnery? Could it conceivably even be, as funeral rites were reduced and infected bodies dumped unceremoniously in common graves, that the meaning was just what you saw, that in the end there *was* no meaning, beyond the fact that people just lived and died and crumbled into dust?

This sense of the uncertainty and fragility of life, which also led to some hysterically wild behaviour, developed into a sense of impermanence that began to colour the culture at that time. It pervades the poetry of Eustache Deschamps or François Villon, as it informs the increasingly grim representations of Christ on the cross, or the widespread theme in European art of the Danse Macabre – the first version of which would appear in Paris at the cemetery of the Saints-Innocents. It was almost, as Vovelle suggests, that people had only just discovered death.[6] It had been so well embedded in the Christian story and so clothed in ceremony as the passage to a higher state, one which could be negotiated by piety and good works, that it could even be seen as a well-earned reward. But the dance of death of the Danse Macabre, with those grinning skeletons leading innocent victims – pope or peasant, king or beggar, regardless – to their shared fate, told a different story. It suggested subversively to this formally stratified monarchical society that all people were equal, and that the only real sovereign was death.

The truce of 1347 at least allowed Paris to perfect its defences, but the war soon resumed, only for the French to suffer another humiliating defeat at the Battle of Poitiers in 1356, especially since

King Jean le Bon (r. 1350–64) was taken prisoner. This left his son, the future Charles le Sage, to continue the war while trying to raise the ransom by increasing taxes and dealing with a rebellion at home, led by Étienne Marcel – who is represented on horseback on a statue outside the Hôtel de Ville. A wealthy draper, Marcel had become provost of the merchants at a time when King Jean was already struggling to maintain his authority and to raise funds for the war. Jean had been confronted at the States General by the demand for a deal whereby they would agree to finance the war in exchange for the dismissal of certain advisers, reform of the justice system, an end to the raising of money by currency manipulation and significantly, since it suggests a certain growing national feeling, a guarantee that there would be no concessions to the English. His son Charles, now suddenly faced with this challenge, indicated initially that he would resist the proposed changes, but within months Marcel had persuaded the States General to approve by statute a comprehensive reform which would in effect have amounted to constitutional monarchy.

Over the course of the next year, the clever but cautious Charles and Marcel worked through a relationship where there seems to have been a certain amount of goodwill on both sides, but which in the dire situation of the country was like a chess match that neither could afford to lose. Marcel had real achievements to his name, since he had built up the defences of the city and organised the population to resist an invasion, but as the States General proved unable to raise the taxes he deemed necessary to combat the marauding bandits ravaging the countryside, a failure for which he blamed the nobles, he overplayed his hand. He led an angry mob to see Charles, did not protest as his armed companions massacred two nobles present and, while assuring Charles that he was safe, humiliated him by exchanging headgear, leaving the dauphin wearing a hood in the red and blue colours of the city. Charles fled the city and started to organise a blockade, while an increasingly isolated Marcel appeared to fall back on the support of Charles de Navarre, a potential claimant to the throne, and even on the support of the English – before walking into a trap, being assassinated and having his corpse trailed through the streets. Historians are understandably divided about Étienne Marcel. For some, such as Jacques Castelnau, he was a genuine precursor of the Great Revolution.[7] For others, such as Guy Fourquin, he was an opportunist who looked rather to the past and 'in no way foreshadowed the 1789 Revolution'.[8] However, it is clearly because the Third Republic in 1888 took the former view that he now sits commandingly on his horse in front of the Hôtel de Ville in Paris.

The city enjoyed a period of relative calm after Charles took over the kingship. He continued Marcel's work in fortifying the city, blending new defensive walls and battlements with tall banks and floodable ditches in an attempt to counter the new weapon of artillery. However, he no longer felt safe in the Île de la Cité and always made sure that wherever he was staying there would be an easy means of escape. This was true of the new residence he built near the Arsenal, the Hôtel Saint-Pol, as it was of the Louvre once he had added a drawbridge, and indeed of the formidable Bastille, which he funded out of his own resources. The Bastille would not only protect Paris against invasion but would provide cover both for his Hôtel Saint-Pol and for the Château de Vincennes, a favourite royal residence on the outer edge of the city. This brief interval of rather uneasy peace coincided with success in the larger war that was going on in fits and starts across the country. The French forces were now led by Bertrand du Guesclin, a proper general rather than the king himself or some nobleman in search of glory, and by the time Charles died in 1380 the English were left with no more than Calais and a few lesser ports.

Obviously, both countries had broadly similar problems. The dynastic system could be shaken by a king dying inopportunely and leaving the throne in the hands of a child, as with the new king, Charles VI, aged eleven in 1380, or the English Richard II, aged ten in 1377, just as his realm had similar internal problems with the Peasants' Revolt of 1381 and the ongoing Anglo-Scottish war. In this situation, the larger war became intermittent or was fought by proxy. However, the forty-four-year reign of Charles VI, although for the first eight years the power was wielded as regents by his uncles the Duc d'Anjou, Philippe II the Duc de Bourgogne and the Duc de Berry, was colourful enough. It began indeed at his father's funeral, when the rival canons of Notre-Dame and Sainte-Chapelle started a fight over who had precedence in the conduct of the royal obsequies, ending in several clerics being injured or imprisoned. And it continued with the revolt of the Maillotins.

A particular complaint of hard-pressed Parisians at this time was the indirect and, in their eyes, stealthy taxes on basic food-stuffs, wine and salt in particular, which raised the cost of living. The king had initially abolished them, but within two years they were brought back. It took no more than a simple incident involving a cress seller in the Halles to start a major riot involving two or three thousand people, who broke into the Hôtel de Ville and armed themselves with the *maillets* (lead mallets or bludgeons) intended for use against a possible English attack on the city. They pillaged the houses of Jews and tax collectors, and went on to break into the prisons and release the inmates. As the trouble spread to other cities, the throne reacted strongly, made an example of Ghent in particular, brought in the army to quell any further trouble in Paris, where it had already executed a dozen of the ring-leaders, and now executed a number of bourgeois supporters. It reinstated the indirect taxes and seized the opportunity to cut Paris down to size by suppressing the municipal structures that had given the city a degree of self-government. The throne was back in control.

Such might have been the case were it not for two factors, the first being that the regents were beginning to plot against one another. A prime example is Philippe de Bourgogne's elaborate attempt to invade England in 1386. He brought together a combined force of French and Burgundian troops with a sizeable fleet of 1,200 ships and waited at Sluys on the Dutch coast for Jean, Duc de Berry, to turn up with his supporting force, but that did not happen until the autumn weather had turned against them and the armies had to turn back again. The second factor was that the king himself, although only in his early twenties, had begun to experience the psychotic episodes which would have him dubbed Charles le Fou. The first was when he was leading troops through the forest in August 1392, when he went berserk, swung his sword wildly and killed four of his own men. Thereafter he had frequent attacks and suffered from the illusion that he was fragile because he was made of glass.

His condition was soon made known to the Parisians by the tragic masquerade that was to be remembered as *le Bal des Ardents* (the Ball of the Burning Men). At a celebratory ball for the wedding of a lady of the court, a surprise event had been planned whereby the king and five young courtiers, disguised as demons or savages, would suddenly appear from nowhere to dance among revellers, uttering strange and salacious cries. Linked by rope, they were dressed in tight linen costumes soaked in pitch or fat on which had been stuck hairs and leaves to produce the shaggy effect. In an attempt to penetrate the disguise of one demon, the king's brother, the Duc d'Orléans, unaware that torches had been kept at a distance for safety reasons, approached with a torch and accidentally set the whole line of savages on fire. Two of them were burnt to death on the spot, two died of their burns later, a fifth saved himself by jumping into a barrel used for rinsing goblets and the sixth, the bewildered king, was saved spectacularly by the Duchesse de Berry wrapping him in the voluminous skirts of her gown. However, this extravagant episode did not enhance the image of royalty in the eyes of Parisians and provided a suitable introduction to the nightmarish confusion and misery of the next fifty years.

Societies need continuity and at a certain stage of development a hereditary monarchy can provide it, especially if it can be sanctified so that the subjects believe in the divine right of kings. Where it throws up a king who is incompetent or mad or a small child, however, it may produce an ongoing disaster, such as happened now as rivalry between the regents developed into a factional struggle for power between the king's uncle, Philippe II de Bourgogne, and his young brother, the Duc d'Orléans. In 1407, following the death of Philippe, his son Jean sans Peur (Jean the Fearless) had his rival the Duc d'Orléans murdered in the Rue Vieille-du-Temple as he was visiting his sister-in-law who had just given birth. This precipitated the civil war between his Burgundians and the Armagnacs – as the Orléanists supporters would be called after the Comte d'Armagnac, father-in-law of the dead duke's son – which would burden the country for the next three decades.

Heavily personalised though the struggle was, there were still ideological differences between the two sides. The Armagnacs were defending the conservative French model of a strong Catholic monarchy and had the support of the alternative French pope, Clement VII, in Avignon. The Burgundians, on the other hand, tended towards the less religiously defined English model based more directly on the middle class, and had the support of the Pope in Rome, Urban VI. Meanwhile Jean sans Peur, helped by a terror campaign waged by the strike leader Simon Caboche, ruled Paris with an iron hand for several years from 1409 until the bourgeoisie swung against him and he was murdered in his turn in 1419. This led his son Philippe III le Bon to concoct a treaty with the English Henry V – who had recently won the Battle of Agincourt – which made Henry the successor to the French throne through marriage to Charles VI's daughter, thus eliminating the dauphin, Charles. So Henry V became king of a new Anglo-French monarchy and, although he would die shortly afterwards, there would be English troops garrisoned in Paris – with

Sir John Fastolf, source of Shakespeare's Falstaff, in charge at the Bastille – until 1436.

Yet there was a twist in the tale. For the dauphin Charles, with the earnest encouragement of Joan of Arc, who described herself as 'Joan the maid, the envoy of the king of Heaven', had rallied his forces and had himself crowned as Charles VII at Reims, the traditional site of coronation for French kings, in 1429. Joan then led an attack on Paris, but was captured after being wounded – ironically, since she saw the enemy as the English, by a French archer, as one writer points out.[9] She was then tried for heresy and for dressing in men's clothes – which she had done for obvious reasons – and although she defended herself valiantly, she was condemned and burnt at the stake. Meanwhile the war went on and gradually turned Charles's way, so that he recaptured Paris in 1436 and was able to enter in triumph in the following year. Having already made a peace treaty with Philippe le Bon, he was now free to act against the English continental possessions and by 1453 he had left them with no more than Calais.

How then had the Parisians been affected by this seemingly unending intermittent war? They had lived through the rioting, pillaging and the bloodshed of revenge killings from both sides, as well as threats to the city from regular armies of one colour or another and even from militarised groups of bandits that had been rampaging freely through the countryside. Again, the war had to a degree exacerbated the natural disasters from which the city routinely suffered. There were floods, the most serious of which were in 1426–7 and 1442. There were the inevitable epidemics at regular intervals, whether of whooping cough, smallpox or mumps as well as syphilis, just as there were the usual droughts and food shortages, notably in 1418 and 1448. Indeed, there were years when hungry wolves, not content with eating the corpses they dragged from their graves in the cemeteries outside the walls, came into the city at night and attacked both dogs and inhabitants – in 1438, when ten people were said to have been killed, the city was offering a reward for each dead wolf. All of this left people uncertain, worried, suspicious of their neighbours and of other groups, producing a divided city with a lack of trust on all sides.

It also created a lingering mutual distrust between Paris and the throne. After entering in triumph in 1437, Charles VII moved the court out of Paris and his three successors followed his example, so that the city would not have its king in residence until 1528, when François I chose it as his capital. This move to the Touraine, like the later move of Louis XIV and his successors to Versailles, would create a certain disjunction between the crown and its frequently fractious capital, eventually leading some sections of conservative opinion to take the old saying *Paris n'est pas la France* to mean that Paris is not part of a 'true France'. Yet there was no question of moving the capital elsewhere, even if the war had changed it in significant ways. Although the population was now partly recovering from the loss of the nobles and wealthier bourgeois who had moved to safer havens in the early part of the century, the absence of the court meant the decline of luxury trades such as goldsmiths and tapestry makers, as well as the bankers and businessmen who had fed off it. So Paris, even as its economic role was diminished, became 'a city of civil servants and lawyers'.[10] Which would create an ongoing tension between the court as the political capital and Paris as the administrative capital.

Nevertheless, even if the cost had been high, the results at the national level were broadly positive. The erosion of the feudal system in which the country had for so long been entangled would enable the progress towards a more unified and centralised state. And after all, France had now emerged as the largest, most populous and – so long as it could maintain peace and husband its resources – the richest state in western Europe.

*   *   *

Among the writers of the later Middle Ages there are two who stand out, both for the value of their work and as contrasting figures from opposite points of the society: the court writer Christine de Pizan and the poet of the lower levels of society François Villon.

Christine de Pizan is mainly of interest today for two reasons, the first being that she was doubtless the first female writer in Europe to live by her pen. The daughter of an Italian physician and astrologer who had been appointed to serve the court of Charles V, she married a royal secretary in 1379, but when he died of the plague in 1389 soon after her father had also died, she was left with the demanding problem of providing for her mother as well as her three children – and this at a time when women had no separate legal status and were taken to be the property of their husbands. Since in that period writers were dependent on patronage, she needed a great deal of initiative and energy, but she remained close to the court and produced dedicated works for many important figures, the Duc de Berry and Henry IV of England among others.

She was remarkably prolific, but the text that has drawn increasing attention is *Le Livre de la cité des dames* (The Book of the City of Ladies), which has been hailed by Simone de Beauvoir among others as a founding feminist text. It is in effect a retort to Jean de Meun's continuation, from around 1280, of the original allegory of love by Guillaume de Lorris entitled *Le Roman de la Rose* (The Romance of the Rose). Reacting against de Meun's presentation of women as lightweight and coquettish, while writing in the same allegorical style and implicitly referencing Augustine's *City of God* in her title, she produced her reply. Citing as examples the qualities and achievements of notable women from past history and the Bible, she imagines a city of women in contrast to what was then, in its values and emphases, a city of men. In effect, she is implying that the depreciation of women – as indeed its compensatory opposite, the excessive idealisation of

Woman – is a function of the gross inequality within society between women and men. To that extent, she is looking beyond her own time.

As for François Villon, the greatest lyric poet of his time, he was not exactly your average man of letters, and what we know about his life comes mostly through his encounters with the law. Born poor and left fatherless at an early age, he took the name Villon from the canon of a church in the Rue Saint-Jacques who brought him up. He completed his education at a then very riotous Sorbonne in 1452. In 1455, he becomes involved in a brawl, kills a priest and flees Paris, but is pardoned and returns, only to be involved with his companions the following year in the theft of 500 gold crowns from the sacristy of the Collège de Navarre. He flees again, returns to Paris in 1461, is arrested after being denounced by one of his accomplices and put in jail at Le Châtelet. Freed after a year on condition that he must pay back his share of the 500 crowns – 120 crowns, which he no longer has to hand – he is involved with his companions only three weeks later in a fight in which a notary is wounded with a dagger. When the notary files a complaint, Villon is arrested, tortured, and condemned to be hanged and strangled, as is reflected in his 'Ballade des pendus' (Ballad of the Hanged Men), but on appeal he is banished from Paris for ten years and disappears from view. We do not know quite when he died or whether he ever had any kind of formal occupation, but he was evidently a man at odds with his society – and possibly to some degree with himself, since in 'La Ballade des menus propos' (Ballad of Small Talk) he concludes, 'I know it all, except myself'.

The first impression given by Villon's verse is one of authenticity. If he writes of thieves in the taverns, or a plump prostitute in a brothel, or the slow horror of the condemned man imagining his hanged body being left dangling on the gibbet for the birds to peck at as it moulders into meaninglessness, you have the sense that he has been there. And this has tended to feed the romantic view of Villon as being a forerunner of the so-called *poètes maudits* (accursed poets) of the late nineteenth century, the idea of the poet as outsider, the isolated authentic voice marginalised by a false culture. But Villon did not spend those years in the Sorbonne doing nothing. He was a sophisticated practitioner, who was clearly familiar with the poetic tradition and with the courtly assumptions that accompanied it – so familiar, indeed, that he could play games with it. It is not simply that in a poem such as 'Fausse beauté qui tant me coûte cher' (False beauty which costs me so much), addressed to the plump prostitute Marthe, he can bury an acrostic of the names François and Marthe, as well as using a double rhyme, but that in a longer, complex piece such as *Le Testament* (The Will), he can treat the tradition seriously or satirically as he pleases. It is this combination of authenticity and artistry that gives his poetry its lyrical power – and gives backing to such memorable lines as *Je meurs de soif auprès de la fontaine* (I die of thirst beside the fountain), or the haunting refrain *Mais où sont les neiges d'antan?* (But where are the snows of yesteryear?)

Paris in the Renaissance:
Humanism and Holy War

....

As the largest city in Europe with up to three hundred thousand inhabitants, Paris in the sixteenth century was bound to reflect the significant challenges and conflicts inherent in what was in effect a turning point in Western civilisation. Not only Christendom, but the traditional view of the cosmos was threatened by this heresy of Copernicus that the earth moved around the sun. And if that made the earth seem smaller, the centrality of Europe itself came into question with Columbus discovering America, Vasco da Gama reaching India and Magellan becoming the first to circumnavigate the globe – were the strange 'barbarians' discovered there a threat to civilisation itself? More immediately, the spread of printing, by encouraging a greater exchange of ideas in society, was threatening the control over opinion of both Church and throne. It made possible the publication not only of heretical books but of seditious tracts and lampoons. More subtle, but even more subversive, was the decline of Latin as the language of both religion and the law – and French would become the official language by the Ordinance of Villers-Cotterêts of 1539. With Luther's German translation of the Bible being the first that people could read in their own language, the truth would no longer have to be in Latin. And with other studies revealing mistakes in translation from Hebrew into Latin coinciding damagingly with attacks on the worldliness of the papacy and the corrupt practices involved in the selling of salvation, the Church and the official tradition were under attack from all sides.

This overhanging uncertainty about fundamentals conditioned the geopolitical context that the French kings would have to try to negotiate. For it would create a split in western Europe whereby Spain became the staunch defender of Catholic orthodoxy, England became Protestant and France, torn in both directions, would have its own wars of religion. The competition between the three countries was personalised by the fact that their three long-serving leaders in the first part of the sixteenth century – François I, Henry VIII and Charles V of Spain – were direct contemporaries and it was complicated by the fact that Charles had also become Holy Roman Emperor. Moreover, in the larger world that was now opening up, this competitive new age of nations was already turning into the age of empires. Portugal, first in the field, was building up an overseas empire including Angola and Brazil, leading to Lisbon becoming the premier port for spices and slaves, Spanish conquistadores were devastating the empires of the Aztecs and Incas in South America, while Sir Francis Drake and others were moving towards creating the East India Company and laying the basis of a British empire. So how were the French kings to fare in this often brutally competitive new world?

Inevitably, given both its importance and indeed its quite vulnerable geographical position in relation to Spain and the forces of the Holy Roman Empire, Paris would become an echo chamber for these interlocking background conflicts and more directly, in the latter part of the century, the stage on which they would be murderously played out.

On the chilly morning of 15 February 1515, the Parisians were hopefully awaiting the solemn entry of the new king. It had not been a great century so far, they might have been reflecting, since it began with the collapse of the Notre-Dame bridge, which saw the provost of merchants and the magistrates clapped in prison for incompetence. Then, of course, there was that student burnt at the stake for ripping the host from the priest in the Sainte-Chapelle in 1503, not to mention those two deadly outbreaks of the plague in 1500 and 1510 – though they had at least tried to make changes at the Hôtel-Dieu by replacing the canons with eight elected lay governors and, in order to avoid infection, by ensuring that patients suffering from syphilis were treated elsewhere. The late king, Louis XII (r. 1498–1515), who had just died, it was said, from his exertions at the age of fifty-two to produce a son and heir with his eighteen-year-old bride Mary Tudor, had been a fair and sensible ruler except for one thing. Just like his predecessor Charles VIII (r. 1483–98), who had died at the age of twenty-eight after absentmindedly hitting his head against a door lintel, he had kept going off chasing dreams of military glory in Italy only to suffer repeated humiliating defeats and pile up debts that citizens had to pay for.

So, it was hoped that this new king, François I, would be an improvement and it would be a real boon if he chose to make his residence in Paris, since no king had done so for almost eighty years. It would bring back the luxury trades, provide more jobs and raise wages if the court and its wealthy clientele came in to the city. It would also tend to make the city safer if there were royal troops on hand to deal with villains such as Esclaireau, Jean de Metz and the like, whose gangs of robbers and looters were terrorising the city at night. Certainly, the municipal authorities had spared no effort or expense to charm this new king, for the city seemed everywhere festooned and garlanded for this official entry into Paris of François I as king of the realm. And indeed, if contemporary accounts vary slightly on points of detail, they all agree that this was a most elaborate and lavish occasion.[1]

In fact, this solemn processional entry of the new king was already something of a tradition for the French monarchy. So François, having already been anointed and crowned at the cathedral in Reims, had first gone to the Abbaye de Saint-Denis to participate in a ceremony and to pay his respects to the sepulchres of his predecessors. He now came on to meet the welcoming party of city representatives waiting outside the Saint-Denis gate: the provost of merchants and the magistrates in their crimson velvet robes, together with representatives of the various trades – always eager to seize the opportunity to submit formal requests. Here, as in the city itself, there were stands for observers to view the proceedings, and all were deeply impressed by this charming new king sitting smilingly astride his horse. He was young, he seemed extraordinarily tall and strong, he wore a glittering silver doublet decorated with diamonds and a fine feathered hat, he was handsome and appropriately kingly with a commanding royal nose. Moreover, his colourful retinue of diamond-studded princes and nobles followed by four hundred archers was magnificent to match.

Once that stage had come to an end with the formal handover of the keys, the drawbridge was lowered and the procession entered the city, to move down the Rue Saint-Denis, cross the Seine and pass in front of the royal palace on the Île de la Cité in order to proceed to the cathedral of Notre-Dame. All along the route the streets were lavishly decorated, there were more stands for spectators, there were arches with welcoming messages, there were allegorical or historical scenes like living paintings being enacted in open spaces, with cheers and the sound of trumpets everywhere. The Parisians, deprived of a monarch in residence for so long, were enchanted by this gracious young king, making his horse rear upon two legs and tossing coins into the crowd on both sides as he passed. However, the tone quietened when the procession arrived at Notre-Dame and clerics emerged bearing crosses, candelabras and censers. The bishop then formally addressed the king, to demand whether he would solemnly agree to guarantee the privileges of the Church and then, the royal assent having been readily given, the central doors opened and the procession entered the cathedral for the celebratory mass.

Afterwards, having granted pardons in cases presented to him and consulted with representatives of the university, he engaged in a tournament with obvious relish and talent. Finally, he and his attendant nobles were the guests of honour at a magnificent banquet in the royal palace on the Île de la Cité. After which it only remained for the city to round off the celebrations by presenting him, on the eleventh of the following month, with a gold statuette of Saint Francis on a plinth representing a salamander, the king's chosen personal emblem. It had been a wonderfully successful royal visit.

And after all that . . .? François made it clear that he intended to make his residence down by the Loire. He would not settle in Paris until 1528, thirteen years later – and even then it would only be because he was short of money.

Louis XII had famously said of this cousin who was going be his successor: 'this big young fellow is going to ruin everything', and it began to look as though he might be right.[2] Brought up in a cultivated provincial court by a widowed mother whom he much revered, François was a lover of women and quite infatuated with all aspects of chivalry, whether the glory in battle and the knightly jousting or the idealised romances, the ceremonial dances and the formal courtesy in behaviour. The trouble was that, in a world facing fundamental changes, he was tending initially to face backwards. He was young, of course, as he was intelligent and curious, but he was also rather innocent and lacking in guile. And he would pay the price.

Having learnt nothing from the self-glorifying and ultimately fruitless activities of his two predecessors in Italy, he started in great style by leading his cavalry to victory at the Battle of Marignano, following which – according to the legend at least – he had himself knighted by his own leading chevalier Bayard. He then visited the Pope, who proposed an agreement whereby François would take over the right to make clerical appointments in France, but at the cost of giving back to Rome the revenues of the large and rich French Church. When the throne of the Holy Roman Empire fell vacant, which opened up the dream of following in the steps of Charlemagne, he manoeuvred to get elected but in the game of bribing the electors – and according to one source he laid out two tons of gold – he was outplayed by the younger and more diplomatically astute Charles I of Spain.[3] Thereafter they were mortal enemies and, since François failed to get Henry VIII's support at the famous meeting of the Field of the Cloth of Gold, the resumption of war became inevitable. In the course of a second attempt to capture Milan in 1525, François suffered a devastating defeat at the Battle of Pavia, was taken prisoner, to be released after some fifteen months and allowed to return to France in exchange for his two young sons. The whole humiliating affair had all but drained the treasury and it is doubtless because it was still in the process of being resolved that François decided that he needed to move permanently into Paris.

Despite these early misadventures and although the conflict with Charles V would continue intermittently, François's reputation rests essentially on his contribution to the development of the Renaissance in France and on his ambition to make Paris the cultural capital of Europe. Always fond of reading, he had been influenced by his mother's love of Italian Renaissance art and been introduced by his tutors to this new humanist trend which, while not straying outside the Catholic ambit, was shifting the focus of interest from God to man. He was also tempted to put his own stamp on this city, now the largest in Europe, which was already beginning to see itself as unique. It was largely in this century, as has been seen, that the mythical origins of the city were being proclaimed and it was variously viewed in glowing terms as the new Rome, the great ornament of the world, or the summit of civilisation – although Henri II would spoil the picture a little in 1554 with his perhaps slightly overstated complaint that the city was full of 'muck, manure and filth'.[4]

The most visible of François's contributions were the new buildings which he enabled. He had of course been active down in the Loire valley, modifying the châteaux of Amboise and Blois and creating the enormous Italianate fantasy of Chambord, but he certainly left his mark on Paris. He remodelled the Louvre, which he had chosen as his residence, getting rid of the medieval fortress, filling in the defensive ditches and ordering the construction of a handsome new wing adorned by sculptures. He commissioned a new Renaissance city hall, the Hôtel de Ville designed by the Italian architect Cortone and built for himself a hunting lodge in the Bois de Boulogne with an enamelled brick façade – though the former would be damaged by fire during the Paris Commune of 1871 and the latter destroyed during the Revolution. To create more space for development, he removed a number of unused royal buildings such as the Hôtel Saint-Pol and the Hôtel de Bourgogne, and took advantage of the sale of a large area by the debt-ridden monastery of Sainte-Catherine to provide sites for those wishing to build luxury homes. This marks the rise of the Marais and several of these buildings have now been turned into public assets, such as the Musée Carnavalet, the museum of the history of Paris, the Bibliothèque de l'Histoire de la Ville de Paris and the Musée Cognacq-Jay, devoted to Paris in the Enlightenment period.

If François did not quite succeed in enticing the influential humanist Erasmus to come to France, he did bring Leonardo da Vinci, who brought with him the *Mona Lisa* and other canvases to feed the royal collection that would end up in the Louvre. With the same lavish financial inducement, he also brought the flamboyant goldsmith and sculptor Benvenuto Cellini, who produced pieces for the royal buildings and gave impetus to the work of the 1,400 goldsmiths working in the city from mid-century onward.[5] Other artists he patronised included Rosso Fiorentino and Andrea del Sarto, while he also employed agents in Italy to seek out high-quality works – not only artworks but also rare books and manuscripts for the royal collection. For there was now taking place a great expansion of printing and engraving in answer to rising demand – the Rue Saint-Jacques alone had some 160 bookshops – and access to knowledge was a fundamental issue in relation to which François aspired to play a leading role.

As royal librarian and cultural adviser, he employed Guillaume Budé, a humanist scholar who had served him as secretary and diplomat. Budé was a multi-talented individual who had produced, among other things, a translation of Plutarch, a dictionary of ancient Greek and a treaty on numismatics. On his advice, François founded the Collège Royal, designed to provide lectures of the highest quality by the best available specialists in the basic subject areas. It was to be free to the public, free of doctrinal interference and free of any degrees or examinations. If the humanists were delighted, the Sorbonne, which saw its complaints about the lack of official theology disregarded by this independent institution, was not. However, the Collège endured and is today the highly prestigious Collège de France, a distinguished independent research centre situated close to the Sorbonne, providing lecture series open to all.

The tension between conservative Catholic opinion and the new humanist current might have been more easily managed had there not been the third and increasing trend of opinion stemming from the Reformation, that of the French Protestants, or Huguenots as they tended to be called – after the Swiss-German *Eidgenossen*, meaning confederates. Already in 1523, a monk called Jean Vallière had been publicly burnt at the stake because of his Protestant convictions and it became formally forbidden to teach or preach Lutheran doctrine three years later. Despite that, in 1533 the rector of the university himself, in an inaugural lecture apparently influenced by Jean Calvin, had advocated the cause of the Reformation, after which he was forced to flee while Calvin himself had to make his getaway over the rooftops of his college. Yet within the year there were tracts attacking the mass appearing all over the city, including one nailed to the king's own bedroom door. Although generally tolerant, François decided that, since he was after all the head of a Catholic monarchy, he was obliged to clamp down on the organisers – which he did by having them arrested and executed. Despite this, the reformist cause was gain-ing ground among those of the educated middle class such as notaries, doctors and printers and, in particular, among the students. In 1542, the works of Luther, Calvin and Étienne Dolet were banned. This was followed by the public burning of Calvin's publications, the arrest of preachers on grounds of heresy and by the execution of Dolet, who was burnt at the stake along with his books on the Place Maubert in 1546.

If it was dangerous to be viewed as Calvinist or Protestant – especially since they could be represented, if generally mistak-enly, as being republicans and therefore the enemies of a Christian kingdom – it could be uncomfortable to be in the middle, as a humanist. One such figure, who also had other ways of enraging official opinion, was the unique François Rabelais. Although not everything is known about his life, he was a monk, a physician and a highly learned humanist who also knew what was going on, since he had acted as agent for the Du Bellay brothers, diplomats involved in royal affairs, who became his protectors – as also did François I himself who, on receiving a complaint that Rabelais's writings were heretical, said they were merely playful and of no offence to God or king.[6] Much of the writing is indeed playful, but he is in effect using an elaborate take-off of medieval romances, with their allegorical stories and fantastical tales, to poke informed fun at the society around him. The result is an extraordinary blend of comical exaggeration, sophisticated wordplay, pastiche, satire, scatological humour and exuberant invention that has dazzled other writers from Jonathan Swift to James Joyce.

The images of Paris with which he leaves the reader are typical enough. In his *Gargantua*, he takes over an existing tall tale about 'a great and enormous giant' called Gargantua and confronts him with this society of tiny people. At one point, annoyed at being followed around by these little creatures underfoot, he sits down on top of Notre-Dame cathedral and thinking, when they will not go away, that they are waiting for him to stand them a drink, he decides to stand them a drink with a vengeance. He undoes his trousers and – in a blend of the grotesque with comic precision – floods the Parisians down below, 'drowning two hundred and sixty thousand, four hundred and eighteen of them, not counting women and little children'. After which, he mentions his sexy derivation for the name of the city, plays with the bells of the cathedral and takes them to string around the ears of his equally gargantuan mare. No explicit message emerges from all this sophisticated buffoonery, unless it be the motto of his imaginary commune: 'Do what thou wilt', but he is implicitly satirising institutional religion and mocking the late medieval world almost to the point of blowing it up from within. He was certainly sailing close to the wind and in dying in 1453, six years after his protector François, he perhaps departed in good time.

Less fortunate was Petrus Ramus. An academic who felt that his own traditional studies at the Sorbonne had been worthless, he discovered – in the bookshops rather than at the university – the new humanist culture based on such figures as Plato, Galen and Euclid. He started his own college, but soon incurred the wrath of the rector of the Sorbonne, Pierre Galland, who, on discovering that his syllabus included a materialist such as Lucretius, accused him of 'vomiting pus and poison'.[7] Nevertheless, since this new wave of Renaissance culture was becoming unstoppable and turning young men away from a Sorbonne largely tied to theology, Ramus was appointed in 1551 to a chair of philosophy at the prestigious new Royal College. Not only did he attract enormous audiences – so many tried to crowd into his opening lecture that several people fainted and had to be carried out[8] – but he proceeded scandalously to 'undermine the honour that had been bestowed upon him, by lecturing not in Latin but in French'.[9] He published widely, became a highly influential figure and was protected for a while by the Cardinal of

Lorraine, but since his criticism of Aristotle was deemed by Galland to amount to an attack on both religion and the kingdom, he was forbidden to teach philosophy. For Ramus, as for others, the pressure would only increase.

Paris did not suffer as many devastating epidemics in this century as it had in the previous two, but there were still regular outbreaks of *la peste* (the plague), the generic term that was used – often for lack of a precise diagnosis – including severe ones that claimed thousands of victims in the 1560s and 1580s. The city authorities were now taking over control of the disease from the Church authorities and, whereas doctors had previously only visited hospitals occasionally, they were now becoming interns. As of the epidemic of 1531–3, public announcements were trumpeted at street corners forbidding the use of the rather notorious public hot baths and the practice of keeping pigs in the city, while doctors who had treated plague victims were forbidden to treat other patients on pain of hanging. General hygiene was marginally improved by insistence on the requirement that each house should have a latrine while, if contagion was not yet well understood, distancing and masking were recommended. Whether by these measures, by banning public shows or by taking over the costs of treating the poor, at each attack of the 'plague' the city did what it could.

Unfortunately, the medical faculty of the university, along with the Church's resistance to surgery, was of no great help. Discoveries in the field of anatomy were in fact being made but being made the hard way by academics such as André Vésale, who had to organise surreptitious midnight visits to the public gibbet at Montfaucon, or the charnel house of the Cimetière des Innocents to acquire corpses for investigation and demonstrations in teaching. One problem was that surgery, in that it involved physical and not just mental activity, was deemed to be low grade and non-academic. That, plus the lack of knowledge, meant that surgical activity developed out of the work of barbers, so that its practitioners were recognised by the university on condition that they dealt only with surface complaints. When François I created a faculty of surgery in 1544, the university refused to recognise it. However, the Parisians themselves were seeking help from these barber-surgeons and by the end of the century there were around a hundred of them. The first dissection theatre would open in 1608, but the university's tie to theology and its inability to accommodate new knowledge were such that it would reject William Harvey's discovery in 1628 of the circulation of the blood and it would not formally admit surgery into the university until 1750.[10]

François I's son, Henri II (r. 1547–59) lacked his father's charm, was seen as melancholy and was more strictly religious. Although married since the age of fourteen to Catherine de Medici, the niece of two different popes, he was drawn rather towards the older Diane de Poitiers, who was something of a mother figure. As rulers go, he was a competent administrator, who carried forward François's building programme so that Paris, with its new wing of the Louvre, its new churches and its new private palaces, was gradually acquiring the look of a real Renaissance capital. He also rationalised the organisation of the state in various ways and is credited with introducing the idea of protecting a technique or process by having it patented. However, he also gave a more rigorously Catholic slant to the throne by dismissing a number of his father's ministers and by drawing close to the Duc de Guise.

In his first year on the throne, Henri set up the Chambre Ardente (Fiery Chamber), said to be a darkened room lit only by torches, in which reformists or suspected Protestants were tried for heresy, seen as treason. Certainly, the reformist movement was growing, with the Huguenots more and more openly declaring their faith, to the increasing anger of many Parisians. In 1557, several hundred worshippers met in a house in the Rue Saint-Jacques, only to be attacked by an angry mob when they were leaving, with the result that over a hundred of them, many from the nobility and some forty of them women, were imprisoned at Le Châtelet. Undeterred, some five thousand Protestants met in May of the following year to sing hymns in the meadow known as the Pré-aux-Clercs, in the Saint-Germain area, which was then closed off. When four city councillors appealed to the Parlement for clemency towards the Protestants, they were arrested. Three retracted under torture, but Anne du Bourg – the man who had committed the other heresy of implicitly criticising Henri's marital infidelity – held out and was publicly hanged and then burnt at the stake before a large crowd in 1559.

These events in Paris mirrored the crisis facing the country. It was not simply that they indicated the threat of a religious civil war, but that they coincided with the larger problem of maintaining peace with the neighbouring powers, England, Spain and the Holy Roman Empire. For, as Babelon points out, the Parisians were constantly in fear of being invaded during the sixteenth century, a factor that naturally sharpened their worry about internal strife.[11] It was obviously the job of hereditary monarchs to manage these situations and Henri had tried to do so in the standard manner, firstly by making a truce with Spain and, secondly, by creating marital linkages with both England and Spain through the double marriage in June 1559 of his sister Marguerite with the Duc de Savoie and his daughter Élisabeth to Philippe II of Spain. And it was all to be wrapped up memorably with public celebrations including feasting, balls, masquerades and a jousting tournament in which Henri intended to compete in person. While the standard practice was for the king to act as judge rather than to participate, he was highly practised in jousting, and it would be useful to demonstrate to the Duke of Alba and other distinguished Spanish guests in particular that he was a man to be reckoned with.

As usual for such celebrations, the city was lavishly decorated and over several days the wedding mass and subsequent festivities had proceeded successfully, so it remained only to round off this grand occasion with the traditional knightly display of gladiatorial jousting. Triumphal arches had been set up at either end of the Rue Saint-Antoine, the street paving had been removed and replaced by sand for the horses to gallop on, there were stands, dressed in rich tapestries emblazoned with coats of arms, for spectators on either side and in the royal box sat Diane de Poitiers, Catherine de Medici and the dauphin's new bride Mary Stuart. At every window, on balconies and on the roofs of the houses, the people responded excitedly to the sound of the trumpets as the cavaliers on their splendid steeds, also in their mailed costumes, entered in turn to salute the royal box and then the ambassadors, before pounding forward with their long lances aimed threateningly towards the opponent in the attempt to unseat him.

The tournament was coming to its end. Henri had held his own in two of his three bouts, but it was past midday in the midsummer sun and he was clearly extremely hot in his magnificently decorated metal armour – now in the Louvre. On the third and final assault of his last bout, both wooden lances broke, and the judges duly declared a draw. When Henri insisted on a replay to settle this last bout, the queen and even his young opponent the Comte de Montgomery pleaded with him to desist, but Henri impatiently rejected their pleas and went back to his starting position to await the joust on his ominously named mount *Le Malheureux* (Unlucky One). Once again, they thundered towards each other, and the ash lances broke again, but this time, since Henri had forgotten to pull down his visor, a long splinter penetrated deep into the corner of his left eye. He suffered in agony before dying ten days later.[12]

This development now left the throne and Catherine de Medici in an extraordinary position. Her life had been strange enough so far. Orphaned within weeks of her birth, taken hostage by rebels at eight, threatened with death during a siege at ten, married off to Henri II at fourteen with the consummation being supervised by François I himself, she had found herself sidelined by Diane de Poitiers and of interest to her husband essentially as a source of male heirs to feed the line. Yet even there she had failed for the first decade of the marriage, so that the new king was the frail François II, aged only fifteen, while waiting in the wings was the next son Charles, aged nine – a situation, she decided, that now required her to take over as regent. These anomalies did not go unnoticed by the great humanist Montaigne, who loved Paris 'warts and all' but was sufficiently aware of a gathering storm to decide that it was wise to 'keep your boots on', just in case. Especially since, introducing a novel and dangerous notion of cultural relativism, he also suggested that, just as Europeans were baffled by the habits of 'barbarians' in newly discovered countries, so those same people might be baffled by grown-up Europeans who chose a child as their ruler – especially since that child was himself then ruled not by a man but by a woman. For 'we all dismiss as barbaric any practices that are unlike our own'.[13]

Catherine's memory lingers in Paris with the Tuileries Gardens, named after the workshops of tilers who used to be occupy the area. The Château des Tuileries which she commissioned would be burnt down in 1871, but the delightful gardens in which she gave lavish receptions, and which stretch from the Place de la Concorde to the Louvre, still give pleasure to Parisians and tourists today. However, her main preoccupation was with sustaining this now vulnerable Valois dynasty while managing the ominously rising religious tensions. In 1560 she issued, through the frail François II, who lasted only seventeen months, the first in what would be a series of Edicts of Pacification in an attempt to find doctrinal compromises between Catholics and Protestants. However, this brought protests from the Pope and Philippe II of Spain, who had direct influence at court through the Catholic faction of the Duc de Guise. A second edict authorising Protestant worship, though only outside town boundaries, created further outrage and, after the massacre of seventy-four Protestant worshippers in the town of Wassy by the troops of the Duc de Guise, the Protestants took up arms in their turn under the Prince de Condé. Which would condemn the country to intermittent religious war from 1562 to 1598.

A further edict of 1563 guaranteed the Protestants freedom of conscience while denying them public worship in Paris, but the largely Catholic population still reacted violently. Although the war now raged outside Paris for several years, the city was besieged in 1567 by a Huguenot army under the Prince de Condé, which ended with a temporary peace in 1570 and further limited concessions to the Protestants. It was now that Catherine made the mistake of thinking that the marriage of her daughter Marguerite to the Protestant Henri de Navarre of the Bourbon line, the future Henri IV, would help to bring about reconciliation of the two sides. Although Henri would later say that her situation was so difficult he was surprised she had managed as well as she did, her failure to appreciate the absolutist nature of the religious passions involved led to the Saint-Bartholomew's Day massacre in the stifling month of August 1572.[14]

Since a number of priests had condemned the marriage, feelings already ran high among the people, and the presence of over a thousand well-dressed Protestant visitors during the three days of the celebrations added to the resentment. While there are contrasting views as to who was responsible at different stages for the sequence of events that unfolded, the violence began with the wounding of the leader of the Protestant representatives, the admiral Gaspard de Coligny, on 22 August. Next day, Catherine tried to reassure the Protestants, who were blaming the Guise clan, but the damage was done; the Spanish ambassador was siding with the Guises, the city's bourgeois militia was lining up with the Catholics and the two sides were heading excitedly for trouble. When Catherine and the unstable young Charles IX met with advisers, was it from fear of a Protestant coup that they agreed to a countercoup? At all events, an organised attack on the leading Protestant visitors was planned and timed for dawn the following morning, 24 August.

It began to the orchestrated tolling of several church bells with an assault on the Protestant guests in the Louvre that would rapidly merge with a general popular uprising targeting local Protestants as well. The wounded Gaspard de Coligny was murdered by the king's Swiss Guards, thrown out of an upper window and desecrated by members of the crowd below, who cut off his head, hands and genitals before dragging his body to the river, pronouncing a mock judgement on him for heresy as they went. This set the tone for much of the slaughter that would continue over the next few days. The small daughter of Nicolas Le Mercier, after seeing both of her parents massacred, was 'baptised' naked in a pool of their blood and warned against ever becoming a Huguenot. A bookbinder was burnt alive on a pile of his own books, in mimicry of the punishment for heresy.[15]

Although there was an orgasmic ferocity to much of the killing, there was often also a religious, ritualistic aspect to it. The largely illiterate rioters, whose information about the world came from priests such as Simon Vigor, who taught that Church and king were indissoluble and that Protestants were heretics, were suffering from shortages and fearful of invasion or the breakup of the society and their belief system. They were also driven by their belief in signs from above, such as the miracle that took place on the very morning of the murder of Coligny, when a white hawthorn – the thorns being suggestive also of the Crown of Thorns – suddenly burst into flower out of season and for the first time in four years in the Cimetière des Innocents.[16] They were killing for the fusion of Church and throne, killing for Christ and king and, when the killing feast was over and the blood of around two thousand murdered heretics was no longer reddening the river, their loyalty and heroism were duly rewarded. Charles commissioned two medals celebrating their achievement on behalf of God and throne, while the Pope marked the event with a jubilee and a commemorative medal featuring an avenging angel smiting the Protestant heretics with a sword.

The total number of those killed in Paris may have around three thousand, but since the violence had spread widely throughout the country, there may also have been ten thousand or more victims elsewhere. Some Protestants prudently switched their affiliation, while others – not including Petrus Ramus who hid in a bookshop but was hunted down – escaped to England or Switzerland. If this weakened the Protestant side, it hardly solved the dynastic problem that Catherine – who may well have had some complicity in the massacre – had been trying to manage. For Charles IX died within two years, the next in line had also died by then and the throne fell to the last possible candidate, Henri III. Henri was intelligent and sophisticated, but he had perhaps spent too long in Venice; he lived a colourful, gay lifestyle surrounded by his bevy of flamboyant young *mignons*, or 'darlings', and he neither presented quite the right image of a Catholic king to the public nor offered the guarantee of a Catholic successor. This meant that the next in line would be Henri de Navarre, whose marriage had precipitated the massacre in the first place and who had reclaimed his Protestant status after switching to avoid being murdered. Accordingly, the Duc de Guise set up a Ligue Sainte (Holy League), financed by the king of Spain, to ensure that heresy would be rooted out and that the kingdom would remain Catholic, which led in turn to the final stage in the wars of religion, covering the ten years from 1584 to 1594.

Since this obviously placed the new king Henri III in a difficult position, he tried for the first few years to placate the Catholic faction. However, he lacked credibility with the Parisians and he was forced to flee to Chartres in 1588 by a popular uprising aimed at deposing him. He arranged successfully to have the Duc de Guise and his cardinal brother assassinated, but the Catholic reaction was such that he was forced into the camp of Henri de Navarre, who was marching on Paris. But as he awaited at Saint-Cloud for events to resolve themselves, he was attacked in his turn in 1589 by an infiltrating Dominican monk – and the king declared on his deathbed that Henri Navarre was now the legitimate king of France, Henri IV. With the joint royal and Huguenot troops, which were only about half of the combined forty-thousand men of the bourgeois militia plus Spanish-funded mercenaries, Henri now tried to take Paris. He blockaded the city, destroying the windmills on the outskirts which provided the flour for bread, but failed repeatedly over eight months, first with a surprise attack on the Left Bank, then with a direct assault, then with a night attack and finally, in January 1591, with a disguised attack by soldiers dressed as peasants leading donkeys carrying flour in an attempt to trick the defenders into letting them through the Saint-Honoré gate.

As it happened, the siege itself had largely won the battle for him. For the price of basic foods in the city had risen tenfold and there were reports of people eating uncooked meat from dogs, animal guts that had been thrown into the gutter, even rats, mice or whatever could be eaten. Some thirty thousand people died in this famine. Also, to the weariness of war that this engendered was added a growing resentment of the Spanish participation in this dynastic struggle. In this situation Henri IV, a shrewd and humane individual who was doubtless all too aware of the damage done to the nation's image of itself and of the extent of the rebuilding facing him if he did become king, decided to employ a peaceful, political approach to the problem. He negotiated with the other side, paid all the bribes that were necessary, and made a deal whereby the Parlement would issue a decree declaring him the legitimate sovereign, while he in return would renounce his Protestant faith and formally embrace Catholicism in the sacred basilica of French royalty at Saint-Denis. As he said famously, 'Paris vaut bien une messe', or 'If what it takes to win Paris is to attend a mass, it is well worth it.'

Having formally embraced the Catholic faith at Saint-Denis and been crowned in the cathedral at Chartres, he made a triumphal entry into Paris in 1594 and made his way immediately to Notre-Dame for the mass. He was scrupulously careful to observe every element of the elaborate ritual of Catholic monarchy, including wearing white and employing the royal touch to cure the king's evil, or scrofula. Outside the cathedral he had arranged for his supporters to distribute tracts declaring a complete amnesty in these terms: 'His Majesty, wishing to reunite all his subjects and have them live in peace and friendship, especially the bourgeois and inhabitants of his good city of Paris, desires and intends that everything that has happened since the beginning of the troubles should be forgotten.' The message was widely welcomed by an exhausted city.

For if Paris, as Henri understood, had shocked the world – including even the Russian tsar Ivan the Terrible – with its Saint-Bartholomew's Day massacre and the murder of its own king, it had also shocked itself. How could this city, with its mythical self-image as the greatest in Christendom, have come to that? Even with Henri IV wiping the slate clean, how could those horrors now be forgotten? It was a delicate problem which would be resolved, as Babelon suggests, by a convenient distinction whereby Paris was of course still the 'queen of cities' and the summit of civilisation, but it was just that the Parisians themselves could tend sometimes to be just that little bit fractious or frolicsome – and with that subtle distinction the mythification could go on even more merrily than before.[17] This fiction suited Henri well enough and, by 1598, he could start to reintroduce some balance into the nation with the Edict of Nantes, which granted Protestants the right to practise their faith in various areas – even if he still felt it prudent to exclude Paris.

The Seventeenth Century: Towards the New Rome

....

Henri IV, or 'good king Henri' as he was dubbed, was a welcome change for most Parisians. Unlike his weak and rather over-refined predecessors, he was a soldier who had come to power the hard way and who operated, as he said memorably, 'with weapon in hand and arse in the saddle'. He had directly seen the chaos and misery inflicted by the religious wars, he was able to talk to people on their own terms and he wanted, as he again said famously, 'to ensure that every peasant in the kingdom had a chicken in his pot of a Sunday'. He was popular also because of his reputation as a *vert galant*, or a 'gay old spark', although it should be said that of his many mistresses the one he really loved and trusted as adviser was Gabrielle d'Estrées, whom he intended to marry but who died in childbirth in 1599 at the early age of twenty-six. Above all, he was popular with the people, despite any lingering doubts about his religious affiliation, because he got things done. And for the royal entry of his second wife Marie de Medici, the citizens of Paris – never knowingly outbid in the matter of genealogical inflation – declared officially on the basis of an admittedly indirect connection with the Greco-Roman god that he was the *Hercule gaulois*, the Gallic Hercules.

Indeed, the task of reviving an exhausted nation may well have looked Herculean and to give himself room for manoeuvre Henri first had to establish peace. Having achieved this internally through the Edict of Nantes, he achieved it externally by defeating a Spanish army supporting the Holy League and securing the Treaty of Vervins of 1598, which he followed up by settling an ongoing dispute with the Duchy of Savoy through the Treaty of Lyon of 1601. He then had to renew the apparatus of government and for this he brought in his old comrade-in-arms and Protestant nobleman the Duc de Sully, who was regarded as a bully but a formidably efficient and hardworking one. To make significant improvements, Henri needed both to eliminate the accumulated national debt and to have access to a steady supply of new money, a task which Sully and his new finance team set about energetically. They made economies by streamlining – abolishing certain traditional posts, eliminating tax abuses or attacking embezzlement – and created a flow of new money by means, notably, of a *paulette* tax. Named after its inventor Paulet, this was a tax whereby the holder of a public office, by making an annual payment of one-sixtieth of what he had originally paid for it, could make it hereditary. There would be disadvantages to this in the longer term, clearly, but in the meantime it provided a steady annual income for the crown.

So, having provided the money, how to spend it? Although Henri was particularly interested in beautifying Paris, he obviously had plans for the country as a whole and, together with the energetic Sully, he set in train a whole range of improvements. Forests were protected, swamps were drained, roads and bridges were constructed and a whole network of canals was planned. Various projects were undertaken to develop agriculture and the silk industry was introduced, along with other luxury trades such as glassware. Of particular interest to Henri, the army was reorganised, with a new cadet training school, a revised pay structure, a more powerful artillery force and a strengthened set of border defences. However, there was also the challenge, especially since Paris was starting to grow again and would do so throughout the century, of developing it as an appropriate capital city. It was a challenge that would persist through the continual building and rebuilding that would mark this new seventeenth century.

For Paris at this time was not the ordered entity that we think of as a city today. It was more like a random conjunction, on the one hand of villages where people lived much as they might have in the country, with a back yard or garden in which they kept chickens, rabbits and even pigs – even if these no longer roamed the streets to run into the legs of a prince's horse and cause his death – and, on the other hand, of the often quite sizeable estates of nobles and clerical institutions. The city was still smaller, of course – you could have walked across from north to south in little more than half an hour. But you would need a sharp sense of direction, for beyond the general order imposed by the river, the old Roman crossroads and the surrounding defensive wall, there was little logic to the layout and only a few of the streets had their names engraved in stone. You might also need sharp elbows since – as can still be seen from a street such as the old Rue Quincampoix in the 1st arrondissement – the streets were narrow, crowded and ill-paved, with carts and horse-drawn carriages rattling over the stones, hawkers crying invitingly to advertise their wares, and everything bathed in the stench of the legendary Paris mud. Above all, you would not choose to walk at night, since there was no street lighting, although even in daylight you would not wish to wander into one of the dozen or so *cours des miracles*, dens of thieves, tricksters, beggars and apparent cripples who, when you were no longer looking, were suddenly and 'miraculously' cured.

It was in this context that Henri's first venture in improving Paris assumes its significance. The first stone for a new Pont Neuf had been laid by his predecessor in 1578, but the civil war had intervened and there had also been technical problems. Henri now rethought the project, used a tax on wine to finance it and produced a bridge that was novel in that it was destined solely for wheeled traffic and pedestrians and had no houses on it. If this provided a splendid view up and down the river not just for Parisians but for Henri himself as he looked over from the Louvre, it caused a problem for the civic authorities, who were banking on raising money through leasehold rents from the goldsmiths and similar merchants who traditionally lived on bridges. However, he solved this problem in the grand manner by combining the bridge with a new triangular Place Dauphine close by on the Île de la Cité, which he named in honour of his six-year-old son, the dauphin, and for which he specified uniform brick and stone façades.[1] There would then be an attractive little garden between the Place and the midpoint of the bridge itself, as well as a new Rue Dauphine driven straight up through the Left Bank to open up that area to further development.

The Pont Neuf was, of course, built of stone, unlike so many former wooden bridges, which were regularly swept away by the river, and it had attractive ornamental features such as the hundreds of different mascarons, or grotesque faces, on the keystones of the arches. It was the first to cross the whole breadth of the Seine since previous bridges connected either bank only with the Île de la Cité. It was also the first to have pavements, called *banquettes* since they were raised well above road level to protect pedestrians from the traffic, and these were enhanced by half-moon-shaped alcoves at the top of each stone pile, where merchants and tradesmen would begin to set up their stalls. In fact, the bridge soon became popular almost as a central city funfair, where – so long as you kept an eye out for pickpockets – you could be diverted by open-air shows, magicians, quack doctors or acrobats while you were viewing the wares of confectioners, flower sellers or whatever. It was here that the *bouquinistes* of the quays originated, after booksellers set up stall in the half-moon alcoves and provided readings to tempt passers-by. However, the new bridge, which would have its equestrian statue of Henri IV, also had a symbolical value in that it drew the city together after all the divisions and, as one writer points out, this was the bridge that solemn royal processions would cross on their way from the Louvre to Notre-Dame, as it would be the bridge the revolutionary tumbrils would cross on their way to the guillotine in what is now the Place de la Concorde.[2] For all that, since Henri was nothing if not practical, it also had attached to it the first functioning water pump drawing water from the Seine for distribution to the city and named the Samaritaine, which in turn would give its name in 1910 to the iconic Art Nouveau department store – recently modernised – on the Right Bank.

Henri also played his part in the continual improvement of the Louvre, which had been the favourite royal residence of his predecessor and where he regularly stayed himself, often throwing lavish parties. He commissioned the Grande Galerie, the wing of record length for the period which stands alongside the right bank of the river and which at that time connected to the Tuileries Palace of Catherine de Medici – he had in mind, obviously, that this would combine well with the new Pont Neuf. He also started a tradition of encouraging high-quality arts and crafts by inviting practitioners to have their workshops on the ground floor of the building. A more significant tradition that he also started was that of the *places royales*, meaning squares either built by the king or built to honour the king, combining the strict uniformity of line and brick and stone façades with a statue of the reigning monarch. To the Place Dauphine, which had the first such statue – they had previously perhaps been considered too much at risk of defilement – was now added in the Marais district the magnificent Place Royale, known since 1800 as the Place des Vosges, which contains the house of Victor Hugo, today a museum.

Henri, of course, had broader preoccupations. He was interested in France's place in the world, stimulated as he was by the accounts of de Vitré, who had explored the Far East, and Malherbe, who had circumnavigated the globe. After a failed attempt to set up trade with Japan, he set up a company in Dieppe on the model of the English East India Company founded by Queen Elizabeth I in 1600, although it was sixteen years behind England in sending out ships. Again, although the country had recently been free from actual violence, there could be no real escape from the religiously coloured politics of Europe at this time and, in 1610,

Henri was threatening to go to war against the Holy Roman Emperor over the disputed succession to the Rhineland principality of Jülich-Cleves-Berg. Indeed, he was on his way to discuss the matter with the ill Sully when his coach was caught up in a traffic jam in the Rue de la Ferronnerie – in today's 1st arrondissement – and a young, red-bearded assassin dressed in green jumped on the running board and killed him with three stabs of a knife.

Was this thirty-two-year-old provincial assassin, called François Ravaillac, who had been refused entry to both the Jesuits and another religious order on the grounds that he was 'prey to visions', just a disturbed Catholic zealot? Or was he being manipulated by the scheming Duc d'Épernon, who happened to be in the carriage along with Henri, as the balance of opinion suggests?[3] For it transpired that Ravaillac had been housed in Paris at the home of d'Épernon's mistress, and it was d'Épernon who would ensure that the full power of the throne would pass, not to a regency council as Henri had laid down, but to the newly crowned Queen Marie de Medici herself, thus opening the door to Spanish Catholic influence.

For twelve days Ravaillac was repeatedly tortured as he continued to claim that he was divinely inspired to prevent Henri from making war on the Pope, and on the thirteenth he was taken to a crowded and expectant Place de Grève – now the Place de l'Hôtel de Ville – for his public execution. This was conducted by the official executioner with the usual scrupulous thoroughness. As a preliminary, Ravaillac was tortured once again, with burning sulphur, followed by molten lead, followed by boiling oil, all of which eased the task of pulling off the flesh with the large pincers. There then followed the prescribed punishment for regicides of being hung, drawn and quartered. This was proceeding correctly until one of the four horses pulling his arms and legs in opposite directions fell badly and had to be taken out, whereupon a young knight saved the day by gallantly offering his own mount. This horse was so powerful that it almost immediately pulled away a thigh to public acclamation, which forced the executioner to begin prematurely to hack away the remaining limbs while the priest earnestly intoned the last rites to the regicide. After which the remains were joyously torn or chopped to pieces by the crowd until nothing identifiable remained for the exasperated executioner, as prescribed, to reduce to ashes.

Henri, who had survived seventeen plots to kill him and observed the Saint-Bartholomew's Day massacre, would hardly have been surprised by any of these events. Nor, since he was all too aware of the thread of violence in French history, would he have been surprised that his remains and those of other kings would be torn from their tombs at Saint-Denis during the Revolution. However, he might have been mildly surprised that one of three skulls auctioned for a mere three francs at the Hôtel Drouot in 1919 should be claimed to be his, and that this would lead to an elaborate scientific controversy following the four-hundredth-year commemoration of his death in 2010 – though he might not have been at all surprised to find it inconclusive.[4]

If intermarriage between leading families was an understandable way of trying to maintain peace across Europe, it had its drawbacks. Marriage became a business transaction, with brides being required to provide a political advantage, a dowry, a capacity to produce male heirs and an acceptance of the king's 'official mistress'. To expect them also, after the assassination of two kings in a row, to be competent regents to small boys – Louis XIII became king at the age of eight, Louis XIV at the age of four – was asking a lot. It was asking too much of Henri IV's second wife Marie de Medici, whom he had married because he was in dire need of money, whom he liked as little as she liked him, and whose seven years as regent turned into lurid melodrama. She was not as bad as she has been painted, but she was lacking in judgement, she was too dependent for advice on her self-seeking Florentine favourite Concino Concini, she squandered public money, she reversed Henri's policy of keeping the militantly Catholic Spain at a distance and she weakened the throne. She made an enemy of her son by refusing to let him take over when he came of age, causing him to have Concini murdered and herself sent into exile, where she fomented several revolts. It required all the skill of the chief minister Cardinal Richelieu to manage this situation, until she ended up banished in 1631 and died destitute in exile.

Nevertheless, Marie patronised the arts, brought to Paris the painters Gentileschi and Rubens, and left her mark on the city with the Palais de Luxembourg, a handsome palace in the French style but with Italianate sculptural features, which today is the seat of the French Senate. With its popular public gardens and large pond where children sail model boats, it is in some sense the Left Bank's answer to the Tuileries Gardens and complements the creation of the Jardin des Plantes, one of the oldest natural history museums in the world, associated with such figures as Jean-Baptiste Lamarck and the Comte de Buffon, which opened to the public in 1640. At this time also, the increase in population led the throne – in a foretaste of the organised urban planning of the late nineteenth century – to combine with private enterprise to develop the Île St-Louis with ordered housing in the manner of the Place Dauphine. This island was in fact an artificial creation formed by the junction of the Île Notre-Dame with a small island used as cow pasture and duly named the Île aux Vaches. The result was an extremely select enclave for a wealthy clientele, a perfectly preserved piece of seventeenth- and eighteenth-century Paris, so distinct and select indeed that at the beginning of the twentieth century some residents tried – unsuccessfully, believe it or not – to declare independence. Nor should Richelieu's own contribution be forgotten, for he built for himself a most attractive palace close to the Louvre, which he left to the throne before his death in 1642 and which we know today as the Palais-Royal. With its cool arcades and its gardens, it offers relief from the traffic in the grey Rue de Richelieu as well as housing the Conseil d'État, or High Court, and the Ministry of Culture.

Richelieu would have been pleased to see justice and culture rubbing shoulders in this fashion, since his conception of his role as controlling chief minister was highly inclusive. For he was much more than the ruthless villain popularised by Alexandre Dumas's *Three Musketeers*, the cold, scheming Red Eminence in his scarlet cardinal's cloak. He was certainly feared and hated by many – and not exactly loved by his 'master' Louis XIII – but he was shrewd, dedicated and courageous, with a wider range of interests and sympathies than the legend suggests. It is necessary to look at the situation confronting him at both the national and European levels and to ask less whether he was hungry for power than what he did with it. At the national level, after dealing with a dysfunctional regency, he had to find a way of consolidating the power of the throne not only against the nobles but against a Huguenot rebellion supported by the English, involving the siege of La Rochelle in 1627, which he successfully led himself. He even, at a time of Catholic revival, had to protect the throne against the Church itself, since the larger European interests of the Vatican could conflict with those of the French state – especially at a time when one strand of the confused Thirty Years War that devastated Europe between 1618 and 1648 was the struggle with Catholic Spain.

Richelieu's answer to these pressures was to create an early model of the modern centralised nation state, if a highly author-itarian one with censorship of opinion and punishment for dissent. This aimed to get rid of any lingering feudal elements and create a coherent national order based theoretically, as Simone Bertière states starkly, on 'centralisation, absolute verti-cality of top-down decisions, abolition of intermediate levels of government, and the sacralisation of the State to the detriment of civil society'.[5] However, Richelieu was a highly cultivated indi-vidual whose vison went beyond narrowly political issues. He built up an extremely large and valuable art collection and had an enormous library, which eventually passed to the Sorbonne. He was a great patron of the theatre and, in addition to religious and political works, he wrote several plays. More significantly, he was not only the *proviseur*, or chancellor, of the Sorbonne, but the founder of the famous Académie Française, the body designed to protect the purity of the French language and arbitrate on cultural matters, whose forty members – the famous '*Immortels*' – sit within the Institut de France on the Left Bank. In short, Richelieu was already seeing the country not simply in political terms but more broadly as a culture or civilisation controlled through the state.

Richelieu was thus preparing the way for the absolutist dream of a totally ordered monarchical society that would characterise the France of the *Grand Siècle*, this developing 'great century' that would be associated mainly with Louis XIV. It implied a controlled order everywhere, in the organisation of society into the 'Three Estates' of nobility, clergy and the rest, in politics, in the language, in personal life, in the arts, in the theatre, in architecture and attendant garden design. As Mousnier puts it: 'unity, simplicity, regularity and order triumph in architecture as in society, as in the State ... Everything proceeded from the King, who embodied the State, and everything was responsible to the King.' Obviously, this was an aspiration rather than the reality and, by ironic juxtaposition on the same page, Mousnier reminds us of the insanitary state of things at this time by telling us that 'Louis XIII relieved his bladder in the corner of the room, the more refined Richelieu drowned the ashes in the fireplace and great ladies did not hesitate to satisfy their needs in their box at the theatre. Whence the lavish use of perfumes and the abundance of sweet-scented flowers.'[6] Yet rather than mocking or diminishing the aspiration, that explains the need for it and the extent of its ambition.

* * *

'To study the Grand Siècle without speaking about the theatre would be a heresy,' declares Pierre Mélèse, and it is true that the best-known and most representative art form of the Grand Siècle is the theatre.[7] However, as compared with London, which had some ten theatres at the start of the century, Paris only had low-level travelling farces before the 1630s and would have no more than five theatres operating at any one time during the course of the century. Nevertheless, the 1630s saw the emergence of a generation of more sophisticated literary dramatists, including Pierre Corneille, vying for production by two permanent theatres, the Hôtel de Bourgogne and the Théâtre du Marais. And over the course of the century the theatre becomes, as another writer puts it, 'an entertainment fit for a polite and refined society'.[8] Which is not to say that the spectators were all perfectly behaved. There were those who were more interested in observing the more prestigious nobles in other boxes than in watching the play; there were younger elements who offered gratuitous and loud advice to the actors, not to mention the gentleman who on one occasion brought along a large dog which forced its way into the dramatic action.

Nor is it to say that actors themselves were seen as respectable, partly because elements of the Church frowned on the theatre despite the royal patronage and would deny the sacraments to actors unless they renounced their calling. Even the great actor-manager and comic dramatist Molière was denied Christian burial until his widow pleaded with the Archbishop of Paris and obtained a grudging and conditional exemption.[9] If that disapproval may have limited audiences to some extent, another factor was that, because of the lack of street lighting, performances were given not in the evening but in the afternoon between two o'clock and four-thirty – whence our word matinee. Any necessary lighting was by candlelight. The theatre would be rectangular, with *loges* (boxes) for the aristocrats and the *parterre* (pit) for the middle classes, which would have seating on either side but where most of the audience could be standing. There would also be spectators

on the stage, where there would be a single set, or several places
– garden, salon or whatever – within one set. Both staging and
costumes were more realistic for comedy, which tended to deal
with contemporary situations so that costumes could readily be
tailored to the social standing of the characters. However, for tragedies set in ancient Greece or Rome, as most were, since there
was an implied assumption that their world was akin to that of
the 'new Rome' that was monarchical France, actors could be
dressed in vaguely Greco-Roman costumes while wearing a wig
and a plumed hat.[10]

The first performance of a play was often given at court, or in
a private theatre such as that of Cardinal Richelieu, and there was
a great deal of patronage, with playwrights duly including in a
foreword or even in the script itself a lavish tribute to the donor.
The patronage may have limited the scope of the playwright, even
if it made for a unified aristocratic and upper-middle-class audience, but for various reasons it was essential. The audience in
relation to the city's population was comparatively small, there
were neither evening performances nor performances every day,
there was the disapproval of the Church and there was the fact
that dramatists were only guaranteed financial returns from the
first run. Even Corneille, who earned a great deal from his many
successes, complained about earnings and retired earlier than
expected. Also, as the great Jean Racine warned his son, playwrights did not enjoy a high social standing, which is doubtless
why, even if he invoked religious scruples, he settled for the steady
income and the status of court life as historiographer to the king.[11]
The theatre faced real constraints at this time, and it is remarkable that it achieved so much.

It is an indication of the monarchical society's concern in the
seventeenth century with redefining itself culturally as well as
politically in terms of order, that there should have been such a
concern with the *règles*, or rules, and so much learned commen-
tary on them – Richelieu, even though he was Corneille's patron,

submitted his famous tragicomedy *Le Cid* to the Académie Française for formal evaluation. For the hallmark of French classical tragedy, which makes it quite unlike Elizabethan drama or Romantic drama, is the preoccupation with observance of the rules: the 'three unities' of time, place and action. These were derived from Aristotle – not entirely accurately, since he is essentially concerned with unity of action and pays little attention to the other two – and implies strictly that the action should take place at one particular spot and the timeframe should not be longer than twenty-four hours. Since such concentration of a dramatic action inevitably raised questions about plausibility, there was much discussion about *vraisemblance*, or verisimilitude. Another concern was that of *les bienséances*, or the proprieties – there was some concern, for example, that Corneille's heroine Chimène, in *Le Cid*, spoke more freely about her feelings than a young lady should. However, that is a secondary consideration that stays with its own time.

The essential feature of this strict concentration on the unities is that it brings about a particular type of tragedy, one in which physical or historical action is subordinated to a psychological conflict portrayed at a moment of crisis. In perhaps the greatest French classical tragedy, Racine's *Phèdre*, this basic conflict combines with a masterly use of the alexandrine verse form to produce what is in effect a powerful dramatic poem. Unhappily, that tends to make it too specific and too dependent on knowledge of the language to travel easily across borders, as evidenced by the National Theatre's presentation of it in London in 2009, with Helen Mirren in the lead role. It was not just that the audience could not feel the horror of Phèdre's guilt at her passion for her stepson as could a seventeenth-century Catholic audience believing in original sin, it was that the free-verse translation could not come anywhere close to the contained, refined power of Racine's original. Nor, it has to be said, does Corneille's opposite assertion of the power of the heroic will over passion commend itself to the modern audience. So, inevitably perhaps, it is the great comic dramatist Molière, since he is dealing with human foibles familiar to audiences in any society at any time, who travels most easily.

'We are highly obliged to Your Majesty for the honour He has done us, and entirely edified and delighted at the care Your Majesty wishes to take of the conduct of His affairs,' said the Chancellor Pierre Séguier, for something to say after Louis XIV had made the startling announcement that, at the age of twenty-two, he intended to operate without a chief minister and govern the country on his own.[12] That roundabout, third-person mode of address is typical of the way in which language reflected the relationship of king and subject. For royalty was real at this time, rather than the decorative historical relic it may often seem today. It is not even enough to say that Louis became king at the age of four years and eight months, it is rather that he was recognised as such at that point, since his kingship came with his birth as part of the divine purpose. As Archbishop Fortin de la Hoguette advised him in his *Catéchisme Royal* of 1645: 'you are the image of God in all His domain. Let Your Majesty never forget that he is both a man and a deputy God here below.'[13] This heavy dual responsibility had dictated the two sides to the education of the child king. The first was religion and Louis performed many ceremonial acts at a very early age, laying the first stone of the Val-de-Grâce church and washing the feet of the poor at the age of six. The second was war and, by the age of seven, he was attending the gathering of troops for the war in Flanders and playing war games in a specially built model fort in the garden of the Palais-Royal.

The psychological effect of such an upbringing on an orphaned child, emotionally over-dependent on his mother and Regent Queen Anne, can be imagined, especially since he had a ringside seat for observing the strains of dealing with war abroad and rebellion at home. In the longer term, France would come out well from the Thirty Years War, since the chief minister Cardinal

Mazarin was able in 1648 to sign the advantageous Treaty of Westphalia, which put an end to the supremacy of the Holy Roman Empire by recognising the independence of the German states and the Netherlands, and which, in effect, marked the start of Spain's decline. In the short term, however, since Spain had withdrawn from the negotiations, a separate and costly Franco-Spanish conflict would drag on and the Parisians were already seething. Mazarin was deeply unpopular since he was of Italian extraction, was thought to be enriching himself excessively and was suspected of being the queen's lover – an accusation spread all over the city by thousands of often obscene pamphlets dubbed *mazarinades*. He was especially unpopular with the middle classes because of the series of stiff taxes he was imposing to pay off the war debts, while the Parlement de Paris – an unelected legal body, but accustomed to offering views on legislation – already felt diminished by the tough new line taken by this upstart foreigner. So, when Mazarin rejected a request from the Parlement to cancel the offending taxes, Paris exploded into a full-scale insurrection, with hundreds of barricades being flung up on the Île de la Cité, around the Halles and in the university area on the Left Bank.

This resulted in the frightened young king, at the age of eleven, having to be smuggled out of Paris along with his mother in the middle of an icy January night in 1649. Anne had decided to make a stand against the rebellion and Paris now found itself besieged by an army led by the Prince de Condé. This ended inconclusively with the Peace of Rueil two months later, but that was only the first phase of the five-year rebellion known ironically as the Fronde – after the sling that children used to play war games or smash windows. For after the middle class it was the turn of the princes of the blood and the nobility to get into the game. The ambitious Condé switched sides and Paris, having been the actor in this drama, would now become merely the theatre of a damaging and confused struggle for control of the throne and the country. With Mazarin having at moments to take a back seat or even leave the country, it fell to Anne to manage the situation. She had Condé arrested, then under pressure had to release him and, at one point, in February 1651 she was preparing for a second flight from Paris when her plan was betrayed and an angry crowd stormed the palace, insisting on seeing for themselves whether the king was there. When she said the king was asleep, they refused to believe her and forced her to take them to his bedroom. Which led to a second unnerving encounter with his Paris subjects for the young Louis as he slept – or pretended to sleep – with dozens of rioters tramping around his bedroom.

By taking advantage of division among the rebels, and by playing up Louis's arrival at his majority at the age of thirteen in September 1651, Anne managed to isolate Condé temporarily. But he left Paris only to gather his forces, and he was back to fight a battle against the royal troops in the Saint-Antoine area just outside the wall of the sealed city in July 1652. He was actually on the point of losing the battle when cannon fire from the Bastille – directed, farcical though it may seem, by the Grande Mademoiselle, Louis's own first cousin the Duchesse de Montpensier, who had aspired to marry him – fell upon the royal troops and, simultaneously, the city gate was opened to allow the rebel army to enter. And with the gates now closed again but against the royal army, Condé found himself in control of the city. He summoned both the civil and the religious authorities to the Hôtel de Ville to outline his proposals, but he handled the audience badly, ran into serious opposition and the meeting developed disastrously into a confused massacre that left around a hundred people dead. If Condé was still able to set up a provisional government, he was now hated by Parisians for provoking this disaster and for causing them to be besieged by the royal army still outside the city walls.

Mazarin, cannily keeping out of the picture, advised Louis to offer a complete pardon to any participant who would lay down his arms. Condé refused but was able to leave the city with his remaining followers and go off to join the Spanish, which enabled

Louis to re-enter the city to cries of joy from the volatile Parisians. The Fronde had been a fiasco. It had sought to bring together in one cause the conflicting interests of different social groups, as well as the opposed interests of individual leaders. If this failure did not immediately strengthen the absolutist monarchy, it at least left a certain tired acceptance that there was no substitute in sight – and it would be almost a century and a half before Paris rose again. As for what the young king learnt from the fiasco, it was not to trust either the volatile Parisians or the nobility. He learnt that he would have to keep sole control, that doing so would require him to work eight hours a day and that he must protect his kingship by glorifying it with statues and great buildings in order, in the manner of Augustus, to turn this capital city into the new Rome. Meanwhile, he moved for greater safety from the Palais-Royal to the Louvre.

Yet there was one last lesson that he had to learn. He had fallen in love with Mazarin's niece, Marie Mancini, and it was clear that they were very close. Mazarin himself was initially flattered by the relationship and the possibility of marriage, but Anne pointed out sharply that, if only because of Mazarin's own unpopularity, the Paris public would be up in arms again. In any event, there was no political advantage to such a marriage. The king finally yielded to her argument but wept as he saw Marie to her carriage for the last time as she was sent away with her sisters to La Rochelle. 'You're in tears and yet you're supposed to be the master,' she is reported to have said to him.[14] He was heartbroken and corresponded with her secretly until the gossip started and he had to stop and finally recognise the obvious, that kings did not marry for love, but for the advantage of the kingdom. Which meant, predictably enough given the war with Spain, that he would marry the infanta Maria Theresa.

Following Mazarin's death, Jean-Baptiste Colbert was Louis's chief minister – he did not have the title, but since he gradually acquired responsibility for every department except war, he was in a powerful position to pursue the twin goals of absolute monarchy and the transformation of Paris into the 'new Rome'. His initial task was to clean up the finances and try to repair the situation whereby the nobility paid no taxes, the Church and the upper bourgeoisie had many exemptions and the burden therefore fell disproportionally on the poorer elements of society. The inequality was written formally into the tripartite organisation of the kingdom into nobility, Church and third estate but, with Louis's support, he made a spectacular start by having the superintendent of finance, Nicolas Fouquet, condemned for embezzlement and dispossessed of his fine château of Vaux-le-Vicomte, which served as a warning to other abusers of the tax system. He also took a strongly *dirigiste* approach to the economy by helping to set up new industries, improve manufacturing standards, develop overseas trade and promote exports. But he was also intent, the more so since he knew of Louis's doubts about Paris, on turning the capital into this new Rome.

Anne herself had celebrated the birth of Louis by commissioning François Mansart to design the impressive Val-de-Grâce church, with its handsome dome inspired by that of St Peter's in Rome. Colbert now set in train the whole set of improvements – presented as glorifying the monarchy – that would continue into the next century. He worked closely with the highly effective Nicolas de La Reynie, the head of the Paris police force, who did much to organise and clean up conditions in the city. So, while there was the new colonnade of the Louvre designed by Claude Perrault or the addition to the Tuileries of the north pavilion designed by Louis Le Vau, there were also new creations designed to serve social ends. One was La Salpêtrière, transformed by Libéral Bruant from an old saltpetre, or gunpowder factory, into a hospice for poor or mentally disturbed women, renowned at the time for its architecture but also unfortunately for its rats, which has since been transformed again into the Pitié-Salpêtrière, now the largest hospital in France. Another was the splendid Hôtel des Invalides, also by Bruant, a commanding building with its wide frontage, its large esplanade, its fifteen courtyards and its church with its handsome gilded dome, which provided a home for retired and injured soldiers and now houses the army museum.

However, the two improvements which did most to change the atmosphere of the city were not buildings. One was the replacement of the old defensive ramparts enclosing the city, now that France was secure following the Treaty of Aix-la-Chapelle of 1668, with the wide tree-lined avenues known as the *boulevards* (not a place for playing *boules*, but from a Dutch word akin to bulwark), which would transform Paris from a fortified city to an invitingly open one. The other was the novelty of public lighting by hanging lanterns, which would gradually be introduced throughout the city and which, impressing foreign visitors as it did, would invest Paris with the title of *Ville Lumière*. But in addition, Colbert, like Richelieu, had strong cultural interests. He possessed a fine private library, supported writers and painters, became a member of the Académie Française and created a number of specialised cultural academies, covering inscriptions and medals, sciences, architecture and opera, in addition to establishing the Paris Observatory. It was a systematic attempt to create the great monarchical society.

And now that the city was becoming larger, safer and with new sights to see, there was a growing demand from the many who did not possess their own coach for vehicles for public hire. The *fiacre*, or rented cab, had been introduced by Nicolas Sauvage in 1617 and, since his premises were in the Rue Saint-Martin in a building with a sign saying Saint-Fiacre, which reflected the local reputation of a Carmelite friar from a neighbouring monastery, he decided to call the new cab *le fiacre* – which explains the oddity that the Paris cab should derive its name indirectly from an Irish saint called Fiachra. It has to be said, however, that the *fiacre* also

developed a less than saintly reputation as a convenient venue –
for Bonnie Prince Charlie in his Paris days, among others – for an
illicit amorous encounter behind drawn curtains. This is celebrated in 'Le Fiacre', a 1939 version of an old *Belle Époque* song
rendered with smooth sophistication by Jean Sablon, in which the
yellow cab is clip-clopping along with suggestive squeals coming
from within when an old gentleman walking nearby realises that
the female voice is that of his wife, tries to stop the cab and is run
over. Whereupon his wife checks that her husband is dead, tells
her lover Léon that there is no need to hide any longer and asks
him to give the driver a fat tip of a hundred cents as a reward –
and the cab goes clip-clopping happily on again as before.

The *fiacres* of that period were regulated officially and were of
two kinds, a two-horse carriage for up to eight persons costing
seven *livres*, and a four-horse carriage for ten persons and for an
agreed distance costing twelve *livres*. This was already a step
towards an affordable public transport system, and in 1662 Louis
did indeed authorise by letters patent the introduction of a much
cheaper service of carriages on five designated routes at fixed
times. The carriages bore the arms of the city, had attractively
uniformed drivers and were an immediate success. The man
behind this proposal – not too surprisingly perhaps, since he was
a scientist and inventor as well as a philosopher and theologian
– was Blaise Pascal, backed by several financiers.[15] However, the
society was not yet ready for such a democratic venture, the Paris
authorities made it ultimately non-viable by forbidding its use by
'soldiers, pages, lackeys and other common workers', and it finally
collapsed in 1677. There was now a return to rented vehicles, the
two most familiar being the *crenan*, named after a partner of
Pascal, and the *vinaigrette*, developed by Pascal himself. The
crenan was a horse-drawn, two-person cab prefiguring the nineteenth-century type of *fiacre*, while the *vinaigrette*, which took its
name from the small decorative silver box containing perfume
made with aromatic vinegar for use when travelling, was a lighter,

man-drawn vehicle suitable for the single, perhaps more fastidious passenger.

Despite all these improvements, Louis did not get over his distrust of Paris. With the death of his mother Anne, any emotional tie to his childhood in the city had gone. He envisioned a place where he could feel safe, impose his vision of kingship and keep those unreliable nobles under his control. He moved officially in 1671 to Versailles and over the next forty-four years, until his death in 1715, he would only return to Paris for short official visits twenty-four times.

Paris versus Versailles

....

At first sight, eighteenth-century France appears to be a paradox. Here was a large and powerful country, the centre of Enlightenment thought and the envy of Europe with its sophisticated salons, its glamorous lifestyle and its trend-setting fashions, a nation so dominant that French would become the language of culture and diplomacy. How was it that it could crumble so dramatically in the Revolution that occurred before the end of the century? While the answer is not a simple one, the paradox itself was already contained in germ in the long reign of the outstanding representative of absolute monarchy, Louis XIV, the *Roi Soleil*, or Sun King, himself. For the paradox is perceptible in the principal areas of his activity, most obviously perhaps in the domain of war, which led to so many paintings of a victorious Louis on horseback on the battlefield.

Military dominance was naturally a central condition of *grandeur*, or greatness, at that time. War was to some extent inherent in the complex system of family connections between the rulers of different countries and Louis had trained for it from an early age. He developed a large standing army and began in 1667 by attacking the Spanish Netherlands, the present-day Belgium, which he claimed as his wife's inheritance, but withdrew with the gain of Lille in the face of a Dutch–English–Swedish alliance. Five years later he invaded Holland and found himself up against a larger coalition in a war that dragged on for six years, but from which he emerged with the gain of the Franche-Comté and with the sense that he had become the greatest ruler in Europe. He now boldly annexed Strasbourg but provoked a Grand Alliance of European powers with which he engaged in a nine-year war and from which he emerged in 1697 with his territory intact, but with the obligation to recognise William III as king of England as well as with serious debts. Finally, there was the long and disastrous War of the Spanish Succession (1701–14), which achieved little more than to plunge the country into further massive debt and to turn public opinion heavily against the throne. Louis had good reason towards the end of his life to tell his grandson that he had been too fond of war.

The same paradox informs the personality of the man himself. 'He was the hardest man in the world to get to know', according to his contemporary, the Marquis de Sourches.[1] He was a healthy outdoor type who could also be a fussy indoor type, a man who could happily hunt all day in all weathers, but who also had the 'vapours' from possibly depressive episodes. He was a man of feeling who wept easily, as was common enough at the time, and who could be kind but often ruthless. He was a basically timid man who had no real taste for public ceremony or display but who performed in public constantly and ballet danced solo at Versailles. He was hardworking and intelligent but not an intellectual, was therefore cautious in dealing with advisers more informed than himself, and often secretive and calculating in dealing with others. Yet none of this is surprising in one conditioned since early childhood to bear the awesome responsibility of being a semi-divine great king, a new Augustus for the new Rome. He was in the extraordinary position of being not only the lead actor in a great monarchical drama, but the creator of the drama and the director of it on a daily basis. If others saw him as egocentric, 'a man for whom nobody counted except in relation to himself', as his contemporary the Duc de Saint-Simon put it, it is hard to see how he could have been anything else.[2]

Given this ambivalence, as well as the heavy pressure that his unusual situation placed upon him, the creation of Versailles begins to seem not only understandable but necessary. He needed not only to direct his own play, but to create his own theatre, a glamorous alternative Paris where he would be free from those dangers that had traumatised him as a child, where he could keep a close eye on those untrustworthy nobles by attracting them with the chance of a government post or a retainer, where he could be the absolute ruler on his own terms. It was a formidably expensive venture, obviously, and it would take time even for thirty thousand workers to build such a large administrative complex. He initially had only his immediate ministerial advisers and security staff on site while many of the government agencies remained in Paris, and it would be eighty years before the operation was completed with the transference in 1762 of the ministries of war, the navy and foreign affairs. Meanwhile, the foreign ambassadors were in Paris, as were many government officials and, like Colbert, not everyone was pleased. For one thing, it was a three-hour journey by carriage to and from Versailles and for another, not every courtier, as Saint-Simon reported, was delighted at being 'stuck permanently in the countryside' away from the more varied delights of Paris.[3]

The impossibility in practice of Louis extricating himself from Paris is brought out by the *affaire des poisons*, and the more sharply since it connected with his celebrated love life, which had three levels of activity. There was the queen, formally respected, who had four children, three of whom died in infancy. There were four successive *maîtresses en titre*, or official mistresses, during the reign, with an acknowledged place at court: Louise de La Vallière, who had two legitimised children by the king; the Marquise de Montespan, who had six of her seven children similarly legitimised; the Duchesse de Fontanges, who died shortly after childbirth; and finally the Marquise de Maintenon, who became Louis's secret morganatic wife. Then at different times there were twenty or more unofficial mistresses, some of them possibly apocryphal. Of course, François I had established the custom of having an official mistress and Henri IV had recognised two of his children by mistresses. Even so, the court of Versailles, so long as surface dignity and formal religious practices were preserved, developed and normalised this situation to the point of creating a kind of royal commune – to the point indeed, as Madame de Montespan's husband kept failing to see the normality of the king repeatedly impregnating his wife, that Louis told Colbert to 'keep a close eye on that madman'.[4]

Beneath the smooth surface, of course, Versailles as the locus of absolute monarchy was a highly competitive playground, for women as well as men. In the opinion of a close observer at the time, there was not 'a single lady of any distinction who did not want to be the King's mistress', since she did not see it as 'an offence to God or her father or her husband to be loved by her King'.[5] But it was not just for the glamour, for the glamour was the face of power and they were often being pushed forward by their family, for whom, as Bardèche puts it, 'the favour of the king was only worth having if it could be turned into actual prizes'.[6] As a prime example of such prizes, Madame de Montespan's father became governor of Paris, her brother became governor of Champagne, a relative of her husband became governor of Guyenne, her friend the Duchesse de Richelieu became lady-in-waiting to the queen and another friend became governor to the dauphin – everybody benefited, in fact, apart from her naive 'madman' of a husband.

The atmosphere was made the more competitive by the king's habit of conferring titles and advantages to the legitimised children of his mistresses, which created envy among his own legitimate relatives. So it was a considerable risk for a woman, who was always in a dependent position in any case, to try to attract the favour of the king. She could be ridiculed, or picked up briefly and dropped, then ignored. Even if she became the *maîtresse en titre*, it would be hard to retain his interest if she was pregnant most of the time. She would be living in an atmosphere of gossip and suspicion. She could be humiliated, rejected and end up in a convent, like Louise de La Vallière. In short, the concentrated world of Versailles as seen from below was vastly different from the innocent vision Louis had of it from above – as he was about to learn from the so-called *affaire des poisons*. Paris had already administered two reality shocks during his childhood, and it was about to administer another.

It began with the sweet-faced, blue-eyed little Marquise de Brinvilliers, the daughter of the governor of Le Châtelet, Dreux d'Aubray, who lived in Le Marais with her spendthrift husband the marquis. She was also the mistress of an ex-officer and adventurer with the saintly name of Sainte-Croix (Holy Cross), an alchemist and healer who dealt in poisons on the side. Tired of failing to control her husband's profligacy and afraid of being reduced to poverty, she decided to correct the situation. With the help of Sainte-Croix and a servant, she arranged for her father to be fed slight doses of poison over a period of eight months, after which he died in agony. However, her share of the inheritance did not last long, so she felt obliged to treat her older brother Antoine, who had succeeded his father as governor, to the same medicine. Yet once again the returns from the operation were disappointing and, since there was presumably nothing to gain from killing her spendthrift husband – which might in any case have drawn unwelcome attention to herself – she decided that she had no alternative but to apply the same treatment to her younger brother François, who duly died in his turn in 1670.

When the poisoner-lover Sainte-Croix died unhelpfully of natural causes in 1672, incriminating documents were found that revealed the scale of this operation of supplying the so-called *poudre de succession* (succession powder) designed to provide clients with a more efficient means of succeeding to an inheritance. With her involvement revealed, the marquise fled to England, but was condemned to death in absentia. She later returned secretly but was discovered to be hiding in a convent in Lille and was brought back under guard to Paris for a regular trial.

At this point the affair began to take a political turn, as it emerged that the marquise was related to several aristocratic Paris families and that she and Sainte-Croix had been close to a protégé of Colbert named Pennautier, the tax collector and financial controller for the French clergy – whose career, it was whispered, had also benefited from several convenient and unexpected deaths. He was arrested, then released after the marquise, before being beheaded and burnt to ashes, declared him innocent. But since she had apparently hinted that certain high-placed figures were also involved in such poisonings, there were rumours of other strange deaths, of strings being pulled and large bribes paid.

With the affair now turning into a damaging scandal, Louis insisted that it be cleared up. But it only got worse with the arrest of a Mlle de la Grange and a priest named Nail for poisoning and forgery in 1676, for this revealed a whole shadowy subculture, mostly in the northern and eastern parts of the city, of servants, ex-soldiers, failed priests and all sorts of marginals making a living as alchemists, forgers, soothsayers, abortionists, dealers in love potions, poisoners, or whatever. La Grange and Nail were executed, but the cases kept mounting and a significant moment came with the arrest of an abortionist who passed by the name of La Voisin and who dispensed 'succession powders' to members of the aristocracy against a background of occult practices such as black masses and the ritual murder of babies. La Voisin and others arrested were now revealing numerous names of clients ranging from high-placed courtiers to the maid of Madame de Montespan or the dramatist Racine, who was claimed – mistakenly in fact – to have poisoned his mistress, the actress Thérèse Duparc. Horrified by the way all this could reflect upon the court, Louis set up a special tribunal to expedite matters, thirty-six of the accused were executed – including La Voisin, burnt alive at the stake – and thirty others suffered either banishment or imprisonment.

However, the greatest shock was the apparent involvement of Louis's former mistress Madame de Montespan, who was said to have been planning to kill his current mistress Mademoiselle de Fontanges and to have been plotting to bring Louis back to her by means of spells and black masses – or else. The accusations were sufficiently grave for him to close down the tribunal and have all archived documents relating to her or her entourage destroyed. The more delicate operation was to have her distanced from court sufficiently gradually to avoid further scandal. However, the affair, with all the gossip and mockery it engendered, cast a cruel light on the contrived perfection of Versailles. It would lead him to question his whole situation and to move towards the safety of a secret marriage with the devout Madame de Maintenon.

Meanwhile, Paris went on displaying the contradictions underlying the regime. On the one hand, the beautification of the city continued with new buildings dedicated essentially to the glorification of Louis XIV and the idea of the new Rome.[7] There were two splendid new *places royales*, or squares with royal statues in the middle. There was the fine neoclassical Place des Conquêtes, now the Place Vendôme and the home of the Ritz and select jewellers, with its equestrian statue of a conquering Louis since replaced by Napoleon, with a column celebrating his victory at Austerlitz. There was also the Place des Victoires with its statue of the king, crowned with his victor's laurels, dominant over four captives representing the vanquished Spain, Holland, Prussia and Austria. Even more eloquent in their tribute to the absolute monarchy were the two triumphal arches, at the Porte Saint-Denis and the Porte Saint-Martin. The first, rather heavy structure, celebrated Louis's victories on the Rhine, while the second, celebrating his victory over the combined Spanish, German and Dutch forces, portrays him as Hercules, naked and wearing a wig. Yet this level of mythification, even as it celebrated his highly personal rule, simultaneously brought home the ruler's absence from the city. And, as far as the Parisians were concerned, time was beginning to run out on Louis.

For the combined cost of building the fantasy capital of Versailles and fighting almost continuous wars meant debts, higher taxes and accompanying economic damage. This combined unfortunately in the 1690s with a succession of natural disasters, which caused bread shortages and a level of poverty in Paris that induced François Fénelon, tutor to the royal children, to write boldly to the king telling him: 'you have destroyed half of the real internal forces of your State in order to achieve and defend empty conquests abroad'.[8] The police lieutenant La Reynie did what he could by organising the distribution of bread at cost price, but the hunger, the riots and the deaths in the street continued up to the terrible winter of 1709, when the ambassador of Venice described Paris as a 'theatre of horror', with the 'cries of the poor and the dying disturbing the peace of the night'.[9] Inevitably, this undermined Louis's authority and resulted in mocking inscriptions being found on the king's heroic statues, along with insulting posters on the doors of churches and public buildings all over the city. The Parisians now wanted bread rather than circuses.

Louis was hurt and irritated by all this, but he now had little room for manoeuvre. He had not improved the situation by revoking the Edict of Nantes – for which, on the tercentenary in 1985, President Mitterrand would offer a public apology. He had done it not only because he was becoming more pious, but because he needed the support of the Church in facing up to Catholic Spain. However, it had forced around half a million Huguenots to emigrate and, since they tended as a group to contain many merchants and skilled craftsmen, he was further weakening the economy. But things were also falling apart at a more personal level. Although he had prided himself that his long reign and his numerous descendants would guarantee that he would not be followed by a vulnerable regency, he lost three of his heirs in quick succession, leaving only his great-grandson to follow him in 1715 as Louis XV at the age of five. Louis had a spectacular reign, but since he was a prisoner of his situation from birth, he could also be viewed as a tragic figure. And it was sad but inevitable that at his death, as Saint-Simon tells us, 'a ruined, stricken and desperate people gave thanks to God'.[10]

At first sight, the economic and political background of France in the eighteenth century hardly seems favourable to the emergence of Paris as the cultural and fashion capital of the West. For the misfortunes continued with the regent, Philippe II, Duc d'Orléans, an open-minded libertine who brought the throne back to Paris and created the relaxed interval evoked in the paintings of Watteau, only to plunge the country into a financial disaster. He encouraged the Scottish economic theorist and adventurer John Law, with a view to modernising the banking system by replacing the old metal coinage with paper money, to set up a new national bank in the capital. All too wildly successful initially, it collapsed spectacularly, Paris was overrun by infuriated investors and Law was lucky to escape with his life. The government had to take over the debt, which meant increased taxes and delayed the modernisation of French banking by a century.

Louis XV, who took over at the age of thirteen in 1723 for another long reign ending in 1774, was elegant and cultivated, but had no driving vocation to be an absolute monarch and made himself unpopular with Parisians by moving the court back to Versailles. Of course, France was still a large country rich in natural resources and with the highest population in Europe. There was progress in industry, as in coalmining and metalworking, there was the development of external trade as with Martinique and Guadeloupe, rich in slaves and sugar, and there was progress on the road network and in education. Yet the familiar problems remained. There was the usual sequence of wars: over the succession to the throne of Poland, then over the Austrian succession, skirmishes at sea with the British navy and the Battle of Fontenoy in 1745 – when the French and British argued elegantly about who should shoot first – all this followed by the Seven Years War, fought on four continents from 1756 to 1763. To keep the finances in balance in such circumstances obviously required heavy taxes, but who was to pay them? Significantly, the main opposition up to now had come not from the bourgeoisie, but from the nobility. The nobility or First Estate had already taken control of the Parlement and was resistant to paying, while the Church, or Second Estate, shared its outrage at the notion that the two superior orders should pay like commoners. The king gave in and the writing – if yet unread – was on the wall. And it was in this uneasy, uncertain historical interval that Paris became the intellectual and lifestyle capital of the West.

Even in the great days of the seventeenth century, with its confluence of royal order, religious orthodoxy and literary classicism, there had of course been figures in the margin such as René Descartes with his doubting, rationalist approach, Blaise Pascal with his heretical Jansenist belief in predestination, or the Huguenot Pierre Bayle with his questioning of the sacred status of the Bible. Not that this had been much in evidence in the literary salons of the Marquise de Rambouillet, who would gather in her Blue Room celebrities such as Corneille or Richelieu, or of Mademoiselle de Scudéry, known as Sapho (Sappho, the ancient Greek poetess from Lesbos) to her friends, who wrote for an international audience long serial historical novels with thinly disguised depictions of court personalities. The emphasis at this time was on the art of conversation with the emphasis on literature or music or even games, and the hostesses were mocked for their pretentions by Molière in *Les Précieuses ridicules*.

However, the tone was already changing towards the end of the century in salons such as that of Madame de La Sablière, who argued with Jean de La Fontaine against Descartes that animals did have souls. Then there was the salon of the colourful ex-courtesan Ninon de Lenclos, in effect an early feminist with a sophisticated Epicurean philosophy of pleasure, who argued for gender quality and who saw romantic love between equals as the supreme good. The tone in her salon in the Rue des Tournelles in Le Marais tended towards religious scepticism and it was here that the same Molière, who played knowingly to different audiences, gave an advance reading of his play mocking religious hypocrisy, *Tartuffe*. She had a large number of distinguished lovers, she was a friend of both Jean Racine and Madame de Maintenon, and is known for such sayings as 'more genius is required to make love than to command an army' – a proposition which few of us are in a position to verify.

Clearly, even if the clientele was from the upper crust of society, and even if a hostess needed social standing and considerable wealth to cater on a regular basis for a group of distinguished people, the salons provided a new platform for women. In fact, they placed them in the forefront and left the husband in the shadows. As the salons moved into their golden age in the eighteenth century, the hostesses were not only moderating group discussion and imposing an atmosphere of grace and civility, but were acquiring a significant power at a time of cultural change. For the clergy and the university were notably exerting less influence, while the Académie Française and the related academies, which had been set up by the throne with a view to perfecting and controlling a single royal and national culture, were becoming less hierarchical and open to a broader range of opinion. Since this was also where fame and a retainer were to be found, there was competition among potential candidates to garner enough support to be elected as a member. Given that the obvious place to display their talents was in the salons and that the hostesses selected their guests, these ladies were acquiring an influential role within the culture.

Madame de Lambert, for example, although her guests in the Rue de Richelieu could include the composer Rameau or the painter Watteau, presided over serious discussions on such topics as the change in philosophical beliefs or the education of children, and was reputed to have secured the nomination of half of the members of the Académie. On her death, her guests migrated to the salon of Madame de Tencin in the Rue Saint-Honoré, whose guests included distinguished figures such as the political philosopher Montesquieu, the scientist Bernard de Fontenelle and the dramatist Marivaux. By now the salons were acquiring an international reputation and receiving foreign visitors such as the philosopher Hume or the historian Gibbon – not to mention the colourful Horace Walpole, author of the Gothic novel *The Castle of Otranto*, who was drawn by the reputation of the Marquise du Deffand, said to have been the wittiest woman who ever lived and who had held court with Voltaire among other major figures in the Rue Saint-Dominique. He found her to be now blind, seventy years of age and – rather inconveniently, since he happened to be gay – passionately attracted to him, but they formed a very close friendship that lasted until she died, leaving him her papers and her dog Tonton.

Certain *philosophes*, such as Claude Adrien Helvétius or Jean-Jacques Rousseau, who was never at ease in high society, found salon discussion superficial.[11] Indeed, Helvétius ran his own more rigorous 'philosophical lunches' on Tuesdays in the Rue Sainte-Anne, while Baron d'Holbach, author of *Système de la Nature*, ran his own largely atheistic salon in the Rue Royale. It is doubtless true that extended argument could be limited both by the formal politeness of the occasion and possibly even – though by now to a diminishing extent – by the fear of having to spend a short time in the Bastille, like Voltaire, if reported as having seditious views. Nevertheless, the effect of the salons was positive. It gave women more space and legitimised their concerns. More generally, the civility was enabling. By standardising the practice of politeness and even of polite dress, it provided a platform on which nobles and the educated bourgeoisie could have civilised discussion about issues facing the kingdom. It enabled the spread of information and encouraged critical thinking. It also provided an outlet for the new breed of writers and thinkers from modest backgrounds, such as Denis Diderot, the son of a cutler, or Rousseau, the son of a watchmaker, as indeed was Pierre Beaumarchais – whose hero Figaro, in the celebrated *Le Mariage de Figaro* of 1778, famously explains to his aristocratic master what is wrong with the class system.

Naturally, the salons reflected the general change in the intellectual atmosphere brought about by the Enlightenment, which sprang from a sense of the need for a new scientific outlook and indeed for a new conceptual model of the world. If in England this was expressed by the empiricism of John Locke or the inductive method and mechanics of Isaac Newton, in France it produced a whole wave of thinkers in various fields, from Buffon examining geological history to Fontenelle studying comparative religion. It led in effect to a fusion of English empiricism and Cartesian rationalism in the search for a new worldview and was most spectacularly expressed in France by the monumental twenty-eight-volume *Encyclopédie* (1751–72), edited largely by Diderot. This highly ambitious project was designed to collect all available knowledge in the 'arts, sciences and trades', and to make it available to the ordinary person. To the extent that it was promoting the secularisation of learning, it was implicitly demanding that education be taken away from the Jesuits, but while the Church condemned it and the government formally banned its publication, it in fact managed to continue.

Of course, all this was not a narrowly political venture, being rather a general attempt to move beyond packaged answers to get back to the questions and the disciplines used in approaching them. The so-called *philosophes* were not philosophers in our academic sense – they included what in modern parlance would be different kinds of scientists, sociologists, historians, geographers and so on. They tended to be multidisciplinary – some of them also wrote plays or novels. Nor did they have a unitary view of the good society, or of religion – Diderot was a materialist,

Voltaire was a deist and Rousseau believed in 'natural religion'. There was no agreed political programme, nor even as yet any organised opposition to the slave trade. Nevertheless, by believing in human reason rather than faith, they were moving – explicitly, with Nicolas de Condorcet, towards the end of the century – towards the idea of progress. And by rejecting the idea of original sin, they were declaring humanity free to create its own happiness in its own way. They did not create the French Revolution – there were broader factors involved – but they certainly helped to create the intellectual climate for it.

At a more everyday level of social activity there were the cafés, which sprouted up during the century until Paris could count around seven hundred of them. The first, opened in 1672, failed to convince clients that the then unsweetened coffee brew was appealing, and it was considered by the medical faculty to be toxic and a cause of impotence. The first to take off was opened in 1702 in the Rue des Fossés-Saint-Germain – today the Rue de l'Ancienne Comédie – by the Sicilian Francesco Procopio dei Coltelli. Still there today, if catering mostly for tourists, it became the Café Procope and was highly successful since it was opposite the old Théâtre-Français. It quickly became a haven not just for the theatre personnel, or spectators wanting to discuss the performance, but for aristocrats waiting in the warmth for their mistresses among the actresses or dancers to emerge. Respectable ladies did not as yet enter cafés, of course, although they might send in a servant to collect a coffee, served in a delicate porcelain cup on a silver saucer, which they would sip discreetly in their carriage.

Diderot and Jean d'Alembert among other *philosophes* frequented the Procope and it was there that the idea of the *Encyclopédie* arose one day, though they spoke in code in case there was a *mouchard*, or police informer, nearby.[12] In fact, the cafés were well-furnished middle-class havens open until mid-evening where people could read the gazettes, meet friends and relax in the knowledge that there was no admission for servants, drunken soldiers or other tiresome commoners. Other cafés of note were the Café de la Régence in the Place du Palais-Royal, now the Place André Malraux, which is still a venue for chess players, the Café du Parnasse, frequented by lawyers, or the Café Militaire for officers in the Rue Saint-Honoré – and indeed the Café des Aveugles, which was not for blind clients, but which had a quartet of blind musicians in the basement. As the century moved towards its violent ending, the cafés became popular and much noisier, to the point that some, like the historian Michelet, wondered whether the consumption of all that 'powerfully cerebral' strong black coffee might be one of the causes of the Revolution![13]

Already in the monarchical regime of Three Estates, or ordained orders of being, you wore what you were and, if you were a bourgeois pretending to be a nobleman or a commoner pretending to be a bourgeois, you could soon attract the attention of the police. Even on the eve of revolution, when a hard-pressed Louis XVI convened the Estates-General in May 1789, he insisted that participants be dressed in the costumes defining their estate. So the hereditary nobility of the First Estate arrived in their gold-trimmed cloaks and hats with white feathers, the clergy of the Second Estate wore their religious costumes, and the commoners of the Third Estate were dressed in plain black with short capes. And since the assumption was that the Third Estate, representing 98 per cent of the nation, could on any issue arising be automatically outvoted by the other two higher estates, it was not a promising beginning. How then, against this background, did Paris achieve such dominance in the field of luxury goods and high fashion in the eighteenth century?

In fact, the impulsion had already been given towards the end of the previous century by Louis XIV himself. By building Versailles and so many buildings in Paris dedicated to his own glory, he was creating a new market for fine furniture, mirrors, tapestries, paintings, metalwork and glassware. And in this prestigious royal theme park, where life was regulated like a complex ballet and where his morning dressing and evening undressing were conducted like quasi-religious rituals, he established a new level of elegance in manners and in dress. To sustain his image of himself as the greatest ruler in the history of the Western world, he practised power dressing with a vengeance. For formal occasions, he wore robes adorned with gold fleurs-de-lys and lined with ermine, while for everyday wear he would enhance an eye-catching outfit with red high-heeled shoes designed by himself – which both concealed his shortness and enabled him to sport a fine leg in white silk stockings.

Louis was pursuing political ends, even apart from creating his own style. By using only French fabrics, which he also distributed to the courtiers, he was requiring them to follow his example and promote French fashion. He ensured that free samples of French fabrics were also made available to local dressmakers and, significantly, he approved the publication of a new periodical, the *Mercure Galant*, which had the novel feature of a regular article on fashion that was soon attracting international attraction. Working in tandem with Louis was Colbert, who gauged that though France might be later than Britain in developing international trade and did not have the gold that flowed to Spain from South America, it could use the prestige of the court to create its own goldmine in the area of luxury goods and fashion.

If Colbert's mercantilist policy of protectionism with state subsidies was less successful in other areas, it did work in this instance. He set up a tariff wall to discourage imports, from Italy and Flanders in particular, and went so far as to send abroad recruiting teams to invite weavers, lace-makers and other workers in the relevant trades to come to France. He bought on behalf of the crown the Gobelins factory in Paris and brought together various workshops to transform it into a major enterprise for the production of tapestries and fine furniture for the royal palaces. By means of subsidies and the granting of monopolies, and by encouraging porcelain manufacturers in Limoges or mirror makers in Saint-Gobain to send their work to Paris for finishing, he contributed greatly to making the city the European capital not only of sartorial fashion, but of luxury goods and trinkets – the so-called *articles de Paris*.

The first half of the eighteenth century saw the emphasis move from male tailors to a new guild of *couturières* or female designers, who were more adept at trimming and accessories.[14] There was also a shift from the private home visit to the pleasant outing to one the new attractively appointed shops in the Rue Saint-Honoré or the Palais-Royal, where it was possible to see a range of fabrics and discuss the latest fashions or adornments. This area soon became 'the capital of the capital', especially since the new street lighting enabled the shops to stay open until late in the evening. The industry had clearly moved rapidly from the idea of supplying a standard costume to that of supplying the latest fashion, which meant a rapid turnover of concepts, novelties and, needless to say, profits. The expansion was such that, by mid-century, no less than half of the shops in Paris sold luxury goods or clothing, while there were fifteen hundred *couturières* to three hundred fruit merchants.[15]

Not everybody was happy at what was beginning to be called a 'mania'. There was anxiety in high circles that the new availability of styles was enabling some to dress above their rank. The irascible Tobias Smollett complained that a British couple arriving in Paris could not venture forth without first undergoing a complete 'metamorphosis' of a makeover from tailor, wigmaker, hairdresser or whoever.[16] Actually, as the century wore on, interest in men's fashion declined notably and attention was directed rather towards the increasing eccentricity, dizzying turnover and cost of women's fashion. There was criticism of either the flimsiness or the ballooning impracticality of certain costumes, there was disbelief at new colour shades called 'flea', 'Paris mud' or 'goose shit', and there was astonishment at the extraordinarily tall, supported hairstyles, some in the case of actresses even representing theatrical scenes. These, which required ladies to stoop on approaching a doorway or kneel when in a carriage, made it difficult to sleep at night. And in his contemporary account, Mercier provides a grisly description of the long hair demanded by fashion being provided by hair taken from the dead, causing skin infections, loss of original hair and much discomfort.[17] The French do say that 'you have to suffer to be beautiful', but that was felt by some to be excessive.

So, if the economy benefited considerably from the surge in this new lifestyle area of fashion, what did it do for women? The answer is not simple, if only because fashion itself is paradoxical: is the woman trying to look different or look the same as others, or somehow look the same and different at once? On the one hand, the surge has been seen as a form of democratisation, with the Paris drapers each year sending to all the provincial centres a large doll wearing the season's latest fashion, to enable aspiring middle-class ladies throughout the country to keep up with the latest trends. On the other hand, since women – the vast majority of women, those of the common people, least of all – did not enjoy economic or political equality with men, was it helpful even to upper-class women to have them wear the same costume, have all exposed skin coloured with the same white makeup and their cheeks with the same bright red? Was it innocently turning them into decorative dolls too?

One writer details sympathetically the pressures of this 'dictatorship of fashion' even on those high-placed women who considered themselves to be the most free from restraints at this time. Not only did they suffer corsets so tight that it hampered their breathing, or from the toxic effects of cosmetics prepared by ignorant apothecaries, which gave them migraines, damaged their teeth and could affect their eyes. They tended to be nervy, to have fits of dizziness, to use smelling salts, consult charlatans and be driven to affectations such as being so sensitive – like the Princesse de Lamballe, a close friend of Queen Marie Antoinette – as to feel quite faint at the sight of a beautiful sunset or the scent of a delicate flower.[18] Although high fashion might have a very different effect in later societies where women had more rights, in the tripartite society of the *ancien régime* it could not provide women with any real freedom.

Ironically, this was true even of the unfortunate Marie Antoinette herself. Married at the age of fourteen, queen at nineteen in a foreign country, disliked because she was Austrian – and called *l'Autrichienne*, which includes the word *chienne*, meaning bitch – she was young, flighty and inexperienced when, as Louis XVI's wife, she automatically became the standard bearer of French fashion. She used the services of the designer Rose Bertin, who became a prominent figure at court as a result of their twice-weekly sessions over many years. Bertin not only produced enormous balloon dresses, but a constant stream of high-hair creations celebrating current world and state events – including Louis XVI's vaccination against smallpox. She also dressed dolls in the latest fashions as gifts. At a time when the nation was facing dramatically mounting debts, all this cost a fortune, resulting in Marie Antoinette being labelled Madame Déficit, to become even more hated than before. And it would be the unfashionable, ordinary women of Paris who would march out through the rain to Versailles in 1789 to bring her and Louis XVI back to the capital and call them to account.

Paris in the Revolution

....

What was it about Paris that led it to become the central stage of this French Revolution that would send tremors across the whole of Europe, would see Lenin viewing it as a guide and almost as a timetable for the Bolshevik Revolution in Russia, and would see its causes hotly debated to this day? How had it changed from the times of Louis XIV? And what was it like to be living there in the late 1780s?

The city was now larger in extent and its population had grown to more than six hundred thousand. More fashionable districts such as Saint-Germain or Saint-Honoré now featured neoclassical private mansions, so that the sight of vegetables growing in a garden had become a rarity. A recent royal decree, specifying a ratio between the width of a street and the height of the houses in it, had been issued with a view to dealing with the narrow, crowded streets in various areas. While the names of streets had tended in the past to arise locally, they were now attributed officially, so in addition to royal names such as Place Royale or Place Dauphine, there were now streets named after ministers such as Richelieu or Colbert, or after writers such as Racine, Molière or Voltaire. More of the streets were now paved and even if the creation of pavements was just beginning – one problem being the existence of so many carriage entrances – it testified to a drive to ease the movement of both people and vehicles within the city. The traffic moved faster now, with better sprung vehicles, including the *turgotines*, stagecoaches designed by the comptroller-general of finances Anne-Robert Turgot himself. Paris, even apart from the two novel balloon flights over the city, was on the move.

It was also more mobile as a society, since visitors were now coming regularly from the provinces and since travel within the country was faster than before – a lawyer or merchant could now come from Rennes or Reims, conduct his business in the capital over a few days and be back home within the week. Also, the population now included a larger proportion of incomers from the provinces, whether drawn by the allure of the capital city, by the hope of finding work or, in some cases, by the need for anonymity. In the provincial setting where people tended to know all about one another, there was no hiding place for an embarrassing secret. It had previously been much the same in Paris, since people had lived and worked essentially within their own *quartier*, or district, but now that the population was larger and that people were often working outside their own *quartier*, the situation had changed noticeably. So an unmarried mother could pretend to be a widow, while a man with a criminal past could present himself as an upright citizen.

The growth in population tended to blur the distance between the elites and the common people, which was already happening due to the loosening of the old feudal ties. The ancient sumptuary laws restricting certain modes of dress had long since disappeared and, with some now choosing to dress as they pleased, it was becoming harder to tell who was who. With traditional ties such as that of apprentice to artisan or servant to master dying out, relationships were becoming simply commercial. If a worker clashed with his employer or landlord, he could now more easily find another. In short, the old connections, or what remained of them, were fading, there was less recognition of formal status and less deference. Paris was a place where people were beginning to judge by appearances. In fact, it was on the way to becoming like a modern city, where some could feel freer but others less sure of their place in the world.

For, mentally also, Parisians were having to live in a larger world. There was now a level of literacy in the population, as measured by the percentage of people who could sign their name on a will, and official notices were now pasted on the walls rather than having to be cried out in the streets. Information was more freely available, as indicated by the introduction of the daily newspaper the *Journal de Paris* in 1777. Businessmen were now seen to be travelling to and from other countries and exotic produce such as oranges and tomatoes was to be seen in the shops. The American War of Independence inevitably drew particular attention, since France was supporting the rebels and since Thomas Jefferson as American negotiator was ensconced in a splendid residence on the Champs-Élysées. And some would have noticed the oddity that, while the Bourbon monarchy was supporting the rebels against the British monarchy, the American Declaration of Independence stated that 'all men are created equal' and talked about 'Governments ... deriving their just powers from the consent of the governed.'

In fact, as one study points out, the development of governmental bureaucracy was of itself leading to the development of consistent and thereby equal ways of treating people.[1] The idea of the rule of law and therefore of equality before the law was beginning to emerge from the normal exercise of government. It was clearly recognised by a more literate and politically aware population and may have been reinforced by a Jansenist trend towards greater independence of mind and social responsibility. These changes went along with economic development in that the bourgeoisie was becoming more important, whence the new mixing between the nobility and the wealthy bourgeoisie and the blurring of distinctions in matters of dress and social behaviour. It was becoming clear that the business and professional bourgeoisie had moved towards becoming the centre of the society – birth was giving way to money. It was also becoming clear, in this capital city of Paris in particular, that this did not cohere politically with the relegation of the bourgeoisie to the essentially powerless Third Estate. Would the country be able to adapt? Would it be evolution or revolution?

*   *   *

At the narrowly political level, the basic problem was obvious. It was the national debt, largely war-related, and the longstanding failure of the governmental system to contain it. Of course, the complex dynastic structures across Europe had made it difficult for a large country such as France to keep out of the conflicts over succession that regularly arose, even though a draining conflict such as the Seven Years War yielded no compensatory advantage. In the end, however, the debt had to be repaid, which meant taxes, which had to be agreed by the Parlement, which was in the control of the nobility. Since the nobility and the Church still held to the old feudal notion that the nobility served essentially by the sword and the Church by the spirit, there was an impasse. Ironically, Louis XV had finally felt impelled to tackle the issue head-on. His chancellor, René Nicolas de Maupeou, boldly abolished the hereditary rights and privileges of the Parlement, replaced it with a new court staffed by judges directly appointed by the state and declared that justice would be cost-free. In parallel with this, his finance minister Joseph Marie Terray was about to institute the requisite wealth tax when Louis was suddenly swept away in 1774 in a smallpox epidemic – to bring in a shocked Louis XVI, aged twenty.

Louis was a plump, rather timid young man, well-meaning but limited, who presented something of a contrast to the lively, flirtatious Marie Antoinette. Having rarely ventured beyond Versailles, he had seen little of the country and his interests were mainly in lock-making and geography. Without the knowledge or personal authority to impose himself on the situation, he began with the irretrievable blunder of dismissing both Maupeou and Terray, which put paid to the project for reform. Under the guidance of the Comte de Maurepas, he did appoint some competent ministers, but he lacked the confidence to back them against the nobility and the clergy, so that the same scenario was repeated time after time. And while he gained popularity from his support of the colonists in the American War of Independence, he was placing himself in an ambiguous situation in relation to the notions of independence and equality as well as adding enormously to an already unmanageable national debt.

The first of his finance ministers to revive the attempt to reform was the bluff liberal economist Turgot, who warned Louis about excessive court expenses. He established free trade in cereals, opened the guilds to free competition and then attempted to introduce a land tax. Since this would have hit the nobles, who owned a quarter to a third of the land and paid proportionately little tax, and the Church, which owned some 15 per cent of the land and paid no tax, the proposal provoked outrage in the Parlement. As a result he was also dismissed – though not without warning Louis bluntly on the way out that 'it was weakness that put Charles I's head on the block'.[2] Next to take on the challenge was the wealthy Swiss banker and Protestant philanthropist Jacques Necker, who made a serious effort to reform the national budget by such means as reducing the number of indirect taxes and abolishing hundreds of superfluous posts and sinecures. He also persuaded the king to free all remaining serfs on the royal domains but could not persuade him to require the nobles to do likewise. Nor could he persuade him of the downside of the involvement in America or of inflated court expenses. He finally got himself dismissed in 1781 by publishing his report on the royal finances, which the king had wanted to keep secret.

His successor Charles de Calonne, having survived for a while on further loans, tried to circumvent resistance from the Parlement in 1786 by calling an Assembly of Notables, a body that had last met 160 years earlier. When that fell through, he was replaced by Étienne Charles de Loménie de Brienne, who dismissed the Parlement after it rejected his proposal for a land tax but resigned after a similar rejection by the Assembly of Clergy in August 1788. Louis had no option but to bring back the now favoured Necker, but the popular mood was worsening. The harvests had been poor for several years – since the great volcanic eruptions in Iceland of 1783–4, in fact – and the price of bread was rising beyond the means of many of the poor. Finally persuaded that some way had to be found to break the resistance to change of the nobility and the clergy, Louis was driven to the last resort of convening the Estates-General. Since that body had not met for 174 years and had merely multiplied divisions between the three orders even then, it really did look like a last throw of the dice.

Why did the nobility and the clergy behave in such a seemingly suicidal fashion, since it is clearly they, rather than the bourgeoisie, who were bringing the regime to the point of collapse? There was a difference of interest between the high clergy and the parish priests working close to the people, just as there was a difference of interest between court nobility and the lesser nobles living on their lands, so it was the most privileged group in the kingdom that was holding out against any sort of reform. If they could not envisage change, neither could they afford to – they had too much to lose.

Two weeks before the Estates-General met in May 1789, a warning of the latent violence in Paris was provided by the Réveillon riot. Employees of the paper manufacturer Réveillon in the Saint-Antoine district, already suffering from hunger and hardship – as well as resentment at being too poor to qualify to vote in the elections for the Third Estate – were incensed by a rumour that Réveillon intended to cut their wages. When their demonstrations were blocked by the police, they turned towards the Rue de Montreuil and pillaged and set fire to Réveillon's home. Armed only with sticks or tools, they were no match for armed police in the battle that followed. Up to a hundred were shot and many wounded, while some were imprisoned and several hanged, including a woman.[3] Meanwhile Necker, taking as his model the British two-chamber system of Lords and Commons, had managed to have the number of representatives of the Third Estate raised to 600, to equal the combined total of the nobles and clergy, who had 300 each. If these two could be merged into a single estate, the objective would be attained. However, he failed to impose the idea and, when the Third Estate met in separate session for the first time on 17 June, they challengingly declared themselves to be the National Assembly.

Over the next two weeks, the king played a tense and confused double game. When he ordered the hall to be closed, the new National Assembly took over a closed tennis court and swore an oath not to disband until a new constitution had been agreed. When he declared that the decisions of this supposed National Assembly were invalid, its president, the astronomer Jean Sylvain Bailly, argued convincingly that its opposition was to despotism and not to monarchy. And when Louis found that members of the two privileged orders – less than 20 per cent of the nobles, but almost half of the clergy – were gradually moving across to join the Third Estate, he saw little option but to order the remaining nobles and clergy to join the Assembly, which they did in grim silence on 30 June. However, he had meanwhile given orders for some twenty regiments stationed in the east and north to move on Paris.

When this news leaked out, there rose a feeling of panic in the city, which was already in a state of feverish excitement whipped up by thousands of pamphlets that were appearing from nowhere and by orators sprouting up at street corners. When the king felt sufficiently emboldened to dismiss Necker on 11 July, the panic increased, especially when it also emerged that he had refused to hold back the troops and to sanction the creation of a bourgeois militia. This led the Assembly, rather belatedly, to set up its own committee and its own militia – partly with a view to controlling the actions of the common people, in the disturbed Saint-Antoine district in particular; the workers there were now fearful of finding themselves in an abandoned Paris; suddenly bereft of police and of being bombarded from Montmartre and the Bastille before meeting the full fury of the avenging royal troops.[4] It was a search for weapons with which to defend themselves that led, almost incidentally, to the first great set piece of the Revolution: the siege of the Bastille.

The Bastille, the most formidable fortress in the city, went back to the fourteenth century and came out of the Hundred Years War. It had long been used as a royal prison, most notably by Louis XIV, who with no formal procedure other than to affix his seal on the infamous *lettre de cachet*, dispatched there more than two thousand offenders and political opponents, including Nicolas Fouquet and the Man in the Iron Mask – who remains mysterious even if we know that the mask was in fact velvet. This absolutist use of power depended on the elaborate secret system of police supervision, which Diderot described as an 'enormous net, within which every subject was caught unknowingly, without realising that his every action or opinion was being reported to the police'.[5] However, the Bastille was convenient not just for removing a Voltaire from the limelight for a period, but as a useful repository where a noble family could put away an incorrigible black sheep to avoid the scandal and possible consequences of a public trial.

One such persistent offender – imprisoned in a cell luxuriously furnished by his hated family[6] – was the notorious libertine philosopher the Marquis de Sade, who abused children of both sexes and had not only whipped and sodomised a prostitute but had tried to force her to deny the existence of God – as of course he did himself, although he also tended curiously to give God hell for not existing. Ironically, he had missed his chance of being released by the siege since he had been removed only a few days earlier to the asylum at Charenton for having shouted down from his window, among other incendiary statements, that the warders were killing the prisoners. It was ironical also that the Bastille was due to be closed and now only held seven inmates, including four forgers who had been placed there temporarily for legal convenience. Nevertheless, it remained a powerful symbol of despotism, and in towering over the working-class area of Saint-Antoine it still carried the threat of destructive cannon fire.

On the morning of 14 July, a crowd of perhaps fifty thousand people, following a – false – rumour during the night of an immediate attack, went to the Invalides and seized thirty-two thousand rifles and twelve cannons, with the complicity of the French Guards, the body used to maintain order but which had moved to the side of the people. They then marched in search of ammunition and gunpowder to the Bastille, whose governor the Marquis de Launay had apparently agreed with a delegation to remove his cannon from the battlements and allow them access through the first courtyard to the arsenal. Whether through misunderstanding on both sides or whether de Launay lost his head is not clear, but when firing began the crowd thought they had been treacherously trapped in the courtyard and fought their way through heavy losses to a second courtyard. At this point, to put an end to the confusion, two officers took charge of the operation and stationed two cannons in front of the inner drawbridge guarding access to the fortress. This might not of itself have been enough to take the fortress, but it gave de Launay cause to reflect on his situation and that of his veteran soldiers.

At five o'clock the governor surrendered, but when the drawbridge was lowered and the heavy doors opened the crowd, still resentful at the apparent betrayal, piled in violently and began to attack the defenders. Although at least one assailant tried to save de Launay, the governor was brutally murdered, and his head would be paraded around by a butcher's apprentice on a pike. The seven prisoners were released, and the four forgers soon disappeared into the crowd. There were ninety-eight deaths, seventy-eight people were wounded and some nine hundred of the victors were awarded a certificate declaring them to be a 'Conqueror of the Bastille'. There are obviously ironies and ambiguities surrounding this event, in that it was in fact incidental to a search for ammunition or to the confusion over the terms of surrender, but it represented the point at which the Revolution came out of committee discussion and became real on the streets. It symbolised the defeat of despotism and acquired the mythic importance recognised by the annual celebration of the *Quatorze Juillet* up to today.

Once again, Louis XVI backed down, withdrew the troops encircling Paris and brought back Necker. He also made a conciliatory visit to the Hôtel de Ville, where he accepted from the distinguished new mayor Bailly – the astronomer credited with the discovery of the satellites of Jupiter – the tricolour rosette of the victorious Parisians. If all this was not enough to persuade some twenty thousand of the wealthier nobles to move into exile, a further impetus was the August decrees. These abolished feudalism, removed the tax privileges of the nobility and the Church, and established equality before the law – ideas embodied in the Declaration of the Rights of Man and of the Citizen, drafted largely by the Marquis de Lafayette. Meanwhile, rising anger due to the increasing price of bread and to the belief that profiteers were limiting supplies, led to the spectacular women's march to Versailles and to the forced return of the royal family to Paris on 6 October. With the king still living in luxury but in effect a prisoner in the Tuileries, Paris controlled the Revolution.

But how far did it control itself? The city council was composed of 144 members, with three being elected from each of the forty-eight wards, but the system was over-complicated by the fact that the list had to be approved by each ward, so that candidates rejected by a majority of wards could be struck off and have to be replaced through further contests. In addition, the abstention rate was as high as 85 to 90 per cent, so that decisions affecting around eighty thousand active citizens could be taken by around ten thousand voters. Not only that, but with a non-secret ballot conducted by open roll call and the option for six wards to combine and force a general assembly of all forty-eight, it was a system whereby a determined activist minority could in practice keep the pot boiling and control the game. In fact, it was ready-made for the *sans-culottes* – workers who wore cotton trousers rather than knee-breeches – and by extension the revolutionary leftists.

For the moment, however, the situation was relatively calm, the 1789 harvest had turned out to be good and in the following July, for the first anniversary of the *Quatorze Juillet*, there was an enormous festival of national reconciliation involving some three hundred thousand people on the Champ de Mars, at which the National Guards swore to remain faithful to 'the Nation, the Law and the King'. However, the tone changed after the Pope objected to the new Civil Constitution of the Clergy, which had in effect nationalised the Church, auctioned off much of its land to pay off the national debt, and taken over the payment of priests. This had been accepted without much difficulty, but the requirement that priests swear loyalty to the state rather than to the Pope created division, gave the dispute an international dimension and was one reason why Louis tried to escape from Paris in June 1791, to join up with loyal forces in the east and seek foreign help.

The night-time escape had been planned by the Swedish Count Fersen, who arranged for the royal family disguised as servants, along with servants disguised as bourgeois, to use two light, fast carriages for the 200-mile journey to Montmédy. But Marie Antoinette, who was making the running since the king had become vague and indecisive, had decided to keep the family together and use a heavy coach drawn by six horses. This was both slower and more conspicuous, especially since Louis chatted to peasants while horses were being changed and also stopped at intervals to satisfy his bulimia, or nervous hunger. The result was that they fell behind the schedule and missed contacts, only to be recognised and arrested at Varennes, some 30 miles from their destination. When they were brought back to Paris under guard some days later, they were met by an ominous silence from a large, expectant crowd lining each side of the streets. For the people sensed what the National Assembly now tried to conceal by pretending that the king, rather than fleeing, had been kidnapped – a vain attempt, especially since Louis had left behind a long statement retracting everything to which he had previously consented. A constitutional monarchy would require a credible king, who would not conspire against his people, but Louis – and even less his Austrian – wife no longer fitted the description. As Lord Gower, the British ambassador, reported to London: 'If this country ceases to be a monarchy, it will be entirely the fault of Louis XVI. Blunder upon blunder, inconsequence upon inconsequence, a total want of energy of mind accompanied by personal cowardice, have been the destruction of his reign.'[7]

It was hardly surprising that war with Austria and Prussia should break out in April 1792, or that the weakened French armies should suffer early reverses. On 10 August, after the Prussian commander, whose army included émigré French royalists, had threatened Paris with 'unforgettable violence' if any harm should come to Louis XVI, an infuriated mob stormed the Tuileries and slaughtered the guards. The royal family managed to escape to the nearby National Assembly, but it was decided that the monarchy should be temporarily suspended so that new elections could be held, and that Louis should be placed under arrest. With the threat of a Prussian invasion of the capital now creating paranoia, a mob broke into the prisons and massacred up to a thousand prisoners whom they considered to be enemy supporters. The situation was only calmed by the victory at Valmy, which stopped the Duke of Brunswick's march on the capital and which, since almost half of the French troops were enthusiastic volunteers, led the German writer Goethe – who was present – to declare that this was 'the start of a new epoch in history'. It also led more immediately to the decision that the king should be tried for treason.

What was the choice facing the revolutionaries? It is clear, with the comfortable perspective of hindsight, that the French Revolution, as Godechot points out, was the political expression of a broad array of societal changes not specific to France that were developing at that time.[8] There was an economic revolution due to the rise of capitalism and the beginnings of the industrial revolution, a social revolution with the rise of commercial and professional middle classes excluded from power, an intellectual revolution with the Enlightenment, not to mention an agricultural and related demographic revolution brought about by more productive techniques. The medieval formula of an absolute monarch by divine right acting as father to his subjects no longer matched the reality. Yet if the obvious next step was a constitutional monarchy, it could not credibly be achieved with a monarch who was not only inadequate but who had colluded with the enemy, as the discovery of his secret correspondence confirmed. However, the interlinking of monarchies meant that any major change in a large country such as France was inevitably seen as a threat to the continental order, especially since it also challenged the supranational Catholic Church. There was no way back, but to move forward risked war with most of Europe.

It also risked conflict within France itself. Within the Convention, as the interim assembly was now called, the two influential groups were the Girondins, so named because of the connection of some of their members with the south-west, and the Jacobins, so called because of an early headquarters in the Rue Saint-Jacques. The Girondins, who were in favour of middle-class parliamentary government, were more moderate and more representative of France as a whole. The Jacobins, or Montagnards since they sat in the higher seats in the Convention, held many Paris constituencies, were more supportive of working-class interests and were in favour of a republic. And this conflict between the moderate nationalism of the Girondins on the one hand, and the Paris-based centralist republicanism of the Jacobins on the other, would have to be resolved within the imminent conflict in which France would be at war not only with Prussia and Austria, but with Britain, Spain, Portugal and the Dutch Republic. It was all too likely to be bloody.

The elaborate trial of 'Citizen Louis Capet', as the former king was officially now called, extended over several weeks until it was concluded on 17 January 1793. Louis was calm and dignified throughout, but he was often evasive in his answers. With the facts against him, the deputies handed down a unanimous verdict of guilty by 693 votes to none. As to the penalty, the Girondins had hoped to avoid or at least defer execution, but their attempt failed and they reluctantly added their votes to the final tally of 387 in favour to 334 against. So on the cold misty morning of 21 January, through a shocked silence that had fallen on the city, Louis was driven in a closed carriage accompanied by cavalry to the Place de la Révolution. An enormous crowd of spectators, controlled by military units, watched expectantly as Louis descended from the carriage, walked to the guillotine, mounted the steps and was starting to address the crowd when a drumroll buried his words. He was tied under protest, was placed on the guillotine and uttered a loud cry as the blade fell. There was an 'awful silence' as his head was held up for the crowd, according to the priest accompanying him, 'until *Vive la République* became the universal shout of the multitude and every hat was in the air'.[9]

Except for the hat of one ordinary Parisian, who just went along to see what the fuss was all about and for whom it was 'like the end of the world'. He had a mist before his eyes and felt unsteady on his feet as he went home, stayed in his room and was 'sick for a whole week'.[10]

The next eighteen months were the crucible of the Revolution. The new Republic found itself in the desperate position of fighting for survival against the superior forces of most of Europe, while simultaneously having to put down violent rebellions inside the country, notably in the Vendée and Brittany. Even as it was abolishing slavery, introducing a post-Christian calendar, creating a cult of the Supreme Being and bringing in equalising measures, it was putting down any internal opposition with extreme brutality. It was the stress of this situation, allied to food shortages and the people's fear of retribution following defeat, that led to the transfer of power to the Committee of Public Safety and to the Terror. And inevitably, as the pressure increased, this do-or-die struggle was reflected within the leadership itself. The more moderate Girondins were dispatched to the guillotine, Marie Antoinette followed, and the Republic was now a Jacobin dictatorship with the single aim of winning this desperate internal-cum-external war at any cost.

And by the end of the year, at the cost of some two hundred thousand deaths in the provinces and around two thousand guillotined in Paris alone, it was working. With mass conscription producing a large citizen army of six hundred thousand men with enthusiastic young officers, France was holding its own on the battlefield. But the Terror had its own internal dynamic and, in this tense climate of fear and mistrust, a split now appeared within the Jacobins themselves, whose leadership was increasingly dominated by the purist Maximilien Robespierre. In March 1794, he dispatched to the guillotine the *Enragés*, or extreme leftists who wanted to increase the Terror, and in April he dispatched Georges Danton and his followers, who favoured some relaxation of the Terror now that the military situation was improving. Robespierre saw himself as protecting the Revolution even against the revolutionaries, but did he realise that, as the last leader standing and with others afraid of being next, he was leaving himself dangerously exposed? Did he not grasp that with the improved outlook for the Republican army – it was about to have a decisive victory at Fleurus on 26 June – the whole picture was changing? Or was he too preoccupied with the Festival of the Supreme Being, an apotheosis of the Revolution that he was planning to present in Paris, the stage on which the national power struggle was being fought out?

This event, on a gloriously sunny day on 8 June, was perhaps the strangest episode in the Revolution. Robespierre was himself a deist and this was expressive of his attempt to impose deism as a middle way between the Christianity of the monarchy and the atheism of prominent figures of the Enlightenment – an almost insanely ambitious project in what was still largely a peasant Catholic country. So all citizens were invited to the Tuileries Gardens, where a large amphitheatre had been set up for this vast affair staged by the painter Jacques Louis David and involving some nine hundred musicians. The Parisians, in their best apparel, were arranged in separate groups of men, women, old and young, while the deputies were in patriotic attire and Robespierre was resplendent in a striking sky-blue costume. There were enormous effigies, with the central one symbolising the monstrous Atheism, which stood on the shoulders of Ambition, Discord and False Simplicity.

After making a speech, Robespierre dramatically applied a torch to the monstrous Atheism, from which eventually emerged to cheers from the crowd – though rather blackened in the event – the serene figure of Wisdom. He now made a second speech, addressing himself directly to the Supreme Being above. Following that, he led the whole crowd in an enormous procession across the river towards the Champ de Mars. There were trumpeters, cavalry and artillery detachments, followed by the twenty-four constituency groups, the deputies, columns of men and women, lines of young and old, a red-draped vehicle pulled by six bulls with gilded horns, white-clad shepherds and shepherdesses, with more bands, constituency groups and cavalry units. And walking alone in his sky-blue costume in front of the parade was Robespierre with an almost ecstatic expression on his face, unaware of the occasional voices among the spectators calling him a dictator or saying that 'not content to be the master, he wanted to be God'.[11]

Over the next six weeks he led what became known as the 'Great Terror', with victims increasing to eighty a day until his frightened colleagues turned on him. It is not clear whether he had attempted suicide, but they found him with a shattered jaw held in place with a blood-soaked neckerchief. After a surgeon was called to dress his wounds, he was held with his ally Louis Saint-Just and others in the Conciergerie. They were tried by the tribunal in mid-afternoon and loaded on to the tumbrils at five o'clock. As they were passing Robespierre's house, a group of women stopped the tumbril and began dancing mockingly around it.[12] They arrived eventually in the crowded, noisy square where the guillotine stood commandingly, descended from the tumbril and silently awaited their turn. None of them, before passing under the blade, attempted to address the crowd. There was a sudden silence as Robespierre mounted the steps, was placed in position, then let out a great agonised roar as the neckerchief was ripped away by the executioner before the blade fell – followed by a storm of cheers and applause as his broken face was displayed to the delighted onlookers. Who already anticipated that the Terror for which he had largely been responsible, and which had possibly saved the Republic, would die along with him.

In the wartime atmosphere of the Terror, Paris had seemed a quite different place. There were no elegant carriages in the streets since they had been commandeered to deliver supplies to the front. Convents and mansions belonging to émigré aristocrats had been turned into factories for manufacturing armaments, while various churches were used for administration or storage, with the result that there were now some five thousand workers employed in state workshops in the city. There were no priests or nuns in clerical garb to be seen in the streets, while the systematic attempt to de-Christianise the city extended to the names of streets with a religious reference. Thus the Rue Saint-Honoré had become the Rue de la Convention, the Rue Saint-Nicolas had become the Rue de l'Homme Libre, the Rue des Capucines was now the Rue des Citoyennes-Françaises, while the name Notre-Dame, in the square, the bridge and the street of that name, had been replaced by La Raison.

With so many workers having gone to the war, the streets were dirty and there were beggars everywhere. But the atmosphere was lively, with armed Jacobins moving around, soldiers passing through and uniformed volunteers filling the taverns or singing in the streets. There was constant discussion and argument, prompted by the patriotic placards on the walls and by such slogans as 'Liberty, Equality, Fraternity or Death!' or 'The French People Against the Tyrants' – and it was not just the foreign tyrants that people had in mind. The general mobilisation itself, in that it treated people on equal terms, was felt to embody a new sense of equality and of the fraternity engendered by equality, which was leading people from different levels of society to begin to address one another with the familiar form of *tu*. The revolutionary workers, now seeing themselves as citizens rather than as subjects, had developed a class consciousness, tinged to a degree with popular nationalism, which was historically new.

Nor was that all that was new. For women had entered the historical process in various ways, by marching on Versailles or by engaging in bread riots, as in May 1793 when they pillaged shops, confiscated grain and kidnapped officials. It was a woman, Charlotte Corday, who murdered the leftist Marat in his bath – she saw herself as a Joan of Arc figure and asked for a portrait painter just before she was guillotined – and it was women of the opposite view who joined in his funeral procession. Indeed, there was a militant leftist Society of Revolutionary Republican Women and then there was the parallel 'Declaration of the Rights of Women and of the Female Citizen' by the Girondin writer Olympe de Gouges, which argued for equality under the law and rights in relation to divorce. For the Revolution's idea of human rights still excluded half of the population.[13]

But as yet these were dreams that the society of the time could not accommodate. The newly class-conscious male revolutionary workers became confused and disillusioned by the unnecessary continuation of the Terror. The revolutionary women were treated as troublemakers by the Jacobins, who banned their organisations, warned them not to interfere in public affairs and told them to go home and look after their families. Olympe de Gouges was executed along with the Girondins, as also was the well-known activist Madame Roland, who on the steps of the guillotine uttered the famous cry: 'Oh Liberty, what crimes are committed in thy name!'

Almost overnight, the atmosphere was transformed, with the sudden sense of relief and freedom leading some to sing and dance in the street. Under pressure from relatives demanding the immediate release of prisoners, the Committee of Public Safety freed 478 people within five days and proceeded to re-establish proper court and legal procedures in relation to witnesses and the rights of the defence. The Convention would also take steps to draft a new constitution aimed at setting up a bicameral parliament, with deputies chosen by indirect election, a property qualification for voting, executive power held by time-limited directors and other measures designed to ensure that the Jacobin leftists and the common people could not again gain control. And that message was rammed home when the bad harvest of 1794, followed by the worst winter in almost a hundred years, led to another uprising by starving sections of the population, which was promptly put down with many arrests.

Indeed, the message was already visible in the city, where the Jacobin workers who had dominated the scene had given way to the dandyish gilded youth known as the Muscadins. Although many of them were in fact middle class, they all affected aristocratic mannerisms as well as an ostentatious new clothing style, with the men wearing very large neckerchiefs under elaborate ringlets and the women wearing startlingly revealing dresses. Royalist by conviction and often by their personal history, they held balls for victims and, in one instance, a ball solely for the grown-up children of victims of the guillotine. For all their foppishness, however, they came in October 1795 to be a threat to the regime, even though the northern border had been secured, an advantageous Peace of Basel had ended the war with Prussia, and peace with Spain had followed shortly afterwards.

Although it had seemed that internal opposition from the western part of the country had also successfully been quelled, the royalists were reinforced by the arrival of the Comte d'Artois, the king's brother, with British and émigré troops in October 1795. With the government forces mostly deployed near the frontiers and Paris only lightly defended, the Convention's forces were heavily outnumbered. Moreover, the Muscadins were seizing the opportunity to organise a royalist rising within the city. With the situation looking grave, a young twenty-six-year-old general was brought in. He demanded full control, had forty cannons brought in after midnight from the west of the city, placed them in commanding positions, repulsed a probing attack at 5 a.m. and was ready for the main assault. When it came at 10 a.m., he led the defence throughout, despite having his horse shot from under him, and within two hours the battle was won, with some three hundred royalists lying dead from grapeshot and musket fire in the streets. Which marked both the effective end of the revolutionary period and the beginning of an illustrious career for Napoleon Bonaparte.

8

Paris under Napoleon

....

After the upheaval of the Revolution, it is hardly surprising that the short life of the Directory, from October 1795 to November 1799, was as hectic as it was unstable. Clearly, the new constitution agreed by the Convention was designed to calm things down, since it set up a two-chamber legislature consisting of a Council of five hundred and a reviewing Council of Ancients of 250 men over the age of forty. The indirect mode of election, subject to property qualification and involving only a third of the seats in any one year, was intended to achieve the same ends. Again, while executive power was exercised by the five directors, they too had been chosen indirectly by the Council of Ancients from a list provided by the lower house. Ironically, the complexity of these safety features would act as a net in which its originators would become entangled. Especially since they were attempting to deal with the reverberations of a violent upheaval in a context affected not only by a stagnating economy but by the changing fortunes of an expensive war, for the Revolution was moving from defending itself against external enemies towards pursuing and attacking them in their own lands. No sooner had the young General Bonaparte put down the royalist insurrection in Paris than he was off leading an army in Italy.

The economy was badly affected by the removal of price controls and by the related fall in value of the *assignats*, government bonds backed by the estimated value of confiscated church property which had served as paper money during the Revolution. This led in 1796 to an uprising led by the journalist and revolutionary egalitarian François-Noël Babeuf, who was banking not only on support from the by now quite disenchanted working people, but on the mutiny of a section of the police force against an order to join the army at the front. He was easily outmanoeuvred and executed. Similarly, a plot to overthrow the regime by the royalists in their turn was foiled when its organisers were imprisoned after being denounced by the army officers approached to carry it out. Despite this, the threat of a comeback by the royalists was increasing. They did well in the election of April 1797, and it began to seem ominous that in the next phase of the electoral cycle in the following year, when another third of the seats would be in contention, they would achieve a majority and bring about a complete reversal.

A strike against the royalists by the army under General Charles Pierre Augereau – sent back from Italy by Napoleon, who had close ties to the director Paul Barras – duly eliminated that threat, with the leaders being deported and the balance restored in favour of the moderate republicans. However, the fading of the royalist threat left room for a resurgence of the neo-Jacobin left and the directors were discovering that the system of a partial election each year was not operating to their advantage. They managed to stop this return of the left by some crude manipulation of the 1798 election, but they were clearly not going to be able to repeat the trick with any appearance of legality in 1799. Yet the country, under economic and military pressure as it was, was clearly not ready to return to the confusion and violence of the past, and it was in this context that the idea of a coup d'état to overthrow the Directory was born. The key figure involved was the self-described 'survivor' Emmanuel Joseph Sieyès, who saw the advantage of using the popularity of Napoleon, newly returned from Egypt, in the operation.

Napoleon had naturally been kept well informed by his brother Lucien Bonaparte, who chaired the Council of Five Hundred, and lent himself to the plot while refusing to be identified with any particular party. The first stage of the plan was to claim that there was a plot against the Republic and, to deter any reaction from the Paris *sans-culottes*, to move the parliament out to Saint-Cloud under the protection of Napoleon's army. The second stage was to paralyse the Directory through the resignation of three of its members – Sieyès, Roger Ducos and the corrupt and dissolute Barras, who was bribed for the purpose. The final stage was for Napoleon, as protecting general, to confront the parliament with this situation and to invite them to resolve it. All this was not without risk for Napoleon, especially since he knew that his invasion of Egypt would ultimately fail, and he had returned while his reputation for military success was untarnished. Indeed, he now had a rough passage with the neo-Jacobins in the Council of five hundred and the day was only saved by a powerful intervention from his brother Lucien, who was chairing the session. Nevertheless, it was agreed to set up a provisional executive of three consuls, Napoleon, Sieyès and Ducos, who were to supervise the drafting of a new constitution.

Sieyès had seen himself as the leading figure, but Napoleon would soon establish himself as First Consul and become the dominant consul. It had been a chaotic transition from the active phase of the Revolution to a period of enforced internal calm, a roundabout and messy way of achieving the obvious. For if Napoleon has been seen as the gravedigger of the Revolution, he should rather be seen as the leader who carried it forward even though, as Lefebvre suggests, it would only really be complete by 1830, with the arrival of a sovereign who accepted its principles.[1] Essentially, the Revolution was a transference of power from a ruling aristocracy to the bourgeoisie and, given that in this preindustrial era there was no organised working class, it could hardly be anything else. And one heavily symbolical step had already been taken towards the secularisation and state funding of high-level educators and civil servants through the establishment of the École Normale Supérieure and the École Polytechnique. With entry by open competition, this was an 'opening to the talents' that would become a distinctive feature of French society in the centuries to come.

*   *   *

To a large extent, Napoleon himself exemplified the great societal change that had taken place. Of minor Corsican nobility and with French as his second language, he was something of an outsider. In good Corsican fashion, he retained his attachment to his family and, despite being an agnostic, would cross himself superstitiously before going into battle. At the military academy at Brienne and then in Paris, he developed independence and displayed ambition as well as high intelligence and a remarkable capacity for work. He was fortunate in that he did not have the aristocratic status to qualify for the cavalry, since it led him to join the more modern branch of the artillery and it was his obvious skill in that area which originally got him noticed. The Italian campaign of 1796–7 was initially seen as a sideshow in the battle against Austria, but Napoleon's brilliant performance was such that he ended up by invading Austria and negotiating the Treaty of Campo Formio. The fact that he was also popular with his men, since he led boldly from the front and never talked down to them, also fed into the growing legend surrounding him back in Paris – which he nourished through regular army bulletins.

For all his considerable qualities, Napoleon had been an inexperienced young provincial and something of a romantic idealist when he first moved into Paris circles. He had fallen passionately in love with Joséphine, a widow with two children whose husband, a general and notorious libertine, had been guillotined. Fashionable and good-looking as well as gracious and kind, she was also the product of the relaxed morals of the times. She was a former mistress of several notable figures, including Barras, and did not take the same strict view of marital fidelity as did the young Napoleon – who was in any event off to battle in Italy two days after the wedding. When he discovered on campaign that she had started an affair with a handsome young lieutenant, he was deeply affected and he was further humiliated during his Egyptian campaign when Horatio Nelson intercepted correspondence about the affair and had the whole story, less than sportingly, spread out across the London *Morning Chronicle*. However, by the time he became First Consul and was ready to assume power, the iron had entered into the wounded idealist's soul, he had started to have the occasional affair himself, and he now had the statesman's colder and more realistic view of the people around him. This mature objectivity would be required as he confronted the task of reordering the much-changed society left by the Revolution.

Certainly, the Paris of 1800 was in many ways a changed place. Some of it had simply disappeared. The Bastille had gone, leaving a large empty area, the Grand Châtelet prison had been demolished and a number of churches had been destroyed. Much of it was for sale, since the homes of émigré nobles had been confiscated and some two hundred religious establishments had been closed, leaving the extensive gardens of monasteries and convents to be chopped up into building sites to be sold off to the highest bidders among the *nouveaux riches* in order to bring in money for a hardstrapped state. The Saint-Germain district, in particular, now seemed abandoned and ripe for redevelopment. And, of course, the church bells had been melted down to make guns, while clerical costumes and the regular religious processions had gone from the streets. Religious references in street names or shop signs had been removed and the Christian calendar itself, with its Sundays and its festivals, had been replaced by a metric version. The religious revolution, as Reinhard points out, had been as radical and as brutal as the political and social revolution itself.[2]

Yet that was only the surface of the change. For religion, after all, had clothed people's lives from the cradle to the grave. It had run the hospitals and charitable institutions, but now the nuns had been eased out of such activities, with the Charité hospice becoming the Unité hospital, and the abbeys of Saint-Antoine and Val de Grâce being turned into hospitals implementing the new practice of having no more than one patient per bed.[3] The Church had run education, but now there was a very explicit policy to make education the responsibility of the state. The Church had lost its control as regards religious practices, with less than half of Parisians now taking communion.[4] Jews and Protestants were free to practise unhindered and the registration of births, deaths and marriages was now primarily a matter for the state. With family matters now tending to be seen as private, there were more divorces and birth rates were declining. And even though there was a degree of popular enthusiasm for the reopening of some churches after 1795, anticlericalism for many had been legitimised by the Revolution and could be seen as patri-otic. In short, religion had become not so much part of the struc-ture of people's lives as a political choice.

For many Parisians, the economy had been turned upside down. The dismantling of the old employment structure of venal offices, or posts which were purchased and could be held for life and even on a hereditary basis as a family investment, was devas-tating for many quite wealthy people. Those affected ranged from magistrates of the Parlement or judicial employees to inspectors of factories or receivers of taxes. Many others, such as employees of the disbanded trade corporations, similarly lost their jobs and the status that went with them, while the *assignats* or government bonds in which many such people would have invested their savings – for want of anything better – had largely collapsed. Again, the flight of the nobles was a disaster for goldsmiths, fash-ion and other luxury trades, while the abolition of the guilds simply meant that more traders were competing in a smaller market. As against these losses, the return of the court and the National Assembly to Paris in 1789 had brought work for lawyers, journalists and printers, together with their servants, while the city also gained from the revolutionary centralisation of the econ-omy. The overall effect of all this was that a society based on hereditary status was becoming a society based on money.

With the army needing ammunition, uniforms, guns and all sorts of equipment, any merchant who could get an army contract could make a killing. The other great source of new wealth was the property confiscated from the Church and from émigrés, which represented as much as a quarter of the land in the northern part of the city. Wealthy merchants, manufacturers, lawyers and other professionals could pick these up for a song and, if they could pay for them with rapidly depreciating *assignats*, so much the better. At a time when the poor were poorer, with 10 per cent being unemployed and the population falling by around 20 per cent, a new commercial bourgeoisie was being created within a changing economy. This brought about unprecedented social mobility, a dramatic reshaping of the old social hierarchy and the reign of the *nouveaux riches*. Wealth was the new nobility.

Nor were the *nouveaux riches* shy of displaying their wealth. They threw large balls, which may have lacked the refinement of the old aristocratic receptions but were no less lavish. The Muscadins were again prominent, with the men wearing such incredible outfits that they were dubbed the *Incroyables* and the women, known as the *Merveilleuses*, to be indeed marvelled at in their pseudo-Grecian near-nakedness under almost transparent muslin. This style so discomfited the somewhat puritanical Napoleon – whose rather stilted receptions at the Tuileries were described by his chamberlain Louis de Beaupoil de Saint-Aulaire as 'more like a formal military review to which ladies had been invited' – that on one occasion he pointedly piled logs on to the fire so that 'these naked ladies' would not feel too cold.[5] Women rejoicing in their new freedom were also prominent in this new get-rich-quick subculture, which saw deals being done even at the open-air balls in the Tivoli Gardens and in the fashionable restaurants and gambling dens of the Palais-Royal, where curious visitors wandered along the arcades among revellers, dealers and prostitutes.

However, this was a marginal and illusory freedom for women, especially for those trying to feed a family amid food shortages while their husbands were away at the war. The militarisation of the society, the new access to officer rank for the ordinary soldier and the fact that military service was now a component of citizenship all worked against equality for women. The Revolution itself had ended up by excluding them from public office and by subordinating them firmly to fathers and husbands. The brief dawn of legal equality between husband and wife from late 1793 to 1796 was followed by legislation reaffirming a husband's control over his wife's body and property. In fact, the problem was once again being dealt with not through the granting of equality but through sublimation, by projecting the Republic itself as a large symbolic female figure with bounteous breasts as in Eugène Delacroix's famous painting *Liberty Leading the People*, celebrating the 1830 Revolution – a neat masculine trick, women might understandably have concluded.

Nevertheless, if still at the symbolical level, it did represent a significant switch from the masculine mythology of the old monarchical system whereby kings presented themselves – as had Louis XVI most recently and most implausibly – as the 'father of the nation', thereby symbolically treating his subjects as children. This figure of Marianne symbolised the Republic from 1792 onwards and still features on French postage stamps and official documents today. It did represent the new sense of national identity that was being fed by the conflict with more traditionally ruled powers, as by the wartime movement of people through the capital from other parts of the country, which gave Paris, now clearly the home of the government, the sense of being the centre of a combined national effort. And as people moved more freely beyond their own district, either as members of the National Guard or because they were looking for work, they were increasingly seeing themselves and their prospects in terms of Paris as a whole.

Yet this tended only to emphasise class differences. The abolition of the corporate bodies and closed guilds, which had protected the members of so many trades from competition, was now forcing them to fight for their livelihood in a competitive free-for-all. Ideas of the equality of rights, of the rule of law and of social distinctions based on merit were becoming the guiding principles of society, but it was a harsher world for many, a world where almost everything had a price. Historically, the middle class was clearly the middle way and was doubtless the better way but, while it offered more opportunity, it still involved a sharp division between the rich and the poor. So this new post-revolutionary Paris, more secular, less deferential, drawn to nationalism as well as to progress, and all this within the overarching threat of a general European war, was about to present Bonaparte with a serious challenge.

Napoleon had been working hard all day and was not exactly keen to go out for the evening. Still, it was Christmas Eve 1800, the world was on the threshold of a new century, and it was the first Paris performance of Haydn's *Creation* with a new French libretto, a reinforced chorus of 250 voices and a special return from retirement of the famous Pierre Garat to sing the part of the Angel Gabriel. Also the ladies were looking forward to the occasion and were all dressed up and ready to go. Or so it had seemed, for there was now a delay of some kind – something to do with the correct way of folding Joséphine's magnificent new Ottoman shawl, or whatever. So rather than be late, he decided that he would go ahead in the first carriage along with the three generals, Lannes, Bessières and Berthier, leaving his handsome aide-de-camp Jean Rapp to escort Joséphine, her daughter Hortense and his own sister Caroline in the second carriage.

It was a dark, rainy evening and as Napoleon's driver César approached the entrance to the Rue Saint-Nicaise, he could see that it was partly blocked by a cart laden with what looked like a load of hay, which was also obstructing a cab that was coming out of the Rue Marceau. The consular guardsman acting as leading outrider rode forward to sort out the confusion and created sufficient space for César, who was aware they were late for the performance, to whip his horses through the gap. He had just turned into the Rue de la Loi when the carriage was rocked by an almighty explosion that smashed its windows and set the horses bolting until he just managed to rein them back in front of the theatre. Napoleon sent one of the escorts back to make sure that Joséphine was safe and to reassure her, and went into the theatre, where it emerged that the explosion had coincided eerily with the orchestra's rendering of the opening description of Chaos.

Joséphine was safe, thanks to the protracted negotiations over the correct way to fold the Ottoman shawl. Of the black horse attached to the cart, only the front half was left, while of the young girl whom the perpetrators had paid to hold the horse only the legs remained. The landlady of the Café d'Apollon, who had come out eagerly to see the First Consul pass, had both breasts ripped off by a piece of debris. In all, seven people were killed, twenty seriously injured, several blinded, and forty-five houses damaged to the point of being uninhabitable. This was serious. There had been previous attempts to kill Napoleon, but this was new. For, as Clayton argues, it was the first terrorist act in the modern sense of attempting to assassinate an individual by means of a bomb that was known to be indiscriminate in its effects.[6] It had been carried out by French royalists, as Napoleon's efficient minister of police Joseph Fouché soon discovered, but they were financed by William Pitt's government in Britain and ferried back and forth in British ships. The enemy was Britain.

Napoleon would become as obsessed by the British as the British were already obsessed by him. An attempt in 1796 to invade Britain, in association with the Irish revolutionary Wolfe Tone, had been beaten by bad weather, leading Napoleon to advise General Hoche that it was better to challenge Britain in the East, only to find himself temporarily marooned in Egypt after Admiral Nelson destroyed the French fleet in Aboukir Bay in August 1798 – and humiliated by the publication in London of his intimate correspondence with Joséphine. However, just months before this attack in the Rue Nicaise he had led his army over the Alps and enhanced his reputation by defeating the Hapsburgs at the Battle of Marengo, leaving Britain alone and reduced to this brutal, if bungled, attempt to assassinate him.

For the British felt the more threatened by Napoleon in that they did not know quite what to make of this unusual new figure on the European scene who, as Semmel suggests, 'unsettled Britons' certitudes about their enemy and themselves'.[7] Britain and France had of course been entangled in wars and rivalry for centuries, but this individual simply did not fit the existing categories of revolutionary, monarchist or whatever. Yet he was finding supporters such as the leading Whig Charles James Fox, or Lord Byron or William Hazlitt, prompting people to reflect that Britain had undergone its own revolution and killed its own king, and causing unease at a time when Britain had, in George III, a Hanoverian king who was intermittently deranged. It was frustration at this situation that led the British to promote attempts at assassination, as Pitt admitted under pressure when he said that 'the idea of interference with the government of France had been implicit since the beginning of the war'.[8]

The problem was that assassination did not sit well with notions of honour and gallantry in war or peace. So the government smiled on the wave of scurrility, far beyond the normal jolly John Bull vulgarity, that was directed at Napoleon. For it was not enough to write him off as the Corsican upstart, adventurer or pirate. To justify the extreme measure of assassination, he had to be dehumanised. So he became an ogre, a demon and, although he was in fact above average height for men at that time, a 'little green monkey of four foot two inches'.[9] James Gillray, encouraged by George Canning, pictorialised all this in his cartoons, whether by portraying Napoleon as a self-important midget agitating in the palm of George III's hand or, in a series called *The Apples and the Horse-Turds*, as a horse-turd floating among royal apples but considering himself an apple. This stream of gross abuse did not incline Napoleon to take a high view of the British.

And with fear and hatred on each side, there was to be no quick resolution to the conflict between France and Britain. In the brief, unreal peace that followed, the British planned another assassination attempt, which would be foiled in 1804, while Napoleon made elaborate plans to invade Britain – with troop-carrying balloons or a tunnel being considered – which would be abandoned as impracticable. The Battle of Trafalgar of 1805 would confirm Britain's control of the seas and, although the resolution of the upheaval caused by the French Revolution would take another ten years, it already seemed clear that, however many war coalitions there would be – and there would be seven in all – the conflict between the land power France and the sea power Britain would be decisive in the outcome.

Once in charge of the nation's affairs, Napoleon proved to be very much a hands-on performer. Autocratic, but intelligent and extremely hardworking, he was often dictating to several secretaries about quite different matters at once. Centralising and controlling in his approach, he began with two significant measures. One was to bring order to a fragmented financial system by setting up the Banque de France as the national central bank. The other was to sign a Concordat with the Pope, which allowed those churches that had not been destroyed or sold off by speculators to reopen, although the clergy would be kept under supervision and the Bishop of Paris would be nominated by Napoleon. This enabled him to re-establish religious freedom on his own terms and to weaken the old link between the Church and the royalists. He also recognised that, while he did not himself have religious beliefs, many in the population did and therefore needed to be incorporated, along with those émigrés who would gradually return, in any new national unity – which he would also seek to foster by replacing the old orders of nobility with the new Legion of Honour, based on merit alone.

As his chief ministers he depended on two contrasting figures, each of whom embodied the contradictions of this disturbed period and with neither of whom he was entirely at ease. One was his foreign minister Charles Maurice Talleyrand, a former bishop and *ancien régime* grandee who had aligned himself with the Enlightenment and the Revolution, but who retained the aristocratic sophistication and the venal practices of the old order. Napoleon was often baffled by Talleyrand, who seemed mysteriously to have contacts everywhere and whom he suspected correctly of thinking that ideas of military glory were really rather silly, but he found him indispensable and perhaps even a useful corrective, to the point that he was the only minister to be granted direct access.

The other strangely contradictory figure was his uncouth minister of police Fouché, who somehow combined being the former teacher and perfect family man with having been the radical Jacobin whose ruthlessness in repressing a royalist rising in Dijon had shocked Robespierre.[10] He was now making up for failing to prevent the 1800 assassination attempt in the Rue Nicaise by capturing the leaders of the British-backed royalist group planning the next one. Ironically, it was in the face of this ongoing threat that Napoleon, despite his initial doubts, was persuaded that to establish his leadership on a par with the usual, hereditary kings and emperors of Europe, he should be declared emperor, which he did in the grand manner by crowning himself in the presence of the Pope in 1804. This left the leader of the royalist plot Georges Cadoudal declaring bitterly as he mounted the scaffold: 'We did better than we expected. We wanted to restore a king and we created an emperor!'[11]

Paris, which he saw as both the face of France to the world and its very sensitive nerve centre, was an immediate priority for Napoleon. He had been present in the city between May and September of 1792 and had observed, from a window in the Place du Carrousel, the frenzied attack on the Tuileries Palace by the revolutionaries. The Parisians, he had decided, were dangerously prone to insurrection, therefore he must bring order, prosperity and a touch of Roman greatness to the city that would keep them quiet and make them proud. This required adequate funding, if only to avoid the financial failure that had brought down Louis XVI, but amid the national confusion taxes had not been properly collected, so to add a little spice to the exercise he decreed that the first Department to settle its obligation in full would have the honour of giving its name to the former Place Royale in Paris, which is why that magnificent square is today called the Place des Vosges.

The administration of the city now became more personalised and professionalised. It was brought under the interlinked control of two prefects with clearly defined functions, one for the Department of the Seine, of which it was the major part, and one for the police. The old *quartiers*, which had been turned into revolutionary sections, were recast as twelve arrondissements, each with a mayor and two deputies. Since all of these officials were appointed rather than elected, Paris was now under Napoleon's command and, with the prime aim being to avoid popular discontent, he kept his eye closely on the availability both of food and of work. With the diet of the poor being so heavily dependent on bread at that time and with harvests being uncertain, there had frequently been bread riots, so in order to prevent this he subsidised the provision of bread at an affordable fixed price. He also set about rationalising the chaotic marketing of food to the capital, which saw produce coming in by barge or cart to be sold in the open on the riverbank or on street corners so that a few days of frost could destroy the lot. He therefore promoted the construction of large covered central markets for perishable goods, wine and wheat, with covered local markets for everyday shopping.

At the broader level of the economy, he rationalised financial dealings by introducing the metric system, based on the franc, and approved the plan for a new Bourse, or stock exchange, although this would only materialise under his successors in 1826. He also encouraged the development of industry, which was helped both by the army's requirements and by the revival of the fashion trade during the empire, with Joséphine setting the tone in a classical style, if one much less revealing than before in deference to Napoleon's puritan prejudices. With the emergence of new industrial enterprises in the form of two large textile mills as well as a chemical plant, a machine factory and a novel sugar-extraction business, Paris was increasingly being seen not just as a commercial but as a manufacturing centre.

However, living conditions in the city, as far as both health and safety were concerned, still left much to be desired. Following a disastrous conflagration during a reception at the Austrian embassy, which revealed the total inadequacy of the small part-time fire service, Napoleon had it reconstituted on a professional, militarised basis with round-the-clock watchmen throughout the city. This in itself was a reminder of the ongoing problem of providing water to Parisians, many of whom were still reduced to buying drinking water from water carriers in the streets. He ordered the construction of an aqueduct from the Ourcq river as well as the creation of a number of fountains to provide free water day-and-night, and began the construction of the Canal Saint-Martin to facilitate river traffic within the city. Beyond that, he brought the hospitals under the administration of the prefect of the Seine, insisted on proper medical qualifications for doctors, created a Health Council to monitor health and safety, insisted that new streets being introduced had a proper sewerage system and promoted vaccination against smallpox.

One spectacular measure of public hygiene arose from the creation of three large new cemeteries: Père Lachaise to the east, which contains the tombs of such figures as Peter Abelard, Frédéric Chopin, Molière and Alfred de Musset; the expanded Montmartre to the north containing among many others those of Hector Berlioz, Edgar Degas and Émile Zola; and to the south the Cimetière Montparnasse, which would not open until 1824 and which holds the remains of more recent figures such as Jean-Paul Sartre and Simone de Beauvoir as well as Baudelaire. And if that does not provide sufficient matter for contemplation, you can visit the Catacombs since, as a measure of public hygiene, the bones from the whole disordered range of small cemeteries across the city were exhumed and moved to abandoned stone quarries, where they line the walls, often in eerily near-sculptural fashion, along miles of seemingly endless, echoing underground galleries.

While Bonaparte appears to have had a hand in everything, among the more visible and enduring of his contributions are, firstly, three new bridges, two of which were named after his victories: the Pont d'Iéna and the Pont d'Austerlitz. The third, the Pont des Arts, the pedestrian bridge linking the Institut de France and the Louvre, was the first metal bridge in Paris. Having suffered damage in each of the world wars and from collisions with boats, it was rebuilt and back in service by 1984. Although it was intended for art displays, it more recently became more of a bridge for visiting lovers, who would engrave both names on a padlock, attach it to the iron railings and throw the key away for ever and ever into the river – all very heart-throbbingly romantic until they found in 2014 that there were soon going to be some seven hundred thousand padlocks and that the weight was threatening the bridge. So saddened lovers now take simple selfies or switch downstream to the footbridge named after the former Senegal president Léopold Senghor, while sedate Parisians are quietly pleased that the bridge looks like its old self again.

Napoleon did not have time to carry out all of his ambitious plans for the city, especially for a whole new set of buildings around the Champ de Mars to provide a proper government district for the ministries still scattered across the city. Nor did he have time to sort out the problems connected with narrow, muddy streets still generally lacking pavements, although this led to the creation of further shopping galleries such as the Galerie Saint-Honoré and the famous Passage des Panoramas, which had all sorts of attractions and retains its charm today. However, he did have time to create the attractive Rue de Rivoli – which had the advantage in his eyes of removing the old Revolution assembly buildings – and several new squares, including the Place du Châtelet and the Place Saint-Sulpice. He was also concerned with replacing the old monarchical celebratory structures with imperial replacements, so he built the Vendôme Column to commemorate Austerlitz in the square of that name, although the gigantic bronze elephant planned for the centre of the Place de la Bastille never got beyond the plaster-mould stage and had to sit there as a white elephant – if incidentally providing a home for the fictional street urchin Gavroche in Victor Hugo's *Les Misérables* – until the locals complained that it was attracting rats and had it removed in 1846.

France, if only because it always had to defend itself against incursions from the east, tended to see itself as relating essentially to the continent and Napoleon followed Louis XIV in cherishing the obsession of transforming the country into the modern equivalent of ancient Rome – even if he did not see himself as possessing a divine right. So with Rome as the automatic reference for impressive monuments celebrating national victories, and just as the Vendôme Column was inspired by Trajan's Column, the famously large Arc de Triomphe was suggested by the Arch of Titus, while the smaller Arc de Triomphe (du Carrousel) by the Louvre was a reduced version of the Arch of Constantine. Similarly, the handsome Temple de la Gloire, designed to display statues of the country's famous generals, although it has since become the Madeleine church, was derived from the well-preserved Roman Maison Carrée in Nîmes. If Napoleon left such a monumental mark on Paris, it is because his sense of his own personal destiny became fused with the pursuit of national greatness and French leadership – *gloire* and *grandeur* – in the broad European context. And when his second marriage, to the Austrian archduchess Marie Louise, produced the desired son and heir, he would be given the title of the King of Rome.

*   *   *

Since assuming power, Napoleon – at Marengo, Ulm, Austerlitz, Jena, Eylau, Friedland and Wagram – had defeated every continental combination in sight. But his invasion of Russia in 1812 was unsuccessful, largely because the tsar's forces refused to play the game and engage, so that he had to trail with his Grande Armée back to France. Then in the bloody and costly battle of Leipzig in October 1813, against the combined forces of Austria, Prussia, Sweden and Russia, he was defeated and forced to retreat with the grim acknowledgement that, whereas a year before the whole of Europe had marched along with him and his army, now the whole of Europe was marching against him. And the reversal was swift. By January 1814, the combined armies of Austria, Prussia and Russia were moving against France with half a million men and by the end of March they were attacking Paris. It took no more than a day of bitter fighting before Paris surrendered, no more than four days for Napoleon to abdicate, and not even a month for a new Bourbon, Louis XVIII, to be brought back to a Paris which now had British, Austrian, Russian and Prussian soldiers camped out on the Champs-Élysées. Napoleon's European dream had fallen back in upon him.

But not quite yet, for even as the Congress of Vienna was considering how to rearrange Europe after his departure, he was bouncing back from exile in Elba in March 1815, a day after Louis XVIII's hasty flight back to England. And for the next 'Hundred Days', he was busy setting up his government again, organising military parades to revive the rather flagging national ardour, holding a referendum that established him on new terms as a constitutional monarch and, indeed, picking up where he left off on his projects for improving Paris – including the new wing for the Louvre and a covered market for Saint-Germain, not to mention the elephant for the Place de la Bastille. However, the Seventh Coalition of European powers was gearing up against him and in mid-June he was off to take on two Coalition armies, one led by the Duke of Wellington, which combined units from

Britain, the Netherlands, Brunswick, Hanover and Nassau, the other being the Prussian army under Field Marshal von Blücher. And although, in the words of Wellington, the Battle of Waterloo was 'the nearest run thing you ever saw in your life', Napoleon was defeated, surrendered and was soon on his way to imprisonment at the hands of the British on the remote island of Saint Helena.

So why did this quite legendary adventure of Napoleon – one that would linger with the Romantics in particular – end in defeat? Was it due to his own temperament, to the temptation to believe himself to be invincible, to think of himself as fulfilling his 'destiny'? Was he too imbued, like so many of his contemporaries, with the myths and glories of ancient Rome? Or could he say, like Louis XIV at the end of his career, that he had been 'too fond of war'? It is obviously tempting to ascribe his decline and eventual downfall to some personal weakness or character defect, forgetting that he had inherited from the revolutionaries a complex European situation and that, under the pressure of circumstances, he was having to make it up as he went along. So if it all had the potential to go wrong when he declared himself emperor – and began to elevate his relatives – he felt pushed into it in order to force recognition for himself and his government from the hereditary monarchies of Europe. And if he had a complex about the British, that is perhaps because they kept mocking him and trying to blow him up. Because, of course, they had a corresponding complex about him and, as Clayton points out, the mutual enmity also took its toll on the British, with William Pitt dying in 1806 of drink, exhaustion and disappointment, while George III became so insane by 1810 that the Prince Regent had to take over.[12]

Viewed objectively, it is clear that in addition to the conflict within the mainland of Europe, there was an ongoing struggle for dominance between a landlocked France and a sea-controlling Britain. Having failed to invade Britain, been defeated at the Battle of Trafalgar and suffered a blockade, Napoleon responded with a land blockade designed to attack Britain economically by cutting off its trade links with mainland Europe – a move which also reflected the outdated mercantilist belief associated with Colbert that the home economy was best protected by discouraging imports. However, his Continental Blockade caused economic distress in a number of countries, was much resented, and resulted in smuggling and open refusals to comply. It was the erroneous attempt to enforce the blockade that led Napoleon into the Peninsular War, the failed invasion of Russia and even the arrest of the Pope in 1809 for refusing to boycott British goods. The personal ironies of the rivalry with the British are obvious – those who sheltered Louis XVIII were the British, Wellington was British, his captors in Saint Helena would be British, it was always the British – but it was the strategic mistake of the Continental Blockade that brought about his downfall.

Napoleon was a unique figure in the political world of that time. He was a conquering general who was equally interested in the numbering of houses or the provision of water for Paris. He was neither a revolutionary nor, until pushed into it by circumstances, a monarchist. He won it all and he lost it all. Yet his career raised new questions about forms of government, he exported revolutionary ideas with his armies, and he largely created the secular state. And since a spectacular career that did not tick the standard boxes of the period was the stuff of legend, he lingered in the French memory as both a shadow and a temptation – there would be another Emperor Napoleon by 1852, who would return his ashes with great ceremony to Paris. And since the gulf between the Catholic conservative right and the republican left would if anything sharpen over the next century, he could be said to have initiated a Bonapartist strain in French politics running through Napoleon III and de Gaulle up to the present time.

The Image of Paris Darkens, 1815–48

To a Parisian of 1815, it might have seemed that the world had been turned upside down several times over. An extraordinary zigzag sequence had seen the seemingly eternal monarchy swept away by the Revolution, to be followed by a Directory, a Napoleonic empire which had conquered half of Europe, an invasion of Paris by the European powers, the return of the monarchy, soon put to flight by the return of Napoleon, his defeat at Waterloo and the second return of the monarchy, with the gentle but obese and gout-ridden Louis XVIII declaring that he was in the nineteenth year of his reign as though nothing much had happened. Yet people had seen a king, a queen and many great figures beheaded in public by the guillotine in addition to many deaths in the wars, carts laden with cultural booty from Italy, Belgium and Germany brought to fill the Louvre and adorn public monuments and, indeed, up to three hundred thousand Prussian, Russian, Austrian and English troops camped all over the city from the Champs de Mars and the Invalides to the Champs-Élysées and the Jardin du Luxembourg – when they were not thronging the boulevards or the fleshpots of the Palais-Royal. Paris, at vast expense since it had to pay for their upkeep, was playing the humbled host to most of Europe.

It was also the venue for daily meetings of foreign ambassadors, running parallel to the discussions of the victors at the Congress of Vienna, where basic questions were being asked about the future and coherence of Europe as a whole. Both sets of representatives, facing the task of establishing peace across the continent after twenty-three years of intermittent war, were concerned not just with stripping France of its territorial gains but of reordering the boundaries between states so as to secure peace in the future. It was a serious endeavour, which coincided with some imaginative longer-term thinking. There was talk of a standing European committee to settle disputes, while a Russian diplomat from a Corsican background, Pozzo di Borgo, saw the 'union of Europe as a truth beginning to establish itself' at the parallel conference of allied ministers and generals meeting every day at the British embassy in Paris. More imaginative still was the influential political theorist and businessman Henri de Saint-Simon – one of a group to be dubbed 'Utopian Socialists' by Friedrich Engels – who not only argued that developing industrial societies should be run by businessmen, but envisioned a structure akin to the European Union of today.[1]

As yet, however, these were but dreams. The victorious European nations did not see beyond the threat to their monarchical structures and were essentially concerned with trying to eliminate, or at least contain, the threat of republicanism and revolution. This would not make for a smooth transition to a modern industrial society in a peaceful Europe over the next century and, for various reasons, Paris would become the stage on which a whole sequence of dramatic events would play out. And not just at the political level, with the revolutions of 1830 and 1848, and the first of three wars against a rising Germany, that of 1871, which gave rise to the Paris Commune, followed by the First and Second World Wars. There were parallel, often explosive developments in the cultural field, with Paris central to the rise of realism and naturalism in the novel form, as to the development of modern painting from Romanticism through Impressionism, Post-Impressionism and Art Nouveau to Fauvism, Surrealism, Picasso and beyond. So what was it that made Paris the epicentre of a changing Europe at that time?

One factor is that the state played a greater role in France than in the rest of western Europe, and that the highly centralised state was associated with Paris to an exceptional degree. And it was in Paris that the originating events – the spectacular guillotining of the royals and the switches from monarchy to empire and back again – had taken place. It was here that society had been shaken to its foundations, leaving all institutions open to question and creating oppositions in all directions: absolute monarchy versus constitutional monarchy, Church versus state, constitutional monarchy versus republic, republic versus empire. To which add the related class oppositions in this developing society: nobility versus the bourgeoisie and the bourgeoisie versus the new industrial working class. Yet all this would be intensified by the specific new factor that the population of Paris, partly due to the disruption caused by the Revolution and the war in the countryside, would in effect double at a challenging speed, from 546,856 in 1801 to 1,053,262 in 1851. This was significant, as Marchand points out, not just because it magnified the difference between rich and poor to a dangerous degree, but because it created a growing imbalance between the capital and the rest of the country, which would have ongoing political consequences.[2] There would be no ready resolution to these problems. With further revolutions, another empire and another struggle for European domination, it was set to be an interesting century.

The restoration of the Bourbons was carried out under the supervision of the allied powers, who prudently imposed upon Louis XVIII a version of constitutional monarchy, if a strictly limited one since only a hundred thousand of a population of some 30 million would qualify for the vote. Within those limits, it still implied for the king and the returning ultra-royalist émigrés the restoration of the old alliance of Church and state, and initially harsh action was taken against enemies of the regime. Several hundred supporters of Napoleon were killed in a 'White Terror', two of his generals were executed, the army and the administration were purged, and a number of well-known figures were exiled, including the painter David and the mathematician Gaspard Monge. Louis XVIII himself was in fact more cautious than his supporters, he had made the gesture to Paris of residing in the Tuileries Palace rather than at Versailles, and he was sufficiently concerned by the popular dissatisfaction caused by these initial measures to dissolve the ultra-royalist chamber and put together a more representative government under Élie Decazes.

However, the assassination in the Rue Rameau of the Duc de Berry, the king's nephew and only heir to the throne, by an embittered Bonapartist saddler in 1820 strengthened the hand of the ultra-royalists, who now forced the resignation of Decazes. And when the death of Louis XVIII in 1824 brought to the throne Charles X, a famous philanderer now turned intensely devout and traditionalist – to the point of reverting to the medieval form of coronation and claiming to cure scrofula with a touch of his hand – they were on a mission to return the country to its pre-1789 state. With their idealised view of absolute monarchy, they saw this complete restoration – including the Three Estates and the privileges of the nobles and clergy that they embodied – as the only way of preserving the Catholic faith. So in addition to the Chapelle Expiatoire, built to atone for the sin of executing Louis XVI and Marie Antoinette, Paris would acquire a number of new churches, including Notre-Dame-de-Lorette and Saint-Vincent-de-Paul. The death penalty was imposed for any act of sacrilege, there was a strong move to recapture education for the Church, a cleric with no scientific or medical background was appointed despite protests to be rector of the Académie des Sciences and a new law was passed to compensate émigré nobles.

Predictably enough, the opposition had been mounting steadily over the years, there had been various public protests, and attempts to limit the franchise had only increased support for the liberal opposition. When the prime minister Joseph de Villèle called an election in 1827, he lost his majority, with the liberals getting 84 per cent of the Paris vote, but he was not allowed by the king to resign until January 1828. After a minor revolt in the Saint-Martin district was put down by the army with loss of life, Charles hesitated, but then defiantly appointed as prime minister the ultimate ultra-royalist, the mystical Catholic nobleman and papal prince Jules de Polignac. When the Chamber of Deputies refused to work with him, the king forced a new election, which merely created an even more hostile Chamber, with Paris leading the opposition once again. Whereupon he issued four ordinances suspending freedom of the press, dissolving the new Chamber of Deputies before it had even begun to sit, reducing the number of deputies heavily while raising the bar for voting even higher, and postponing the next election by two months. But when the newspapers *Le National*, *Le Globe*, *Le Temps* and *Le Journal du Commerce* all published protests and the police were sent in to smash up the presses, the printworkers initiated a rebellion.

So began, in a late July heatwave, the *Trois Glorieuses*, or the Three Glorious Days of the 1830 Revolution which, significantly, was mirrored in Belgium and other parts of Europe. The printers were soon joined by other workers and by students, barricades were set up, an armoury was pillaged, and a confrontation with soldiers around the Palais-Royal left several protesters dead or injured. On the second day, the barricades spread to the city centre, the Saint-Antoine district and the Latin Quarter, with the army – while being fired upon by snipers from the rooftops as well as suffering desertions – removing them only to see them set up again. By late afternoon, the insurgents had taken the Hôtel de Ville and the army had withdrawn to the Louvre and the Tuileries. The third day saw thousands of fresh barricades being raised across the city and the defection of two army regiments from the Place Vendôme, which led the commander Auguste de Marmont to replace them by withdrawing troops from the Louvre. This merely enabled the rebels to take both the Louvre and the Tuileries Palace so that by mid-afternoon, with Marmont forced to retreat to the Champs-Élysées, they were in control of the city. And although the rebels suffered some six hundred fatalities and the army about 150, that was all it took to send Charles X, who had been sitting it out at Saint-Cloud, on the well-trodden path back to exile in England.

Coincidentally, that same hot month of July saw the trial of the first *vespasiennes*, grandly named after the Roman emperor Vespasian but more familiarly known as *pissotières*, which lingered on as a defining feature of the Paris boulevards until late in the 1950s. They were metal male urinals consisting of a central column providing three stalls within an outer column which also provided a surface for public notices and advertisements. It would be thirty years before a more discreet version for women emerged, but in practice women tended to use the facilities of the larger cafés until the emergence of the modern unisex version in the 1980s.[3] Meanwhile, in the Three Glorious Days of July 1830, these conveniences were especially convenient for providing metal sheets with which to strengthen the barricades. However, they also provide a reminder that, for all the political disruption, the improvement of the city was still continuing more or less normally, the more so since the centralised Napoleonic administrative system, including most of its personnel, was still in place.

For Paris was seen increasingly not just as a world capital but as capital of the world. Already in the previous century, when its Enlightenment salons had made it the home of civilised discourse and French had become the international language of diplomacy, it had been seen as the new Rome. But now that the recent momentous events had made it the centre of a whole European entanglement, it was seen as the place where the problems of Western civilisation converged and where they had to be resolved. For Alfred de Vigny, in his poem on 'Paris', it was the 'axis of the world', while for Balzac it was 'without equal in the universe' and for Edmond Texier it was 'the brain of the world, the epitome of the universe, humanity made city'.[4] And if these descriptions seem rather exaggerated, it should be recognised that the runaway increase in population of the city, as well as its attractions and its anonymity, made life there quite different from that in the provinces – Balzac, originally from Tours, found the place baffling.

All of this obviously made Paris a pole of attraction not just for provincials but for quaintly dressed foreigners, notably the British, who complained about the muddy streets but loved the salons and the restaurants, some of which now offered English menus. They were known either as *les Goddam*, due to their mode of swearing, or *les Bifteck*, due to their dietary habits. The theatres were buzzing, and not just the state-supported 'royal theatres' such as the Opéra, the Opéra-Comique, the Théâtre-Français or the Odéon, but the smaller theatres offering lighter entertainment such as the Variétés, which produced take-offs of high-toned tragedies, or the Gaîté, which belied its name by presenting heart-stopping, gut-wrenching melodramas. All this jollity at the upper level of society led to heavy gambling and the odd spectacular suicide as well as to much prostitution, although there was a sophisticated version of this at a clothing shop at the Palais-Royal, where the attractive assistants all wore ribbons of different colours in their hair – a gentleman would order an ell of cloth of a particular colour to be delivered at a certain time and the appropriate assistant would turn up on schedule to deliver herself along with the cloth.[5]

Apart from existing entertainments such as the circus or fierce animal fights, not to mention public executions on the Place de Grève, there were now novelties such as the popular Tivoli Gardens amusement park or, indeed, the new 'novelty shops', forerunners of department stores. But the more obvious developments were in the area of transport, starting in 1816 with the arrival of a paddle steamer with a hundred passengers aboard, coming from London via Le Havre and Rouen. As an alternative to coach travel, these large-wheeled steamers were soon in use by businessmen, by British and even some American tourists as well as by Parisians who could use them for an outing to the Parc de Saint-Cloud or the races at Longchamp. Commercial travel via the river was also facilitated by the completion of the Ourcq and Saint-Denis canals and particularly by that of the Canal Saint-Martin, inaugurated in 1825. New quays and storage facilities for coal, timber, cement and other raw materials from the provinces would now further industrial development in several districts on the eastern side of the city.

Complementing the river steamers, there was a new attempt at a public transport system in the form of the *omnibus*, a horse-drawn carriage that could take up to twenty passengers. The first ran every fifteen minutes and from 7 a.m. to 7 p.m. between the Madeleine and the Place de la Bastille, and soon there were a hundred in service, covering eighteen different routes, with the busiest being the one that ran along the boulevards. Like Pascal's ill-fated attempt in the seventeenth century, the service ran into financial difficulties – partly because the conductors were not always competent or honest – but it managed to survive and did improve life for Parisians. A more individual form of transport to be seen regularly in the Luxembourg Gardens at this time was the *draisienne*, named after its German inventor Karl von Drais. This was an ancestor of the bicycle, one without pedals, rather like the tiny version very young children use today as introductory machines. They were for gentlemen only, of course, who could apparently paddle along impressively at up to 15 kilometres an hour – so long as it was not uphill.

At a more down-to-earth level, the long-serving prefect of the Seine, the Comte de Chabrol de Volvic, continued successfully with the unending work of expanding the sewers, paving the streets and increasing the number of pavements to make life more comfortable for pedestrians. However, the office of the prefect of police, if only because there were several of them during this period, was less successful. It was not until Louis Marie Debelleyme was appointed in 1828 that it was realised that, with the police being dressed in civilian clothes, it was all too easy for criminals to simulate them for all sorts of nefarious purposes. He kitted them out in fine blue uniforms, but as ex-army men they were not necessarily loyal to the king and with that in mind the force had been kept relatively small – far too small in the event to meet the challenge of the uprising of 1830.

Another event which coincided with the 1830 Revolution – not too surprisingly since the earthquake of the French Revolution and its aftermath had affected every aspect of the society – was the cultural revolution represented by the riotous triumph of Victor Hugo's play *Hernani*. In a time without shared radio or visual media, the theatre played a significant role by projecting issues facing the society, as can be measured by the fact that by 1829, in addition to the regular reviews in sixteen newspapers, there were nine newsletters in circulation dealing solely with the theatre.[6] Indeed, actors could become as involved as audiences – the famous actor François Joseph Talma, in the lead part of a play called *Germanicus* by Antoine Vincent Arnault, started a riot which got the play banned after its very first night by coming on provocatively dressed as Napoleon.[7]

Hugo's *Hernani* – better known today through Verdi's opera *Ernani* – had an improbable plot situated in a fictional sixteenth-century Spanish court and featured the typical new Romantic hero as a man estranged from society and driven by a dark mysterious force towards an unknown destiny. The triumph in the 'battle of Hernani' lay in the fact that in the very sanctuary of the French classical establishment, the Comédie-Française, he had publicly smashed the famous Three Unities and challenged the whole underlying worldview. It was a triumph against considerable odds, for the actors themselves disliked the play and it became notorious even before it was presented. Hugo refused the services of the theatre's regular *claque* of paid clappers, who were unlikely to simulate enthusiasm too convincingly, and decided to line up his own support with the help of the composer Hector Berlioz and the writer Théophile Gautier, who was the leading light of a group of young Bohemian writers and artists.

They certainly did not let him down, for hours in advance of the opening performance at four o'clock, according to a contemporary account, the Rue de Richelieu saw the build-up of

> a throng of strange wild creatures, bearded, hairy, dressed in every conceivable fashion so long as it defied fashion, in tunics, Spanish cloaks, Robespierre-style waistcoats, with Henri II headgear, flaunting every century and every country on their heads and shoulders, and this in central Paris, in plain daylight, while respectable passers-by stood still in astonishment and indignation. Monsieur Théophile Gautier, in particular, insulted one's sight with his scarlet satin waistcoat and the thick hair reaching down to his waist.[8]

And evening after evening, they piled into the gods to wage war with the conformists below, with every exchange on the stage being either clapped or booed in this noisy battle, which would affect the course of French theatre.

Yet there was an innocent and paradoxical aspect to this victory, implicit in Gautier's insistence that he had certainly *not* been wearing a scarlet satin waistcoat, but a pink satin doublet, since 'the red waistcoat would have had a political, republican shade of meaning, but there was nothing like that about it – we were just medieval'.[9] Of course, the invocation of the Middle Ages – as with the German return to the *Nibelungenlied* – was a feature of the European Romantic movement at this time. Yet it was not so easy to be 'just medieval' and non-political in the fractious Paris of this time, since literature and politics had become so intertwined that, as Mansel suggests, this 1830 Revolution had in part been both provoked and won by writers.[10] Beneath the defiant, showy individualism of these young Bohemians there was often a Romantic pessimism bordering on despair. This was due not simply to the sense, as with the hero of Stendhal's novel *Le Rouge et le Noir*, of having missed out on the great heroic moments of the revolutionary and Napoleonic age, but to the feeling of being at odds with their whole changing society.

It did not help that they were embedded in that society and that their relationship to it could be ambivalent. Their attempt to live as outsiders defying middle-class values was often sustained by access to middle-class family money and, moreover, they were still living in an age of royal patronage, which would continue beyond 1830 under King Louis-Philippe. The monarchy sought to win support by granting a sinecure of some kind – a post of librarian or historian in a ministry or some royal château, or whatever. Of the more famous figures, Alphonse de Lamartine, the Vicomte de Chateaubriand and Hugo himself received pensions at one time or another, while those obtaining a sinecure included Alexandre Dumas and Alfred de Musset, who was notionally keeper of the library of the Ministry of the Interior. Since this was the world they were living in and they were trying to build a career, it was not easy to break away from this system.

However, with the rise of the novel as the dominant literary form of the century and the accompanying increase in the number of publishers and bookshops – there were 580 licensed booksellers in Paris in 1828 – the situation would start to change.[11] Novels could obviously reach more people than the theatre, especially since they were regularly serialised in the newspapers. Also, whereas *Hernani* had been engaging symbolically with society at a historical remove, the novel could do so more directly and explicitly. This changed the situation of the writer since it was now possible to make a living from book sales alone and become independent of court patronage. And with a national and even international audience hungry for accounts of contemporary life, there was a ready market for novels set in this cosmopolitan 'queen of cities' where historic changes were taking place: Paris.

The most noteworthy among novelists who depicted the society of that time is doubtless Honoré de Balzac. An extraordinarily prolific writer, he created a whole parallel world in the vast series of novels that he grouped under the title *La Comédie humaine* and, while he also dealt with provincial situations, he was particularly fascinated by Paris. He saw it as a strange new environment, almost as a hell in which people's lives were driven and often deformed by a lust for gold and pleasure. On the very first page of *Le Père Goriot*, the 1835 story of a retired vermicelli manufacturer who has impoverished and humiliated himself in order to get his ungrateful daughters married into high society, he even suggests that the story may not be understood beyond Paris. He begins by describing in great detail the boarding house in which old Goriot has ended up, its owner Madame Vauquer and the villainous Vautrin. His approach is similar in *César Birotteau*, the story of a provincial who comes to Paris and works his way up to the point of becoming the wealthy owner of a perfume business and a knight of the Legion of Honour, only to speculate in an effort to expand and lose the lot. Here again Balzac begins by describing at great length the furniture and pictures in the apartment. In seeing the characters as belonging to and even deriving from their habitat, he is intuitively anticipating the social scientific approach. If *Hernani* was attacking the old worldview underlying the Three Unities, Balzac's imaginative vision was similarly suggesting that the human personality was socially determined rather than deriving from God or nature.

The swift success of the 1830 Revolution, which had been due to a combination of middle-class elements and workers, had raised the uncomfortable question of what was to follow. However, after some fast manoeuvring involving Talleyrand, a compromise figure was produced in the person of the fifty-seven-year-old Duc Louis-Philippe of the Orléanist branch of the dynasty. He was successfully presented by the ageing Lafayette at the Hôtel de Ville draped in the tricolour, the symbol of the French Revolution, and proposed as the 'King of the French' rather than the 'King of France', to emphasise that he would be a constitutional ruler whose sovereignty came not from God but from the people. Thus began the July Monarchy of 1830–48, which is also referred to as the 'Bourgeois Monarchy' since in effect it represented the transfer of political power to the upper middle class. And in surrounding himself with bankers and merchants, Louis-Philippe clearly demonstrated that he recognised the source of his power.

Since neither the traditional monarchists nor the republicans nor the rising socialists were reconciled, this was not going to be an easy ride. However, the new king scrapped much of the royal ritual and adopted a reformist line, promoting religious equality, empowering the citizens by re-establishing the National Guard, and reforming the peerage system. Yet the reform of the electoral system, if it increased the overall number entitled to vote to around two hundred thousand, still left 99 per cent of the population unable to meet the property qualification, while in 1834 Paris itself only gained a municipal council of thirty-six indirectly elected members. Since this arrangement served mainly to strengthen the hand of the bourgeoisie against both the nobility and radicals, it caused dissatisfaction, as also did the appointment as prime minister of the banker Casimir Périer, who shut down a number of republican societies and newly formed labour unions following rioting prompted by an anniversary memorial service for the Duc de Berry.

The situation was dramatically worsened by a cholera epidemic, which lasted from March to October 1832 and which claimed almost twenty thousand victims, including Casimir Périer. This revealed the social differences even more sharply since – with the honourable exception of the king himself – the rich and most of the deputies left a panic-stricken Paris, where the Pont Neuf served as a collection point for patients on

stretchers lying alongside those already dead. The police disin-
fected with chlorine those houses affected, but when they tried to
improve hygiene by removing the contaminated refuse from the
streets, the ragpickers, who made a living by sifting through it,
created riots that were only broken up by cavalry charges.
Although the authorities were doing their best, wild conspiracy
theories were rampant: that cholera was really poison, that the
epidemic was designed by the government to starve the people, or
even that the whole thing was a hoax. With much hysteria abroad,
a number of people who looked 'evil' or 'different' were attacked
and killed in the street. More seriously, as described by Victor
Hugo in *Les Misérables*, there was a lengthy insurrection involving
both republicans and Bonapartists following the funeral of the
liberal General Lamarque in June. Although this was eventually
put down by the army, it had seemed to be touch-and-go for the
new regime.

Louis-Philippe was brave and well-meaning, but he tended to
see himself as leading an improved version of the Restoration
monarchy rather than an alternative to it and, as he aged, his
outlook hardened. This inflexibility was reflected in the reaction
of the then education minister François Guizot to complaints
about the amount of income required to qualify for the vote when
he said famously: *'enrichissez-vous'*, or 'make more money and
then you will qualify'. Obviously, Louis-Philippe's task was daunting given the tangle of conflicts within an evolving society with
contending traditional monarchists, constitutional monarchists,
republicans, socialists and Bonapartists. He became unpopular
and was caricatured by Honoré Daumier as well as being mocked
in the satirical review *Le Charivari*, the model for the London
equivalent *Punch*.[12] Nor did the situation improve as the disturbances continued, with a republican insurrection bloodily put
down in 1834, a failed bomb attempt on the king's life leading to a
score of deaths in 1835, a failed republican plot in 1838 and further
insurrections or riots in 1839 and 1840. The opposition may have

been too diverse to get organised, but this was like a slow-burning revolution.

The most obvious indication that Paris was moving into a new era was the arrival of the railway stations, with several having later to be enlarged or moved to create what we know today as the Gare Saint-Lazare, the Gare d'Orléans, the Gare d'Austerlitz, the Gare Montparnasse and, finally, the Gare de Lyon. Since the government was pursuing a pro-business laissez-faire policy and gifting contracts to its supporters, there was no overall planning involved, their siting was haphazard and travel between them was inconvenient. Nevertheless, within these constraints the Comte de Rambuteau, the prefect of the Seine, made a number of useful improvements. He opened up the cluttered and unhealthy central area by creating the wide street that now bears his name to connect the Marais district to the central markets. He reorganised some hospitals, built a new prison and rebuilt several bridges as well as continuing the routine work of paving the quays and creating new pavements.

However, since this was not yet the age of systematic town planning, Louis-Philippe followed the monarchical tradition of creating embellishments in the form of monuments celebrating the regime. Given that the recent history had been rather contentious, this called for some judgement, so while the Goddess of Liberty was removed from the Place de la Concorde, it was acceptably replaced by a large obelisk from Luxor, with the long and difficult journey from Egypt being followed with great interest by the Parisians. Balancing that was the inauguration in 1840 on the Place de la Bastille of the July Column dedicated to the martyrs of the July Revolution. In that year also, as a rather risky gesture of reconciliation towards the Bonapartists – who had jeered at the king during the inauguration of the finally completed Arc de Triomphe – Napoleon's ashes were brought from Saint Helena and deposited with due ceremony in the Invalides.

At a more practical level, with the lingering memory of how wide open to the enemy Paris had proved to be in 1814 and with tensions arising again with Britain and the German states, the decision was taken to surround the city with a new defensive wall. This heavily fortified Thiers Wall, as it was called after the prime minister Adolphe Thiers, was 34 kilometres in length with a ring of ramparts and trenches 250 metres wide – its eventual disappearance would provide a readymade circular route for the present Boulevard Périphérique. Meanwhile, a significant advance in the secularisation of education and the elimination of illiteracy was made with the decision in 1833 to make attendance at primary school compulsory. New secular primary schools were established and, along with the remaining Church schools, were put under the control of a single board of management.

Industrialisation was beginning to change the appearance of the city, with the new railways in particular requiring steel products and indeed steam engines, although 80 per cent of the latter were made outside Paris. Since the chemical industry was also expanding in various fields, new mills and factories were being created in the outer suburbs and along the banks of the river. A large proportion of the businesses were workshops employing no more than ten workers – a feature of the comparatively backward French economy which would in fact last right into the twentieth century. The funding came from private banks, including several new ones, but most notably from that of James de Rothschild, who made loans to the government as well as to the railway network and to mining companies. The wealthiest man in the city, a baron and a renowned patron of the arts, he entertained lavishly in his magnificent mansion in the Rue Laffitte such prominent figures as Balzac, Rossini and Chopin.

With the city maintaining its reputation for luxury goods and the fashion trade, wealthy foreign tourists mingled with visitors from the provinces, often attracted by the idea of a trip to Paris on one of the new trains. For beyond the specialist perfume or jewellery shops in the Place Vendôme or the Rue de la Paix – so attractive in the evening since it was the first street in Paris to be lit by gaslight – there were the covered galleries with all their offerings and the new 'novelty shops' selling a wide array of different articles, including novelties such as mini-cigars wrapped in fine paper, which were apparently called 'cigarettes'. And then, as a change from the theatre or the opera, one could visit the new luxurious Moorish-style Deligny baths floating close to the bank on the river, with its large swimming pool, its 340 well-maintained cabins and its restaurant. It did indeed give pleasure to very many Parisians until an unfortunate collision with a trawler on the river saw it sink slowly beneath the water in 1993.

In the cultural sphere, the Romantic trend was beginning to yield to some degree to realism. If the most prominent painter at the annual Paris Salon tended to be Delacroix – although his famous allegory of the 1830 Revolution, *Liberty Leading the People*, was not allowed to be shown in public until 1848 – the arrival of the realist Gustave Courbet at the 1844 Salon was a sign of changing times. As for the Romantic writers, if Gautier and Gérard de Nerval were still living the Bohemian life, former royalists such as Victor Hugo and Lamartine were turning republican. And it is a sign of the changing attitudes of the time that we find Lamartine, before the National Assembly of which he was a deputy, attacking the practice of duelling as 'the last trace of barbarism in our customs' and arguing that it should be made illegal. Barbarous or not in an increasingly middle-class society, some famous names were attached to this feudal hangover – and not only political figures such as Louis Blanc, Adolphe Thiers or Georges Clemenceau.

The young Alexandre Dumas, in dandyish buccaneering attire, finding himself mocked by a soldier playing billiards in a café, swept the balls dramatically off the table and issued his challenge. When they met in a quarry near Montmartre on the early morning of a freezing January day and his opponent nevertheless insisted that they strip to the waist, Dumas's trousers fell down. He recovered, managed to touch the soldier on the shoulder with the tip off his sword, the soldier tripped backwards over a tree root, they agreed it was too cold, and honour was satisfied. As the century progressed, duelling became more theatrical than dangerous, with the solemn *Annuaire des Duels* announcing that of the 422 duels recorded in the fifteen years from 1875 to 1890, only twelve had resulted in a fatality.[13] By 1897, when we find Marcel Proust challenging Jean Lorrain for insinuating in a hostile review that he is gay, it has become gestural to the point of being comical. For Proust was indeed gay, but so too was Jean Lorrain. And if Proust was frail and heavily asthmatic, Lorrain had syphilis and suffered from hallucinations. Nor had either of them spent much time with a pistol so, at dawn in the Bois de Meudon, they contrived somehow to miss each other. Since the old practice of duelling was largely killed off by the impersonal, mechanical nature of death in the First World War, there was astonishment and some derision when a duel between two members of the National Assembly was reported as late as 1976.

Beneath the glittering surface of this city so often seen as the prototype of European civilisation, deep fractures were developing due to the interaction of two factors. The first was that, as tended to happen in the early phase of industrialisation, the rich seemed to be getting richer and the poor poorer. And indeed, even though the wealth of Paris was estimated to have doubled between 1820 and 1847, the living standards of all but a minority of workers had deteriorated.[14] As early as 1828 the moderate *Journal des Débats* could describe 'the shocking contrast of abject poverty in the midst of wealth and abundance, of idleness and vagrancy in the midst of the most active industry and the most perfect civilisation'.[15] The second factor was clearly the explosive doubling of the population, which propelled the increasing division of Paris, with the middle class moving towards the north-west of the city and the enlarged working class expanding towards the new industrial areas in the east. Parisians were now divided by class.

Certainly, the condition of the working class, originally laid bare by the cholera epidemic and worsening over the years, was grim. It would become manifest again from 1846 onwards by an economic downturn due to bad harvests, leading to increased joblessness, sabotage in factories and the looting of bread shops. Two-thirds of the population, some seven hundred thousand people, too poor to pay taxes or to have a vote, lived in heavily overcrowded conditions, often six or more to a room, with the lack of water or other amenities leaving them continually exposed to disease. These conditions led to infanticide, abandonment and street prostitution as well as to the spread of rickets and tuberculosis. If the imaginative Balzac's often nightmarish view of Paris gives no picture of this lowest level of society, to which he had no access, it is not surprising that the authorities were unable adequately to understand it, let alone deal with it. So the division was left to lead to mutual mistrust, mutual fear and even mutual hatred. And the image of Paris was being damaged in the process, to the point that even some of the poor were beginning to leave the city.

People were hurling mud or rubbish at passing carriages, middle-class men were arming themselves to deal with robbers or angry vagabonds in the streets. As early as 1832 the *Journal des Débats* had warned of an 'invasion of barbarians' and Paris was now beginning to be seen not as the 'queen of cities' but as a new Babylon, a place that had lost its identity because of the invasion of these strange, inferior, unhealthy 'nomads': 'vile, appalling beings' in the words of Henri Lecouturier, 'a weeping wart on the face of this great city', as he wrote in 1848.[16] Yet even if in the alarm and confusion some were veering towards racist and anti-Semitic language, political analysis was increasingly being conducted in terms of class conflict. Even Guizot, now prime minister, proclaimed his mission to be to ensure the preponderance of the middle classes in France – although by limiting the franchise he was in practice only serving the wealthiest section of that class – but the most notable proponents of economic change at this time were the socialists, 'Utopian' or otherwise.

Saint-Simon, as already mentioned, argued that society should be scientifically reconfigured and governed by financiers, industrialists and scientists rather than by traditionally privileged figures with no relevant experience. Pierre-Joseph Proudhon, famous for having said that 'property is theft', argued that control of the means of production should be in the hands of the workers themselves and that they should organise themselves to achieve this. Charles Fourier, who is said to have hurried back to his home in the Rue Léon Cladel at noon every day in the hope of a visit from the millionaire who would turn up to finance his proposals, influenced the communes that later developed in America and is credited with coining the word 'feminism'.[17] Karl Marx arrived in Paris in 1843 in order to work with the German revolutionary writer Arnold Ruge, who saw Paris as the 'great laboratory where world history is being formed'. Friedrich Engels came over from England to meet him and they had their first lengthy session at the Café de la Régence in August 1844 – although when Louis-Philippe decided that he had 'had enough of German philosophers', Marx was obliged to move on to Brussels.

In July 1847, the opposition launched a series of open-air banquets to demand reform of the electoral system. When the government issued a ban against any further such demonstrations and called upon the National Guard to enforce it, the Guardsmen made clear their agreement with the reformists, leaving a tense stalemate. Yet at the start of January 1848, at the reception for the annual goodwill visit of the foreign ambassadors, Louis-Philippe was in optimistic mood. In expanding on the general outlook for peace and prosperity, he declared that two things were henceforth impossible in Europe: war and revolution.[18] How could he seem so out of touch? Was it that he was now in his mid-seventies or that, having survived in a difficult situation for fifteen years, he assumed that he could continue? Or was it rather that, having constantly seen the avoidance of war as 'the guide and polar star' of his political conduct, he felt that he had done the essential by keeping France – and Europe – out of further bloody entanglements? Whatever his reasons, it took only seven weeks and another violent clash in the streets for the monarchy to crumble and send Louis-Philippe – disguised as an unshaven, wigless 'Mr William Smith' – back to England and exile in leafy Twickenham. It was the end of monarchy in France.

The New Paris of Napoleon III

....

Paris was now accustomed to leading the dance of historical change not only on behalf of France itself but of Europe as a whole. And once again, when the monarchy fell at the end of February 1848, it would prompt the series of upheavals commonly called the 'Springtime of the Peoples', which would affect almost all of mainland Europe, especially Austria, the German states, the Netherlands and Italy. Although the situation obviously varied from country to country, and the background reasons were often conflicting, the revolutionary movements involved were essentially liberal and democratic in character. They reflected a changing Europe in which the early stage of the industrial revolution was beginning to create a new class structure, in which the popular press was beginning to spread political awareness along with knowledge of other countries, and in which new drivers such as socialism and nationalism were coming to the fore. As for the immediate triggers of the disturbances across Europe, there was the economic crisis brought about by crop failures starting in 1845, due mainly to the potato blight that struck northern Europe, particularly Belgium, Prussia and the Netherlands as well as killing over a million people in Ireland. There was also, of course, the unwillingness or inability of the conservative ruling class in the various monarchies to countenance liberal reform.

Insofar as the Paris revolution may have served as a model for others, how then did it proceed? It began as an insurrection, with fifteen hundred barricades made up of square paving stones, chopped–down trees, omnibuses or whatever was to hand. No sooner had Louis-Philippe gone than it turned into a carnival. The Palais-Royal was invaded, and royal paintings were ripped to pieces. The Tuileries Palace was similarly pillaged, with the royal family's clothes and ornaments being shared out and worn mockingly in the street. The throne itself was carried out and paraded through the city by a crowd sporting royal accoutrements as far as the Place de la Bastille, where it was ceremonially burnt beside the July Column. Others among the revolutionaries, making use of the royal wardrobe and playing at being monarchs, remained in the Tuileries for up to ten days, getting drunk on the royal wines and ordering the royal cooks to prepare elaborate royal banquets. With armed men everywhere but no police in sight, there were groups parading or talking animatedly in the streets, children running around with flags or letting off fireworks and everywhere a state of joyous excitement that was prolonged well into the night.[1]

However, the crowd was soon demanding that the carnival be translated into political action and the radical leaders were already laying plans at the Hôtel de Ville. Under the pressure of this situation the Chamber of Deputies, led by Lamartine, joined them at the Hôtel de Ville and eventually constructed a broad provisional government incorporating several of the radical leaders including the socialist Louis Blanc. Quite revolutionary decisions were now taken – that there would be a national election on 23 April for a Constituent Assembly charged with setting up a republic, that there would be universal male suffrage creating 9 million new voters, that all citizens would be guaranteed the 'right to work', and that National Workshops would be set up to that end. However, problems were soon mounting. When the stock exchange reopened on 7 March, the shares had lost half of their value. Money, like many of its wealthier middle-class owners, was fleeing abroad, banks were not paying out, shops were closing, unemployment was rising, and the National Workshops system was both costly and ineffective. In consequence, the government was having to take the highly unpopular step of raising taxes. As the writer Charles Augustin Sainte-Beuve expressed it ironically, if with some exaggeration, 'the wealth of France was completely swallowed up in two weeks, and all in the name of equality and fraternity'.[2]

There was indeed a rather grim irony in this situation. While the working-class radicals had relied for support, or at least toler-ance, on the lower middle classes, their interests were now diverg-ing with the economic downturn and the new taxes imposed by the government, as evidenced by a protest march of traders and others on 10 March. Similarly, the working-class radicals now found themselves at odds with the peasants and small farmers in the provinces, who were resentful at having to pay what they saw as 'Paris taxes' caused by the large sums being spent on the National Workshops. Beginning to fear a poor result in the elections for the Constituent Assembly, the radicals tried to obtain a postponement in order to allow the inexperienced electorate to educate itself to the political realities, but their appeal was rejected. The result was that a quite conservative body emerged, with some five hundred bour-geois republicans, three hundred constitutionalist monarchists and only eighty radicals and socialists, no more than a tenth of the total. The revolutionary element was now at odds not just with the Parisian lower middle class and the peasantry, but with the National Assembly and the very universal franchise for which it had been pressing. Revolution was not turning out to be easy.

Yet it was under the influence of Paris that a broader revolu-tionary movement had come alive across Europe. An uprising had occurred in mid-March in Vienna, forcing the Austrian chan-cellor Klemens von Metternich to flee to London, and it had been followed within days by insurrections in Rome, Berlin and Milan. Indeed, Paris had become a home from home for a collection of continental radicals – to the point that there had been Poles, Germans and Hungarians supporting their comrades on the barricades – and there was particularly strong support from Chopin and Victor Hugo among others for the cause of Polish independence from Prussia. In mid-May, an enormous manifestation took to the streets, broke into the National Assembly, demanded a declaration of war against Prussia and Russia for the sake of Poland, then dissolved the Assembly and proclaimed a new provisional government under the revolutionary leaders Auguste Blanqui, Armand Barbès and Louis Blanc. Just as the Polish issue was largely a pretext, so the ease with which they captured the Assembly – given the ease with which they were defeated, and the leaders arrested – suggests that they may have walked into a trap.[3] What is certainly clear is that they had strengthened the hand of the conservative forces in the chamber, where a 'Party of Order' was now in command.

There was still one last, desperate throw of the dice with an uprising during the 'June Days' of 23–6 June, provoked by the closing of the National Workshops. It involved a core of some fifteen thousand workers supported by elements of the National Guard, and it developed into a ferocious street battle in the eastern districts and the Latin Quarter. The minister for war, General Eugène Cavaignac, had been given full powers and he used them with a vengeance, since he had artillery at his command and was now able to use the new railways to bring up rapid reinforcements. With no quarter given on either side, some one thousand six hundred soldiers and perhaps three thousand civilians were killed, around a thousand were arrested and four thousand transported without trial to Algeria. Many Parisians were as horrified by the brutality of the insurgents as by the viciousness of the repression and were sobered by having to remain in a scarred city under army control until October. Unless, of course, they were able to leave on the first ever 'holiday train' in France, which left for Dieppe on 1 August – as though to emphasise that Paris had lost its political ascendancy over the nation due to the combination of universal male suffrage and the arrival of the railways. It could already be said, as it has so often been said since, that as far as politics is concerned, 'Paris n'est pas la France.'

In fact, Paris was the only place in Europe where the 1848 Revolution had formally succeeded, at least to the extent that it had removed the monarchy. But it had run ahead of the country in terms of historical development and left a splintered society that was going to be difficult to govern. The monarchists themselves were divided between traditionalists and constitutionalists, the upper middle class between traditional and *nouveaux riches* as well as from the lower bourgeoisie – although many shopkeepers and merchants among the latter were wiped out by closures caused by the insurrection and the curfew. The industrial city workers not only lived in a different world from the peasants but had seen working-class recruits to the army and sections of the National Guard fight against them with nationalistic ardour in street battles. On top of all that, the fact that churches were not badly treated during this insurrection reminds us of the complicating factor, not immediately related to wealth or class, that political viewpoint may be influenced by religious affiliation. Indeed, in traditionally Catholic France as opposed to historically Protestant Britain, the Church was closely aligned to the political right until the mid-twentieth century. Meanwhile, the situation was so confused as to seem to call for a solution from above or without.

Which is eventually what happened. The victorious Cavaignac was put in as temporary head of state by the Party of Order, and he stood in the presidential election in December. The other candidates were the radical democrat Alexandre Ledru-Rollin, the revolutionary working-class candidate François Vincente Raspail and Napoleon's nephew Louis-Napoleon Bonaparte, who had only recently returned from exile. In the event, Louis-Napoleon won by a landslide, obtaining almost three times more votes than the other three candidates put together, the shock of which led to the well-known saying, by a French reporter of the period, that 'the more things change, the more they remain the same', and to the famous observation of Karl Marx that 'history repeats itself, first as tragedy and then as farce'. So was this simply a rejection of the revolution and the Republic itself, or was it not also the desire to escape from confusion and even to get back to a sense of national pride?[4] It was sufficiently unexpected and ambiguous for the Assembly to treat the new president with icy silence when he presented himself, and for wise heads to say that he would never last.

He lasted for twenty-two years. Initially elected for a four-year term, he proceeded cautiously, approving a variety of measures agreeable to this conservative assembly. He agreed to proposals to reduce the electorate and to restrict the freedom of the press, as well as approving plans to give the Church back its hold over public education. He hoped to obtain a constitutional amendment that would enable him to continue beyond the four-year limit, but he never quite convinced the traditionalists in the Assembly, who kept him financially on a short rein, and it became clear that the extension would not be granted. Spurred on by his advisers and by the army, he staged a coup in December 1851, held a plebiscite under the wider franchise and obtained 72 per cent of the vote. The stock exchange leapt, the opposition fell silent and within a year, by another plebiscite in which he obtained 92 per cent of the vote, he had become the Emperor Napoleon III, head of what became known as the Second Empire.

The reputation of Napoleon III was for long overshadowed by his defeat by Prussia with the loss of Alsace-Lorraine in 1870 – he was famously dismissed by Victor Hugo, in contrast to the greater Napoleon, as 'Napoleon le Petit' – but he has been viewed more favourably in recent times. Not that he is an easy figure to label. He had a romantic sense of destiny, which inclined him to take risks, but he was also unsure and cautious. He was intelligent, but his mind often seemed to be elsewhere, kind and well-disposed but rather distant in manner. Yet these inner conflicts reflect the contradictions of the situation in which he found himself, not just as a virtual newcomer assuming control of a large and troubled country with the support of the people and against the political establishment, but as a man strongly influenced by the ideas of the utopian socialist Saint-Simon now taking on the powerful role of emperor.[5] If his contemporaries had some difficulty knowing what to make of him, he could have been pardoned for not always knowing quite what to make of himself. However, he did know what he wanted to make of Paris.

This was, after all, his third attempt to become emperor. In 1836, at the age of twenty-eight, with the support of an artillery general, he attempted to raise an army revolt in Strasbourg in the name of Napoleon. It was a flop, which had him arrested, although Louis-Philippe had him shipped off to New York to avoid any unhelpful publicity arising from a trial. Four years later he mounted another, equally unsuccessful attempt at a military take-over with the help of army units based in Boulogne. This time Louis-Philippe had him tried and condemned to life imprisonment in the royal fortress of Ham in Picardy, where he spent almost six years studying to clarify his project and publishing, in particular, *L'Extinction du paupérisme*, or the abolition of impoverishment. Arguing that it was no longer possible to govern without involving the people, who must be given a stake in the system, he advocated combining a universal franchise with a state-directed, reformist approach run by a strong leader possessing extensive powers.

In May 1846, when refused permission to visit his ailing father, he shaved off his beard and moustache, borrowed the clothes of a workman, threw a plank over his shoulder, walked out of the fortress – a trick borrowed by André Malraux, the future minister for culture, when captured in 1940 – and made his way to London. Enjoying the social scene after the years of imprisonment, he had a brief affair with the famous actress Mademoiselle Rachel (Elisabeth Félix), who was touring in *Phèdre*, before falling for the beautiful heiress Elizabeth Ann Howard who, when the idyll was interrupted by the outbreak of the revolution and he felt that he ought to return to France, was fortunately able to finance his plans. Once in Paris, though still officially banned, he set up an office with his supporters and it was noted that his luggage included a scroll containing a large map of a transformed Paris, with new streets and other features indicated in a range of different colours. For although the changes would be attributed to Haussmann, the prefect of the Seine, he himself insisted in his memoirs that he had 'merely been the one who had implemented it'.[6] The conception, the basic plan, the will and the patience to drive it through came from the emperor.

If few at the time anticipated the transformation of Paris that Louis-Napoleon had in mind, there were increasing signs that changes were needed. The cholera epidemic of 1849 had just killed some sixteen thousand people and it was clear, as the microbiologist Louis Pasteur with his germ theory was pointing out, that this had much to do with lack of hygiene and overcrowding. It was also a concern that these unhealthy poor areas with their narrow streets could become embattled areas of insurrection. More broadly, Paris had become not just the political and fashion capital of the country, but the point of convergence of the new railways, the place where banks and major companies generally had their headquarters and indeed, if a little surprisingly, as the prominent entrepreneur Émile Pereire declared, 'the principal manufacturing city in the kingdom'.[7] Yet, in this new age of steam and industrial innovation, Paris was still basically a collection of medieval villages with an overlay of royal and aristocratic embellishments that depended for its design on little more than the river. And it not only needed order and coherence, but it also needed proper housing, clean drinking water, adequate sewerage and fresh air.

This enormously ambitious project called for a high range of professional skills and Haussmann, chosen because he had made a reputation for himself in Bordeaux, was well supported by qualified people: architects for planning and construction, engineers for sewers and aqueducts, horticulturists for new parks and gardens, and a sculptor for new monuments. It also called for freedom and speed of action in taking over the properties designated for demolition to make way for new developments, and authorisation to proceed could be obtained by simple imperial decree. Above all, since it would involve up to three thousand workers and since the expropriated owners had to be compensated, the project called for a vast amount of money. The 50 million francs provided by the parliament were not nearly sufficient, but Haussmann devised a way of making the project partly self-funding by taking advantage of the added value that reconstruction would bring. He would reimburse at the current market rate, then sell off unused spaces at the new higher rate. Despite this there would also, as the enterprise proceeded over the years, be a need for bank loans, notably from the new investment bank of the Pereire brothers, the Crédit Mobilier.

The first stage was the creation of a new north–south and an east–west axis, which would both open up the city for the anticipated rise in traffic, and provide a high degree of uniformity and architectural distinction. There had been a version based on the original Roman axis, involving the Rue Saint-Jacques on a north–south axis and the Rue Saint-Honoré on an east–west axis, but they were by now hopelessly narrow and crowded. The new east–west axis to go along the Rue de Rivoli and the Rue Saint-Antoine was given priority, so that the Rue de Rivoli and a new Grand Hôtel du Louvre could be completed in time for the Universal Exhibition of 1855. Work then began on the north–south axis, involving notably on the northern side the Boulevard de Sébastopol, which meant what Haussmann happily called the 'gutting' and cleansing of one of the poorest, most crowded and most disease-ridden areas of old Paris.[8] The southern side involved creating the Boulevard Saint-Michel and continuing via the Rue d'Enfer up to the Porte d'Orléans. The crossing point of the two axes was the Place du Châtelet, where two theatres, now the Théâtre du Châtelet and the Théâtre de la Ville, were built on either side of the square.

In 1858, owners of properties designated for demolition obtained a judgement whereby any unused land should be returned to them, so Haussmann lost their resale value and had to rely more on bank loans. However, he contrived to make these both indirect and long term, enabling the next phase to be even more ambitious than before. The aim now was to create a network of new boulevards to connect the inner city both with the new railway stations and the existing outer circle of boulevards created under Louis XVIII. These new developments, to mention only a few, included the boulevards Magenta, Malesherbes, Raspail and the present Boulevard Voltaire, plus the squares Place de l'Europe (now Simone Veil), the present Place de la République and the present Place Charles de Gaulle, which was redesigned with new avenues radiating from the Arc de Triomphe as from a star. A central aim for Haussmann was the complete recasting of the Île de la Cité, where he preserved the Sainte-Chapelle and the Conciergerie with its revolutionary associations, but cleared a square in front of Notre-Dame and demolished the unhealthy old medieval streets. The work here included two new streets, two new official buildings, the Préfecture de Police and the Tribunal du Commerce, and the rebuilding of two bridges.

Yet all that was only part of the plan, for Napoleon III also annexed those outlying communes, such as Ménilmontant, Vaugirard and Montrouge, which were formally outside Paris yet within the outer ring of fortifications. This increased the population from around 1 million to almost 1.7, raised the number of arrondissements to the present twenty and raised the tax income for future projects, which more than provided for the extra connecting thoroughfares involved. Taken overall, the range of Hausmann's activity within the framework of this new and larger Paris is extraordinary. There are new or renovated government buildings, as well as schools, hospitals, the new central market and churches. There are the new sewers, as well as the modern aqueducts and reservoirs required for a clean water supply. There are the twenty-four new public squares within the city as well as four newly created major parks at the cardinal points of the compass: the Bois de Vincennes, the Bois de Boulogne, the Parc des Buttes-Chaumont and the Parc Montsouris. With ongoing projects such as the Opéra to be finished after Napoleon and Haussmann had left the scene, this was a monumental effort of urban reconstruction.

Needless to say there were complaints, most damagingly about the cost and the indirect mode of funding which, in combination with a resurgence of the republican opposition in the election of 1869, brought about Haussmann's resignation. Inevitably also, there were complaints about the inconvenience caused by this unending construction work, about the loss of historic old medieval areas, about the resulting rise in property values and rents, or about the fact that with rich and poor no longer living in the same streets the classes were being distanced even further. There were complaints about the bourgeois appearance of the new buildings, even about what Jules Ferry, a republican opponent of the emperor, called their 'triumphant vulgarity and materialism'.[9] Yet while it may sometimes seem that there is a certain sameness about those fine wide streets stretching out from Place du Général de Gaulle, or that the appearance of the apartment blocks verges on the grand bland, the value of the transformation brought about by Napoleon III and Haussmann is not to be underestimated.

It was indeed an attempt to rationalise, make more liveable and beautify an increasingly middle-class city, and indeed the typical apartment block, with its six storeys becoming slightly less luxurious as they rise up towards the servants' rooms at the top, seems like a cross-section of a middle-class society. However, Haussmann's approach is classical, and its success is due to his ability to balance different considerations and achieve a harmonious whole from quite different elements. He combines the structural uniformity of the blocks with variety in the details, just as he balances a run of streets with squares and attempts to balance street life with open spaces so that the citizen will ideally be within ten minutes from a park. But perhaps the greatest merit of the Haussmann transformation is simply that it was built to the human scale. There is a proper relationship between the height of the buildings and the width of the streets, while the buildings themselves are of a comfortable fixed height. It is telling to note the outrage in the early 1970s at the appearance of the skyscraper the Tour Montparnasse – it was said grimly that its sole merit was that it was the only place in Paris from which you could not see the Tour Montparnasse. Since this finally provoked a ban on buildings over seven storeys in central Paris, it is clear that the Parisians were at ease with the city as conceived during the Second Empire.

Paris may have been dethroned politically in that it no longer led national opinion in elections, but it was in process of being recast as a model of modernity and the European capital of high bourgeois style, fashion and pleasure. The Universal Exhibition of 1855 – there would be another in 1867 – was designed to establish that reputation. While the new railways were already bringing in over two thousand visitors a day, the exhibition brought in over 5 million and, equally important in enhancing the status of the regime, it brought a very successful official visit by Queen Victoria, the first by a British sovereign since the Hundred Years War. There were specially constructed viewing galleries in various areas for different activities including: a Gallery of Machines displaying new machinery of various kinds in operation, a Rotunda displaying luxury products such as Sèvres porcelain, Baccarat jewellery or tapestry from the Gobelins factory, and a Palace of Industry displaying a range of stylish treatments of public and domestic utility goods. Inevitably, there was also a Palace of Fine Arts displaying some five thousand pictures from twenty-eight countries, with the retrospectives of Ingres, Delacroix and other French painters being particularly appreciated. Altogether, it was a highly elaborate, financially burdensome yet successful enterprise of which the new empire could feel proud.

Obviously, the visitors needed somewhere stay, so in addition to the new Grand Hôtel du Louvre with its seven hundred rooms and its palatial salons – to be followed by a sequence of Grands Hôtels at regular intervals from 1862 onwards – there were over two hundred more moderately priced hotels around the railway stations and in the area between the Rue de Rivoli and the Grands Boulevards. The visitor might start by going shopping, especially since 1852 saw the birth of the *grand magasin*, or modern department store, with the Bon Marché, which aimed largely at a feminine clientele. This introduced the novel features that there was a vastly increased selection, that prices were not only reasonable but fixed to avoid uncomfortable haggling, and that shoppers were able to wander freely around and touch or compare articles at their leisure. The Bon Marché was followed by Le Printemps, which pioneered seasonal sales, and by a series of other such stores. On the way back to the hotel with the shopping, the visitor might call at one of the new photographers who were sprouting up and advertising with studies of the emperor, the empress and celebrities such as the actress Sarah Bernhardt or the poet Baudelaire. Indeed, the emperor's photographer Disdéri was churning out hundreds of visiting cards bearing the purchaser's portrait every day.

In the evening, the action was on *le Boulevard*, as the Parisians familiarly termed the entertainment district of the Grands Boulevards. That is where the glamorous cafés were to be found, with the Boulevard des Italiens alone boasting the Café Riche, lauded for its high cuisine by the writers Gustave Flaubert and Guy de Maupassant, the Café Anglais, described by Balzac and

Proust, the Café Tortoni, famous for its ice-cream dishes, and the immensely elegant Café de Paris, with its fine old mirrors and magnificent carpets. And *le Boulevard*, of course, is where the shows were to be found, whether melodramas, satirical comedies or opera, both serious and light. The Opéra itself ranked with La Scala of Milan as one of the most prestigious musical theatres in Europe and was therefore politically significant, so it was important for the emperor to support it and he and the empress were duly seen regularly on opening nights. But for Napoleon, as for most of his prominent supporters, it was more of a social requirement than an artistic pleasure. The Paris audience's taste at this time went rather towards the lighter French 'grand opera' with its ballet interludes and, while Verdi's *Don Carlos* received a polite if hardly warm welcome, Wagner's *Tannhäuser* met with the impatient stamping of feet.[10] Napoleon himself, like the empress, was more at ease with the lighter comic opera of Jacques Offenbach who, with such pieces as *La Belle Hélène* or *La Vie Parisienne*, had a glittering career in Paris. Indeed, Offenbach's operettas – tuneful and amusing while poking harmless fun at the regime – seemed to incarnate, for locals as well as for visitors such as the Prince of Wales, the knowing *joie de vivre* of 'gay Paree' at this time.

Napoleon was acutely aware of the role the court could play in keeping the citizens happy while integrating them into the orthodoxies of the empire. He was fortunate also in that the Empress Eugénie, the Spanish countess whom he liked to say he had married for love and not for political reasons, was seen as a charming and highly accomplished hostess. Since she was also pious, she could ensure – or try to ensure, for the emperor had what he called his 'little distractions' – that the tone of entertainments did not offend the religious and conservative forces supporting the regime. Indeed, in its pretentions to propriety as in its strictly organised routine, the imperial court might have been modelled on that of Louis XIV. In the Tuileries Palace, even a family dinner with perhaps a few friends was a sumptuous, processional and tightly timed affair, with the emperor leaving the others at 10 p.m. sharp to go back to work. As for the elaborate annual programme of balls, involving up to four thousand guests, banquets, receptions and dinners for particular groups, this was organised by the grand chamberlain and scrutinised by the empress to make sure that no one who was anyone, including foreign visitors in town, would be left out. Since the lesser royal palaces and the more prominent grandees were also encouraged to organise festivities, the *beau monde* of Paris from November to May seemed to be enjoying one large party.

And so, it need hardly be said, were the fashion designers, the shoemakers, the hairstylists, the jewellers, the florists and the purveyors of gloves and ribbons – indeed, there was one view that, if you were wearing the right shoes, gloves and ribbons, the dress became a mere accessory. In any event, the whole outfit could cost from 700 to 1,200 francs, equivalent to the annual income of many families and the reason why people often hired their costume, especially if a fashionable lady felt that her reputation would not survive appearing twice in the same dress.[11] Another reason for the high cost was that this was the age of the crinoline, the large hooped skirts in multiple layers that had originated in England but now ballooned in France. They created a nice contrast with a fashionably narrow waist, but they became so large – bordering on 3 metres wide – that the palace was forced to limit the number of invitations to the ball at one point. It was the empress who set the tone for fashion and her personal designer, the Englishman Charles Frederick Worth, who dominated the scene by going beyond the traditional way of ordering a costume. At his superb premises in the Rue de la Paix, he presented various new fashions worn by models who paraded among the clients, who could then choose one, but have it made in a different fabric or colour. Since he also allowed the department stores to copy his styles for the middle-class customer, he found himself leading an industry employing some sixty thousand workers and supported by around forty fashion magazines.

The empress was particularly fond of historical fancy-dress and masked balls, especially those imitating the masquerade balls of Venice and those patronised by Marie Antoinette in the reign of Louis XVI. Indeed she herself, when she was not appearing as Diana the huntress, a mythical shepherdess or an ancient Egyptian princess, masqueraded as the ill-fated Marie Antoinette and as the wife of a Venetian doge. One reason for the popularity of the masked ball was inevitably that the disguise enabled guests to engage in flirting and arranging trysts – though the unmasking sometimes led to comically unwelcome discoveries – and the emperor, who liked to appear as a Venetian grandee, was not unappreciative of the opportunities presented.[12] This aspect did not enhance the reputation of the court in the eyes of some monarchists and traditionalists, who saw it as vulgar. As for the workers, who despite the emperor's creation of some improved workers' dwellings already felt pushed to the margins by Haussmann's reforms, they tended to be repelled by the obvious extravagance and the rumours of licentious activity in imperial circles.

One persistent rumour involving the emperor, who seems to have been genuinely fond of his wife but who needed his 'little distractions', concerned his dalliance with the legendary young beauty Virginia, Countess of Castiglione. She came to Paris in 1855 with her older and irritable husband, to whom she had been married off at seventeen, and the count elected to live in a street bearing his own name, the Rue de Castiglione. Blonde, with eyes of varying colour, she was not the beautiful but uninspiring young thing that the emperor at first glance took her to be, since she was bright, spoke several languages and was in fact a spy. Her relative the Count of Cavour, prime minister of Piedmont-Sardinia, was seeking an alliance with France against Austria in support of the unification of Italy and had sent her an unambiguous message saying: 'succeed, cousin, succeed by whatever means you care to use, but succeed'.[13] So at the next ball in the Tuileries, when she made a sensational entrance looking, as Princess Metternich put it, 'like Venus descending from Olympia', she achieved an invitation to a select party at Villeneuve-l'Étang, where the emperor took her in a rowing boat to see the island. They returned many hours later, looking relaxed but rather rumpled, to the visible distress of the empress, who was eight months pregnant, and the affair continued rather damagingly for Napoleon's reputation until the countess left in 1857, having given her all for the cause of Italian unification.

By the time of the Paris Universal Exhibition of 1867, which saw the arrival of so many kings and emperors that it was said that only the Pope was missing, Napoleon might well have reflected that he had successfully managed the delicate balancing act of being at once progressive and imperial, of promoting both the prosperity and the international standing of the country. His achievements on the progressive side of the balance, apart from having given so many more people the vote, were obvious enough. He had brought about the modernisation of Paris by Haussmann and, even in this heyday of the middle class, he had promoted hygienic housing for workers and controlled the price of bread. As an enthusiastic supporter of new techniques in industry and agriculture, he had embraced the industrial revolution. He had supported the growth of modern banking to encourage savers and to provide investment for the new mechanised production and for the new railway network supporting it, which would grow from 3,000 to 18,000 kilometres of track during his tenure.

As emperor, he had also engaged with the trickier business of promoting France's position on the international scene. He had greatly increased France's colonial empire since, even if his Mexican venture had turned out badly, he had established colonies in Africa, Indochina and the Pacific. He had also promoted the successful French project for the Suez Canal, due to be opened by the empress in 1869. The European context was more challenging and his broad aim here was to break up the system established to contain France at the Congress of Vienna in 1815. Victory in the Crimean War of 1854–6 was doubly helpful in that it isolated Russia and enabled him to cement a useful alliance with the British, which was celebrated at the Paris Peace Conference of 1856, when he was able to present his own vision of a peaceful, progressive and prosperous Europe of free nations. It was true that there had been a gradual increase in political opposition at home, largely caused by a deterioration in the economy, but he had met it with various liberalising measures, and he could feel that this great Paris Universal Exhibition would make the whole nation feel proud.

Certainly, the exhibition of 1867 was a most ambitious and elaborate affair, which attracted fifty-two thousand exhibitors from forty-two countries and some 10 million visitors. The entire area of the parade ground of the Champ de Mars was taken up by an enormous exhibition hall 500 metres long, rectangular in form with rounded corners, which had a domed pavilion in the centre surrounded by garden displays. There were seven large galleries covering Food, Arts and Crafts, Extractive Industries, Clothing, Furniture and Furnishings, the Liberal Arts and Works of Art, each offering either a thematic or a geographical pathway. In addition to some ninety smaller and often picturesque buildings scattered around the park outside – ranging from the copy of an Egyptian bazaar to a worker's dwelling and a lighthouse – there was an international exhibition of painting and sculpture named the Palais des Beaux-Arts. There was a museum of the history of work, reflecting a new interest in social concerns and workers' living conditions, there was extensive coverage of the colonies and there was a large, annotated display of rare medicinal plants. But the greatest attraction was the whole area of the new industrial practices, whether new materials such as aluminium or new techniques such as American telegraph technology. From a gallery in the roof space, to which they ascended by a lift, the visitors could see these machines destined to bring change to the world – not just the one designed to hollow out the isthmus of Suez for the new canal pioneered by the Frenchman Ferdinand de Lesseps, but the enormous 50-ton Krupp cannon of the Prussian display, representing the other side of modernity.

As regards the art section, apart from the novelty of the Japanese prints that would influence Claude Monet and Vincent van Gogh among others, the public response was neutral at best and many of the artists themselves were outraged. The organisers, perhaps understandably at a time of rapid economic and social development, displayed little awareness of the profound changes that were taking place in the domain of art. For the Second Empire did indeed, as Mainardi argues, mark the end of the traditional world of art as it had existed in France for two centuries and it was in the transition towards our modern industrial and cosmopolitan society that modernism was born.[14] An additional reason why the art on display was unexciting was that it was conceived as retrospective, which left little room for the current crop of rising talents. A concurrent exhibition of working painters in the regular Salon was intended to compensate for this, but since it failed to find room for such as Cézanne, Pissarro, Renoir or Monet, it was clearly selecting according to the same criteria and failing to understand the profound change in the context in which art existed at that time. In protest, both Gustave Courbet and Édouard Manet set up their own private exhibitions.

The whole purpose and meaning of art were changing under the pressure of new developments. Photography was depriving it of its magical ability to provide the image of an individual lasting far beyond the grave. With political changes, art was no longer tied closely to religious and monarchical power, so that painters were not dependent on government commissions or honours. The background intellectual influences were no longer just the

Church or traditionalists, but the sociologist August Comte, the physiologist Claude Bernard or the aforementioned Louis Pasteur. With the rise of the bourgeoisie and with American and other foreign buyers coming in, there was now a larger and increasingly international market, dominated by private galleries and dealers. Inevitably, in this situation the Académie des Beaux-Arts, the Salon and even the Universal Exhibition were losing their authority, with the result that the traditional hierarchy of categories, according to which historical painting had the highest rating, was breaking down.

Yet it was not easy for the public to move away from the idea of art as a privileged domain where life was distanced and idealised beyond common reality. There was mocking criticism of Pierre-Auguste Renoir for putting a folded newspaper in a painting and then there was the major controversy over Manet's *Olympia*.[15] This was a reworking of Titian's nude *The Venus of Urbino* of 1538 and was found offensive mainly because the model was now looking directly at the viewer, so that she seemed not just 'nude' but naked and was taken to be a prostitute. However, realism and genre painting were already moving towards Impressionism, which would flower under the Third Republic, establish the image of Paris for the world and indeed turn it into the capital of world painting.

The 1860s marked a decline in fortune for Napoleon III. In the first place, his health was failing markedly. He suffered increasingly from a very painful gallstone, which was treated with opium so that he often seemed lethargic and unable to cope. Since this did not prevent him from chain-smoking or indeed from indulging hopefully in his 'little distractions', and since so much depended politically on his health, the empress was often in despair – already at one point she had burst in upon the actress and courtesan Marguerite Bellanger to tell her 'Mademoiselle, you are killing the Emperor!'[16] In the second place, it was becoming clear that his progressive vision of a peaceful and prosperous Europe was dangerously naive, that assertive nationalism was on the rise and that Otto von Bismarck's Prussia was bent on leading a unified Germany that would seek to dominate Europe. If that 50-ton Krupp cannon at the exhibition had not alerted him to the danger, Prussia's defeat of Austria in 1866 certainly should have.

Matters came to a head in 1870 when France, fearing encirclement, felt obliged to object to the nomination of a Prussian to the vacant Spanish throne. In fact, the nomination was withdrawn, but Bismarck doctored the relevant 'Ems telegram' to disguise the fact and make it seem grossly insulting to France, with the result that Napoleon, although in no condition to take to horseback, was driven by the nationalist outrage at home to declare war. The superiority of the Prussian army in every department soon made itself manifest, the French were outmanoeuvred and Napoleon, encircled at Sedan, felt obliged to surrender in order to avoid heavy losses. The sheer suddenness and the humiliating nature of a defeat which so diminished France within Europe shocked Paris, drove the defiant Republican deputies to declare a new Republic which refused to recognise the defeat, and had the city under siege by the formidable Prussian army within two weeks. The situation could not have been worse.

Except that it could – and it would. Paris was in for what became known as *l'année terrible.*

The Paris Commune and the 'Good Old Days', 1870–1914

The defeat at the hands of the Prussians caused consternation in Paris. It was not simply that the French army had been comprehensively defeated on strategy, tactics and weaponry, with the French copper cannon looking out-of-date alongside the Krupp steel artillery – all of which cast a dark shadow over the future by suggesting that the major power on the continent was now Prussia. It was the humiliation of seeing the emperor, who was described as having been wandering vaguely around the battlefield, surrendering in such an ignominious fashion. He may have done so in order to avoid pointless deaths when the battle was obviously lost, but the empress herself was shocked that he should have failed to behave like an emperor and fight to the death. Her humiliation, like that of the Parisians who had become quite nationalistic over the war, may have been coloured by the fact that she had encouraged him to stand up to Prussia. At all events, the shared sense of catastrophe was such that no sooner had news of the capitulation reached Paris on 4 September 1870 than the imperial government had collapsed, and the crowd was marching on the Palais-Bourbon to confront the Assembly.

With the downfall of the empire assumed to be inevitable, the Republican deputies of Paris, in a replay of 1848, proceeded to the Hôtel de Ville and proclaimed a new Republic. They then set up a provisional Government of National Defence, presided over by the moderate General Louis Jules Trochu, with the radical Léon Gambetta as minister of the interior, Étienne Arago as mayor of Paris and Jules Ferry as prefect of the Seine. Having satisfied

themselves that they had created a balanced governmental structure that would also marginalise the revolutionary fringe, they
turned their attention rather innocently to negotiating peace
terms with the Prussians, whose armies were marching on Paris.
They were all the more shocked when Bismarck demanded not
only a compensation payment of 5,000 million francs but the
handover of Alsace and much of Lorraine. Since that was totally
unacceptable, it transformed the war from being a quarrel about
the Spanish throne into a struggle for national identity, thereby
legitimising the Republican government in its decision to resist
the Prussian demands, even after the city found itself under siege
by the Prussian forces on 19 September.

With the elaborate fortified wall built under Louis-Philippe
and with the two months of supplies that the government had
laid in just in case, Paris was confident of being able to resist an
attack. However, the Prussians, playing the cleverer hand yet
again, did not attack, leaving political differences within the city
to fester to the point that there was an insurrection by the revolutionary elements at the end of October. This was quickly
suppressed, and the government strengthened its hand by holding a plebiscite and gaining a large majority. Nevertheless, with
news coming in only sporadically by pigeon mail, and with
Gambetta's escape by balloon failing to bring in support, the
situation was worsening, as underlined by the failed attempt at
an armed breakout on 30 November, which cost a thousand
casualties. A bitterly cold December now combined with the
shortage of food, heating and medicines to make life very difficult, with people reduced to eating birds, cats, dogs, rats, horses
and the two much-loved elephants Castor and Pollux from the
zoo in the Jardin des Plantes. Bismarck now decided that a few
days of bombardment would settle the issue and although it
took three weeks of shelling and another failed outbreak by the
National Guard to drive the point home, an armistice was signed
on 28 January 1871.

But the disaster was far from over since Bismarck, no doubt fore-seeing that it would produce a conservative majority, insisted as a condition that a national election should be held in order to ratify the armistice. And indeed some four hundred monarchists were elected as compared with a hundred and fifty Republicans, whereas the picture in Paris was the reverse, with thirty-six of the forty-three seats going to the Republicans. This left Paris in the paradoxical position of being the capital city and the accepted seat of government while being politically at odds with the country as a whole. It also left the new government led by the seventy-four-year-old Adolphe Thiers, the experienced moderate Republican and long opponent of the Prussian war who was considered to be the best equipped to negotiate the peace, in the difficult position of having to cope with a largely unrec-onciled Paris – and this at a time when Prussian troops were camped and parading to general dismay on the Champs-Élysées.

The radical discontent in Paris was growing and its National Guard, consisting of one hundred and eighty thousand men who had retained their weapons, had now set itself up as a federation ready to defend the republican ideal against any attack. To create a safe distance from the city, Thiers moved the government to Versailles and attempted to establish its authority by suspending two radical newspapers and by proposing to remove the 227 copper cannons left over from the siege. Clemenceau, on behalf of the radicals, proposed a compromise, but the guns became a symbolical issue even within the government until Thiers, feeling that he could not be seen to back down, ordered a surprise incur-sion by the army to remove them. The surprise, as it turned out, was for Thiers and his government when the troops were met with missiles from furious Parisians as well as armed resistance from the National Guard. Some of the soldiers refused to obey, others deserted, barricades were thrown up against them every-where and, with the capture and shockingly violent execution of two generals, the situation soon reached the point of no return. Thiers was forced to order the immediate evacuation of all regular forces and government agencies from Paris to Versailles and left to ponder how to retake the city. This was no longer a war about succession to the Spanish throne, or even about a humiliating defeat by the Prussians. This was the French fighting the French, the Republic fighting Republicans for the delectation of those same Prussians sitting comfortably on the sidelines.

Meanwhile, the central committee of the National Guard had taken over the Hôtel de Ville and was organising elections for a new governing council. The revolutionary elements won no more than forty-two of the ninety-two seats but were still the dominant group in a divided assembly and it was they who imposed the name of the Commune, with its revolutionary associations. The new Council adopted an ambitious, radical and egalitarian social programme – even if women, although active, were still not treated as equals – and set up nine commissions to deal with the administration and defence of the city. Despite the initial violence and some arbitrary arrests, the leaders of this extraordinary experiment in democratic self-government – men such as Eugène Varlin and Édouard Vaillant – were cautious, moderate and respectful of property. Their belief in a secular, self-governing democratic society which abolished child labour, created proper working conditions and educated girls would hardly seem strange today and it was supported by significant figures of the time, such as Clemenceau and artists including Corot, Courbet and Daumier.[1] But in the immediate historical context it represented an unworldly dream, which would soon be shattered by confrontation with the state.

It was shattered in what became known for its shocking violence as the Semaine Sanglante, or the Bloody Week. Although the Commune's defences had been fraying at the edges during April 1871 as the government troops began a bombardment, the decisive attack did not come until 21 May. The Versaillais, as they would now be called, had relatively little difficulty in taking over the middle-class western parts of the city but, as they approached the working-class areas a few days later, they came up against barricade after barricade and ferocious resistance. The battle raged for days until it came down to hand-to-hand fighting and a last stand in the Père Lachaise cemetery, where 147 defeated Communards were shot in front of what has become famous as the Mur des Fédérés and thrown into a common grave. The Commune lost up to four thousand combatants, while the official figures for the army were 877 dead, 183 missing and over six thousand wounded. The Communards had set fire to the Hôtel de Ville, the Tuileries Palace and the Palais de Justice as well as executing some five hundred hostages, including the Archbishop of Paris. Yet the correspondent of the London *Times* was struck rather by 'the inhuman laws of revenge under which the Versailles troops have been shooting, bayoneting, ripping open prisoners, women and children during the last six days. So far as we can recollect, there has been nothing like it in history.'[2]

Of the ten thousand prisoners appearing before military tribunals over the next five years, many were sentenced to execution, life imprisonment or deportation to New Caledonia in the Pacific, and it was ten years before the Republic felt it safe to declare an amnesty. Whether or not the excessive violence on both sides had to do with the shame of serving up this fratricidal battle as a feast for the conquering Prussians, the Paris Commune has remained something of an embarrassment for the French. Needless to say, this did not prevent it from being mythologised at both the right and left ends of the political spectrum. The right tended to see the Communards as degenerate, worthless dregs of society and their women supporters as prostitutes, a view reinforced by the building of the great white basilica of the Sacré-Coeur on a site directly overlooking the battlefield – in order, as the government decree of 1873 had it, 'to expiate the crimes of the Communards'. On the left, the Marxists seized eagerly upon the Commune, with Marx himself describing it as 'the glorious harbinger of a new society', and Engels presenting it as 'the very image of the dictatorship of the proletariat'.[3] It produced the 'Internationale', the anthem that begins 'Arise ye workers from your slumbers', and it was embraced by the Communist Party, which instituted a pilgrimage with lilies of the valley to the Mur des Fédérés on May Day each year.

Each of these interpretations is simplistic and opportunist. The right-wing version does no justice to the human qualities and aspirations of many of the Communards involved. The left-wing version, as Marx himself soon realised, did not recognise that the 'communalism' of the Commune, with its democratic republican practices and its respect for private property, did not conform to the orthodox communist model. It enabled the French Communist Party to situate itself sentimentally within the national revolutionary tradition going back to 1789, but it was less the 'glorious harbinger' of the Russian revolution than, as one historian puts it, 'the culmination and end of the French revolutionary saga of the nineteenth century. Dusk, not dawn.'[4] For, as another writer points out, 'the physical power of the State had been greatly increased by modernisation and its political authority strengthened by universal male suffrage'.[5] The Commune was a great national tragedy and the sadness it generated is movingly encapsulated in the ballad with which it is associated, 'Le Temps des Cerises', or 'Cherry Time', but the utopian city state could not prevail against the unitary national state – even one weakened by a humiliating defeat – in the Europe of nations of the time.

How on earth, you may well wonder, did Paris, after such a humiliating defeat, with much of the city in ruins, with its signature public buildings gutted, with so many citizens slaughtered and the remainder of those on one side harbouring rancorous thoughts about those on the other side, proceed towards what is called its Belle Époque, the 'Good Old Days'? In the first place, it was only in retrospect, after the four draining years and far greater death toll of the First World War, that the period before 1914 came to be seen nostalgically as the innocent time before the outlook became wider and more disturbing. In the second place, the Good Old Days were not necessarily secure, stable, happy days – rather the reverse.

The city had been left bitterly divided politically and its situation was now a highly paradoxical one. It had already lost its political leadership of the nation and it had now been further cut down to size. Its National Guard had immediately been abolished and replaced by an army garrison to render any further disturbances unthinkable. A new constitution introduced in 1875 limited the representation of Paris and other potentially fractious cities in elections. The National Assembly continued to sit in Versailles until 1879 and, significantly, self-government under a mayor was replaced by the old Napoleonic method of control by a perfect of the Seine and a prefect of police, a system which continued right up to the 1970s. When General Charles de Gaulle made his triumphal entry into liberated Paris in 1944, he made a point of not engaging in the traditional appearance on the balcony of the Hôtel de Ville to receive the acclamation of the Parisians, even though the local Resistance had contributed much to the Liberation – *Paris n'était pas la France.*[6]

Yet Paris, after 1879, was still officially the capital city and the seat of government. Not only that, but it was the banking and financial centre of the country as well as being the cultural and fashion capital of France and indeed of the Western world. All the major national academic and research institutions were in Paris, all the important institutes, libraries, archives and museums. It was the centre of publishing, as of professional training for art, music and theatre. Until the latter part of the twentieth century the ambition of a professional in any field was to end his or her career in Paris – *monter à Paris* was the standard phrase. Nevertheless, this representative capital city had lost its political power. So Parisians could agitate and rebel all they liked – and since it was still an unstable society they certainly would – but they would get nowhere, it would all be make-believe, pure theatre.[7] So the Good Old Days would be not so much a contented time as an exciting time. But then happy, stable societies are unlikely to generate much fun and contradiction makes for drama and theatricality, even if the result is not so much tragedy as melodrama and even comedy.

There was indeed a degree of comedy involved in bedding in this new Third Republic. When Adolphe Thiers proposed a republican constitution in 1873, he was replaced as president by the strongly Catholic Marshal Patrice de MacMahon, who had played a leading part in putting down the Commune. MacMahon ensured that the new constitution of 1875 provided for conversion to a monarchy, the only problem being that there were two claimants. There was the Comte de Chambord, grandson of Charles X of the Bourbon line, and the Comte de Paris, grandson of Louis-Philippe of the Orléanist line. This required extensive discussion, in which the Vatican became involved, and the ingenious idea was finally mooted that the dilemma could be resolved by having both claimants, but in succession. The older Comte de Chambord, who was conveniently childless but has a pink rose named after him, would go first, die and be succeeded by the younger Comte de Paris, who would come over from Twickenham. However, there was another problem in that, symbolism being of the essence, they could not agree on the colour of the flag, the Comte de Chambord insisting on the Bourbon white and the Comte de Paris on the tricolour. The unreality of these debates was brought home by the increasingly anti-monarchist tone of the clear Republican majority in the election of 1876. MacMahon fought back by appointing as prime minister the hardline clerical conservative the Duc de Broglie, who suppressed even the word 'Republic', but by 1879 the Republicans had gained a clear majority, MacMahon had gone, the parliament was back from Versailles and the Republic had survived the lengthy melodrama over its legitimacy.

It was now time for Paris to demonstrate that, even it was neutralised politically at the national level, it was still at the centre of the excitingly progressive new Western world. And it would do so by three successive Universal Exhibitions, or World Fairs, the first of which was in 1878 and involved thirty-six participating countries, with Germany and Turkey not invited. The main building, an enormous structure some 700 metres long on the Champ de Mars, sported a statue named *The Republic* on its façade and contained a vast array of attractions, the most notable being the 'street of the Nations' for which each country provided the façade of one of its typical buildings, with the English manorial style rubbing shoulders with the Italian palace style and the Eastern pagoda style. A second pole of attraction was a large new Trocadéro Palace, containing exhibitions of ancient artefacts, a large ceremonial hall and, in the gardens sloping down towards the Seine, a series of national pavilions of Eastern and Western nations, as well as an aquarium. Thomas Edison demonstrated his phonograph, Alexander Graham Bell his telephone, and on show was the head of the Statue of Liberty, ready to be shipped off to New York. The exhibition lost money, but it signified helpfully to its 13 million visitors that Paris was back.[8]

The World Fair of 1889, by contrast, received 32 million visitors and made a profit of 10 million francs. Timed obviously to celebrate the 100th anniversary of the Revolution – which offended some European monarchies – it aimed to show how the Republic had taken advantage of a recovering economy to consolidate itself. Education was now free, compulsory and removed from Church control, Paris had the first *lycée* for girls, there were women doctors in the hospitals, there were new museums and the start of a new Sorbonne. All of these developments had been celebrated in annual Bastille Day celebrations, as by the enormous crowds that had followed the funeral of the great Republican Victor Hugo to the state hall of fame in the Panthéon. At a more everyday level, Paris now had a telephone directory, electric lighting on the boulevards, obligatory flush toilets, sports facilities at Racing Club de France and the Stade Français, not to mention compulsory dustbins named, not necessarily to the delight of his descendants, after the prefect, Eugène Poubelle. Inevitably, all this had created a reaction among monarchists, the new conservative Catholic daily newspaper *La Croix* was gaining influence and, with nationalism rising even in the working class, a new Bonapartist populist had appeared in the form of General Georges Boulanger, a former minister of war who had been threatening to turn a simple border incident into a full-scale war with Germany, which earned him the name of 'Général Revanche' or 'General Revenge'. He had been posted out of the way to Clermont-Ferrand, but the atmosphere was tense, and the shadow of a possible coup d'état hung over the exhibition.

The site was truly vast this time, the emphasis was on the use of steel in construction, and the star attraction was this enormous Eiffel Tower, the more astonishing since it was meant to be temporary – and there were pedantic purists who hoped that it would be temporary. There were eighty pavilions on the Champ de Mars exhibiting, among other attractions, a typical Cairo street, restaurants from various countries and a whole set of reconstructions of buildings from all over the ancient world, from the Etruscans to the Incas. There was the huge hall of machines celebrating new industrial processes, a hall of liberal arts with large sections on photography and medicine, and in the fine arts hall an extensive retrospective of the work of the previous century. And the festive atmosphere was well maintained, notably by the visiting Wild West show featuring Buffalo Bill and the sharp-shooting Annie Oakley. This second World Fair was very successful, and the success was soon cemented by the spectacular collapse of the threat from General Boulanger, who was being pushed increasingly towards a coup d'état. When the government issued a warrant for his arrest, he got cold feet, disappeared and ended up in Brussels, where he shot himself on the grave of his mistress two years later. His fall left the traditionalist and royalist sections of opinion seriously weakened.

Nevertheless, it was indicative of the volatile and confused society of the time that such a hollow figure, who was not even a good speaker, should have drawn support across the board from monarchists, Bonapartists and working-class nationalists. And the fractious 1890s would turn out to be a decade of scandals and colourful political events. There was the assassination of President Sadi Carnot by an anarchist in 1894 and scattered attacks over several years on restaurants and a church in Paris by anarchists such as Ravachol. There was the Panama scandal, revealing that de Lesseps, who had successfully built the Suez Canal, had run into difficulty in his effort to construct the Panama Canal and been bribing government ministers and deputies to conceal the fact, so that the investors had continued innocently to invest – and had lost over a billion francs. Since the Radical leader Clemenceau was also involved and the two men distributing the bribes had Jewish names, it provided a feast for Édouard Drumont's new fiercely anti-Semitic daily newspaper *La Libre Parole* and set the stage for the notorious Dreyfus case. When it emerged in 1894 that military secrets were being passed to the Germans, the Jewish staff officer Alfred Dreyfus was condemned and dispatched to Devil's Island. Even after the guilt of another officer was demonstrated, and writers such as Zola and Proust had waded into the fray, the 'honour of the Army' was defended to the point that Dreyfus was merely given a hurried 'pardon' in 1899 to avoid too much attention to the issue from the world press on the eve of the third World Fair of 1900.

This was an enormous enterprise, involving fifty-eight countries, eighty-three thousand exhibitors and 51 million visitors to the exhibition itself but, since it related closely to urban improvements, it also meant over 100 million travellers passing through the new Gare d'Orsay, the new Gare des Invalides and the enlarged Gare de Lyon. Also, while most of the new buildings were temporary, it left Paris with the two monumental exhibition halls off the Champs-Élysées, the Grand Palais and the Petit Palais. It aimed to provide a retrospective view of the nineteenth century, with separate exhibitions of everything from the arts to the progress in electricity or criminology – as before, the strong emphasis on the new technological developments also led to useful commercial contacts. There were forty national pavilions from every continent, colonial pavilions celebrating in particular the French colonies in Africa, the Caribbean and South-east Asia, an agriculture pavilion and *le vieux Paris*, an elaborate re-enactment of life in the city in past times. Also, Paris being Paris, there were entertainments of all kinds, with a *palais des fêtes* seating fifteen hundred and offering music or ballet, a typical 'Paris street' offering everything from jazz or comedy to marionettes and an upside-down house. Not to mention the famous Serpentine dances with enormous silk scarves of the American Loie Fuller being filmed by the new miracle of motion pictures.

Alongside the exhibitions in this archetypal capital of culture and pleasure, there were all the other entertainments of the theatre, the boulevards, Montmartre and indeed the associated cafés – where the waiters, as one writer reminds us, were called *garçons* because at that time they were in fact boys.[9] Indeed, simultaneously with the 1900 exhibition, there was the great Sarah Bernhardt in the premiere of *L'Aiglon* by Edmond Rostand, for which the visitors could hardly get a ticket for love nor money in order to weep over the sad and lonely death of Napoleon's son the Duke of Reichstadt, amid the empty grandeur of the Schönbrunn Palace in Vienna. Already aged fifty-five when she played this young man of twenty-one, she was one of the first actresses to play male parts and indeed had played Hamlet in the previous year in both Paris and London – using for the graveyard scene a skull given to her by Victor Hugo. Illegitimate by birth, she originally wanted to be a nun, but was led to become an actress and eventually developed her own more refined version of the declamatory style of the period, assisted by her gracious movements and by what Hugo – one of her many presumed lovers, including the Prince of Wales – called 'the Golden Voice'. After she had a leg amputated in 1915 following a stage accident in *La Tosca*, she played seated parts. She also featured in several early voice and film recordings.

Montmartre was obviously a must for the pleasure seeker. On a hill, with its windmills, its vineyards, its quarries, its old houses and its narrow winding streets, its countrified appearance provided a contrast to Haussmann's modern Paris. Also, it was cheap, so it was easier for artists such as Amedeo Modigliani, Kees van Dongen and Pablo Picasso to set up in an old building called Le Bateau Lavoir, so called because it resembled the old laundry boats on the river, which is where Picasso would paint *Les Demoiselles d'Avignon* – the building was replaced by a replica after a fire in 1970. It was also easier for entrepreneurs to set up a dance hall such as the Moulin de la Galette, one of the two remaining windmills and now a restaurant, but famous in its day and made more so by the painters Renoir and Van Gogh. There was also the cabaret Au Lapin Agile, meaning 'lively rabbit' but a play on the name of the sign painted by André Gill and a more inviting name than the original Cabaret des Assassins. This establishment was popular with struggling poets such as Guillaume Apollinaire and artists such as Maurice Utrillo, and still sees itself as the repository of French song. Nor should we forget the Moulin Rouge, the haunt of the diminutive painter Henri de Toulouse-Lautrec, where patrons could see Mistinguett doing the Apache dance or Jane Avril dancing the can-can.

Outside Montmartre, on the 'Boulevard', there were all the other entertainments, ranging from opera or theatre to the music hall, the *café chantant* and the circus. One famous cabaret music hall is of course the Folies-Bergère, named rather improbably given the often erotic nature of its shows after a nearby street called Bergère, meaning shepherdess. Originally offering operettas, popular songs and even gymnastics, it was later slanted towards female nudity and Josephine Baker would famously dance in the 1920s in a costume consisting of little but a string of bananas. Since the barmaids at the time of Manet's well-known painting of 1882, *A Bar at the Folies-Bergère*, were often presumed to be sexually available, he shocked respectable opinion by presenting a pretty barmaid with a slightly sad expression looking straight at the viewer. One is reminded also of his painting *The Luncheon on the Grass*, which depicts two perfectly dressed gentlemen sitting casually with a naked woman, who again is looking directly at the viewer. In a nineteenth-century city routinely described as the 'capital of pleasure', it is hopefully not to spoil the party unduly to recognise that, in a situation where women did not get the vote until after the Second World War, the pleasure was mostly for men.

The latter half of the nineteenth century and the early years of the twentieth century also represented the golden age of the novel. Paris, with its wars and its revolutions, was passing through a dramatic historical period while simultaneously undergoing an industrial revolution that was changing the class system and the conditions of life for so many. Moreover, all this was creating new political alignments and oppositions, while the physical city itself since the Haussmann reforms had been changing before people's eyes. Paris, insofar as it was seen as being in the lead in regard to these disconcerting changes, was bound to be seen as a prime challenge for the writer. And there was certainly a growing audience for the novel along with the parallel increase in demand for newspapers, with the two being often interconnected through publication by instalment. Without television or photographs in the newspapers, provincials – and even locals who knew only their own milieu – relied upon the novel for their understanding of this exciting new Paris, so that a lengthy description of a building that might today seem tiresome could be read avidly by the audience of the period. This was the novel's time.

It had been a little slow to get there, since it was not until Restif de la Bretonne's *Le Paysan Perverti* of 1775, a loosely written tale about a provincial sinking into crime in the city, that Paris began to assume any real importance in fiction. Even in Eugène Sue's serial novel *Les Mystères de Paris* of 1842–3, or in Victor Hugo's treatment of the 1830s in *Les Misérables* of 1862, reality is blurred by fantasy. Paris only became the heart of the novel with Balzac, whose almost hallucinatory vision of the city and its effect on individual lives were backed by detailed description. But by the mid-1850s the intellectual background was changing, it was now the age of Charles Darwin and of the sociologist Auguste Comte, and it was no longer accepted that a person's character was simply God-given, but that it must derive from heredity, culture and social conditions. Paris being such a self-consciously intellectual city, this led to an often confused theoretical debate about realism in the novel as indeed in the paintings of Courbet and others. There was realism, supported by Duranty's review *Réalisme* and Champfleury's collection *Le Réalisme*, which then led to the more explicitly determinist naturalism, firmly tied to heredity and milieu-conditioning, followed by a reaction from the mid-1880s onwards. And the development can be traced in three outstanding and contrasting novelists of the period: Gustave Flaubert, Émile Zola and Marcel Proust.

Flaubert's novel *L'Éducation sentimentale* of 1869 is set in the Paris of the monarchy of Louis-Philippe and the 1848 Revolution. Against this backdrop, he describes the career and disappointed loves of the young Frédéric Moreau in what amounts to a story of disillusionment, of life finally just ticking by. There are some fine moments and painterly descriptions in the novel, but it never quite comes alive. It is so obviously autobiographical that he often seems to take the hero for granted, does not project him fully or integrate him adequately with the background. So why was it less successful than his famous novel *Madame Bovary* of 1857, the story of a frustrated provincial wife who is driven to suicide following an affair and blackmail? The fact is that in this novel Flaubert – almost accidentally, since he was intellectually more of an idealist than a realist and was trying to make his harsh story beautiful – had brought about a mutation in the form. Until that point the novelist had been like a dramatist wandering among his own characters on stage, offering comments or reflections on this and that, and constantly showing his hand. Flaubert had devised the technique of getting the writer off the stage in order to let the story work by itself and give the novel the apparent separate existence that characterises high art. The novel cannot provide 'reality' since it is bound to reflect an individual viewpoint, but it can give what Maupassant called the 'illusion of reality' and gain in persuasive power through the techniques of impersonality. And if Flaubert faced an absurd charge of immorality over his heroine's infidelities – hardly shocking in that hypocritical society – it is precisely because his lack of comment made them the more real and the more disturbing.

Émile Zola, the leader of the later naturalist group of writers, was not only a prolific novelist, but a leading defender of Dreyfus and his death, from intoxication due to a mysteriously blocked chimney, may possibly have been murder. He was also close to the painters Manet and his old school friend Paul Cézanne. He conceived of his vast *Rougon-Macquart* cycle of novels as a controlled 'scientific' experiment, tracing the combined effect of heredity and environment over several generations. Such an ambition may well seem naive today, but it provided a convenient framework and not only did he back his plots with thorough research but, above all, he had the essential gift of creating larger-than-life characters. Although he did not confine himself to Paris, he covers many areas of the city. In *Le Ventre de Paris*, or *The Belly of Paris*, he depicts the life of the workers in the new central markets and there is a memorable evocation of the scents of different cheeses. In *Nana*, based on close research of an actual star performer living in a threesome relationship, he describes the rise of a streetwalker to become an operetta performer and high-class prostitute – if she becomes a destructive force, it is because her true nature has been damaged by her background. In *Au Bonheur des Dames*, or *The Ladies' Delight*, he sets the story in one of the new department stores, giving a full account of its innovations and internal workings. Elsewhere he deals with the Commune and in the late novel *Paris* of 1897, he brings out the political strains and the social inequalities of the city. In combining his mirror of society with an epic imagination he too tends, if less than Balzac, to mythologise Paris as a startlingly new and almost self-devouring force.

Marcel Proust's *In Search of Lost Time*, published in seven parts totalling over three thousand pages, is one of the monuments of the Western novel. It is as famous for its depiction of the upper-class life of the Boulevard Saint-German towards the end of the Belle Époque, as for its central theme of involuntary memory, one famous episode being the taste of the little shell-shaped cake known as the *madeleine*, which unleashes a whole train of memories and offers the hope that the past is never lost. This sense of a past embodied in the present leads to an imprecise chronology, as well as to almost unending sentences that seem designed to relate each thing to everything else and to make the world stand still. It also coheres with a certain mystery about this rather theatrical and hypocritical society in which the hero – also called Marcel – is seeking to establish himself but discovering the impossibility of love. Proust was torn between worlds. Although he came from a scientific family background, he was really more drawn towards the increasing current of idealism and, in emphasising the underlying continuity of the self, he is coming close to a secular version of the Christian soul. Also, as well as being part Jewish and a supporter of Dreyfus, he was gay but could not be accepted as such – as evidenced by the publisher Gallimard's dismissive comment when approached about a monument after Proust's death, that he already had his monument, the public convenience on the Champs-Élysées. In fact, the teasing Albertine of the series is a disguise for Albert and the cover slips at moments, as when her 'pussycat nose' is accompanied by a 'powerful neck with big moles'. One may not agree with Marcel that love is a tragic illusion, but there are some unforgettable characters and descriptions of nature in Proust. If he was himself once dazzled by this fading aristocratic Saint-Germain that left him so disillusioned, he illuminated its glamour and its pretensions, and in this vast fictional enterprise finally, and with some brio, brought it down about his own ears.

Over the last century and a half the image of Paris throughout the world has been coloured by the painting of the Belle Époque, with its remarkably large number of artists, many of them world famous. Naturally, they did not confine themselves to painting Paris, although there were several who were particularly drawn to city scenes, whether Camille Pissarro with his plunging views of the Boulevard Montmartre both by day and by night, or Utrillo with his documenting of bistros, churches and very ordinary streets. However, the leading painters normally trained and, for at least part of their career, lived in Paris, where they could rub shoulders with other practitioners, get the feel of a moving international market and meet dealers. So we have Monet's rendering of a smoke-filled Gare Saint-Lazare or of the Boulevard des Capucines under snow; Renoir's treatment of the Grands Boulevards, his scenes of boating on the river or the wonderfully lively and colourful dance at the Moulin de la Galette; Gustave Caillebotte's view of a Paris street in the rain, or of everyday people and a dog on the Pont de Europe; and of course Degas's indoor scenes of the orchestra in the Opéra, of a dance class, or of the actress Ellen Andrée sitting silently in a café looking apathetic as a result of regular recourse to the notorious 'green fairy' absinthe in the glass in front of her, which was eventually banned as dangerous in 1915.[10] These few examples already give a sense of what the city looked like at this time.

Given the intensity of cultural and political life in Paris, any major change in style was likely to divide opinion. Traditionalists could be offended by the depiction of the seamy side of the city, as by the casual treatment of nudity in everyday situations. Some on the left, by contrast, could feel that Impressionism soon turned into 'the house style of the haute bourgeoisie', as one writer calls it.[11] It is certainly true that the increasingly international art market was a monied one and that buyers tended to prefer the more attractive subjects, just as it is true that the painters in Paris worked essentially on the Right Bank and in Montmartre, where they tended to live and where the dealers were. Nevertheless, there is a number of pictures showing ordinary people at work, such as Caillebotte's three carpenters stripped to the waist as they strain at planing a parquet floor, or Monet's darkly stylised view of labourers unloading coal from a barge under a bridge. There were also those who were implicitly challenging the official view of the society, such as Manet in his more confrontational mode or such as Georges Seurat, contrasting the stilted formality of upper-class couples with relaxed working-class figures in his treatments of Sunday afternoon outings on the riverbank.

This concentrated cultural life also meant that the painting of the Belle Époque, with its rapid succession of proclaimed styles, was as subject to the same intense background influences as the novel, while its socially limited application only made the issue the more confusing. However, the basic question was simple: what was painting for? The old official historical subjects had lost their status while the advance of photography, by taking over the role of objective representation, threatened both portraiture and land-scape painting. This would lead to a sequence of loosely defined groupings, starting with the Impressionists such as Monet, Degas or Renoir, for whom painting would change from being the measured record of a scene or the appearance of an individual towards being a moment in time or an 'impression'. Understandably, under pressure to explain this new trend, some of them were led – as also were some later art historians[12] – to defend their approach in terms of the current theories of perception and equate their activity with a methodical scientific approach. However, since science obviously implies objectivity and impersonality, whereas their activity was necessarily subjective, the question of what painting was about remained open. So would the answer emerge from the runaway succession of movements and sub-movements that Paris would see over the next half-century?

This began with the Post-Impressionists, who reacted against the Impressionists' preference for naturalistic light and colour. Among these could be counted Henri Rousseau, whose artfully childlike and often colourful compositions have the effect of half-forgotten memories; or Toulouse-Lautrec who, if he was not busy painting Jane Avril dancing the can-can, was painting girls on horseback in the circus; and especially the influential Cézanne, who spoke of treating nature in terms of basic shapes such as the sphere or the cone and moved towards a more ordered, architectural approach, providing a bridge between the tradition and the future Cubists. But first there would be the Symbolists, such as Gustave Moreau with his love of the macabre, plus an offshoot in the form of the secret cult of the Nabis (or prophets, in Hebrew), who answered the question by insisting that the true artist was the agent of a higher power. Then came the Fauves (or wild beasts), the significant figure being Henri Matisse, who combined simple forms with vivid colours and painted numerous versions of Notre-Dame from his studio window. The last of this group of avant-garde movements – there would be others – were the Cubists, notably Picasso and Georges Braque, who portrayed objects broken up and reassembled in semi-abstract fashion to be viewed from different angles. The key picture here, influenced by his discovery of African masks, is *Les Demoiselles d'Avignon*, which

Picasso painted in 1907 – the reference is to a brothel in a street of that name in Barcelona, but the title was added later.[13] On a very large canvas, he portrays five outlandishly tall, gaunt, dark, depersonalised staring women in a semi-abstract setting. That stare looks forward eerily to his own stare in the grim-faced, ape-like self-portraits he produced just before his death. When it came to the question of the meaning of art or life, Picasso knew that there were no easy answers.

The early years of the new century promised a new world. There was the new Métro line from the Porte de Vincennes to the Porte Maillot and the first electrified surface line in Europe from Les Invalides to Versailles. There was the first aircraft factory in the world at Billancourt, the first aerodrome at Juvisy and the first flight over the English Channel, by Louis Blériot. There were petrol-driven buses and, above all, there were almost five thousand 'automobiles', a noun that the learned members of the Académie Française after due consideration had decided should be feminine. So there was the luxurious Salon de l'Automobile, the Monte Carlo Rally and agitated traffic police, now with whistles, trying to bring order to the traffic. Georges Méliès and the Lumière brothers had created the cinema, Pathé was thrilling them with *The Perils of Pauline* and Gaumont was starting to synchronise film with sound. There was the first successful identification by fingerprints in a criminal case, even the first licensed woman lawyer and the first licensed woman taxi driver. And sports were blossoming, with the first cycling Tour de France, the first Five Nations rugby championship and the first World Tennis Championship, during which spectators could relieve the intensity by smoking one of the new official Gitanes or Gauloises cigarettes. Paris, which was also now the capital of a large empire, was in the van of progress.

It was also fragmented politically, with the municipal election of 1900 producing thirty-six Nationalists, nine Conservatives, ten

Radicals and twenty-two Socialists, although the broad divide between right and left was underlined by the creation of the nationalist and royalist Action Française and the first socialist newspaper *L'Humanité*. Following an attempted right-wing coup d'état by the jingoistic Paul Déroulède, a physical attack on President Émile Loubet and other provocations, a combined republican government retaliated decisively. It closed down the newspaper of the Assumptionist Catholic order, *La Croix*, which had become the voice of aggressive monarchist and army elements, and went on to complete the separation of Church and state. While freedom of worship would be guaranteed, the state would no longer pay Church salaries and it would lose its place in public education. So in 1905 France, a century and more after the 1789 Revolution, finally became a secular republic. There was still some concern about relations with Germany, of course, the loss of Alsace and Lorraine still rankled and nationalist hotheads talked loosely of revenge. However, the situation had been stabilised by the Franco-Russian Alliance of 1894 and, in particular, by the Entente Cordiale with Britain, which had been eased into place by a visit from Edward VII, who could speak fluent French from his playboy days in Paris. There was anger in Berlin at this 'racial betrayal' by the Anglo-Saxons in lining up with the decadent French against their Nordic cousins, but this new Triple Entente promised security for all three powers.[14]

The downside of such an alliance was that a relatively minor incident could lead to wholesale conflict, which is what happened. A young Bosnian nationalist assassinated the heir to the Austro-Hungarian throne, so Austro-Hungary and Germany declared war on Serbia, so Russia came in on the side of Serbia, so Germany declared war on Russia and France and attacked France via neutral Belgium, so Britain came in to support Belgium. It was all a little unreal. But not for long.

The First World War and the 'Crazy Twenties'

....

On Friday the last day of July 1914, the Socialist leader Jean Jaurès, who had been trying to organise an international movement against the war, was dining in the Café du Croissant in the Rue Montmartre when he was shot twice in the head by Raoul Villain, a student associated with the nationalist and royalist Action Française. Next day, 1 August, the National Assembly voted through a bill authorising the mobilisation of 3.6 million soldiers, and over the following weeks there were cheers and kisses for the provincial recruits as they passed through Paris on their way to the front. That was until 26 August, when the first wave of haggard refugees from Belgium arrived at the Gare du Nord, to be transferred immediately to the Cirque de Paris to ensure that the bad news did not spread too widely among the population. But by 2 September it was learnt that the Germans were no more than 30 miles from Paris, casualties could be seen being brought back from the front, several bombs had been dropped on the city and the government, after rapidly appointing General Joseph Gallieni as military governor of the city, was being immediately transferred to Bordeaux along with the gold of the Banque de France.

It had long been obvious that the position of Paris in the north of the country rendered it vulnerable, but it had hardly been anticipated that the Germans would simply disregard Belgian neutrality. They were in fact implementing the Schlieffen Plan drawn up in 1905, which was designed to exploit that vulnerability by storming through neutral Belgium and taking Paris from the west within six weeks – before having to contend on their

eastern front with France's ally Russia. Gallieni aided the departure of around half a million people and prepared the city for a
siege, closing most of the gates, organising the outer fortresses,
setting up field cannon, arranging anti-aircraft batteries and even
arming the Eiffel Tower with machine guns and a cannon.[1] On 6
September, to help General Joseph Joffre mount a counter-offen-
sive to drive the Germans back toward the Ardennes, he requisi-
tioned five hundred Paris taxis, which rushed four thousand men
to the front and helped the French win the First Battle of the
Marne. Since this episode not only removed the risk of invasion
but demonstrated the unity of soldiers and civilians, *les taxis de la
Marne* became legendary.

By mid-January 1915, with the war settling down to become a
static struggle in the trenches, the government was back in Paris,
the stock exchange had reopened, and the city was regaining an
outward appearance of normality. The novelty was that women
were now replacing men in the workplace, as teachers, post-
women, ticket collectors, bus drivers and even munitions workers. For with industrial areas of the north being now unavailable
and the production of armaments, ambulances and other army
equipment having been taken over by Renault at Billancourt,
there were many more jobs to fill. The wages were less than those
earned by the men but were still much greater than the allowance
for the wife of a soldier on active service, while the work offered
the opportunity for greater freedom and camaraderie with shorter
working skirts and the easing of corsets to match. The freedom
for some was soured by the fact that, while emergency leave, or
permission, was granted for special cases as of March 1915, a regular short six-day break from the front was not introduced until
July. Since the government was all too aware of France's demographic deficit in relation to Germany, it was believed that this
was in order to maintain the birth rate – and suggested jokingly
that this particular *permission* should be called a *spermission*.[2]

Soldiers on leave from a world of discomfort and death at the front were often taken aback by what they found in Paris. It was not that people did not know about the war, since the wounded tended to be directed towards the city as having the highest concentration of medical services, and the Grand Palais itself had been turned into a temporary hospital. However, they might be startled by the ease with which theatres, *café-concerts* and the whole entertainment sector had resumed, even while paying formal deference to patriotism. They too, however, could be tempted by the great novelty of the cinema, attendance at which doubled in the first ten months of 1915.[3] The cinema, in that there was no competitive social display as in the theatre and that people sat more closely together, had a more democratic atmosphere, it offered cliff-hanging crime series such as *Zigomar* and *Fantômas*, and of course it showed regular newsreels giving reports from the front. The soldier on leave might be sceptical about the happy scenes in the trenches contrived by the army's film unit, but the combination of censorship and the apparent authority of film kept audiences largely satisfied. Charlie Chaplin and other American imports, especially after the US troops entered the war in 1917, did the rest, to the extent that by 1918 some 80 per cent of French screens were showing American films, leaving some intellectuals complaining about a cultural takeover.

Living conditions gradually deteriorated as supplies of food and heating materials became more difficult to maintain. The authorities, at both the national and the municipal level, took a range of counter measures – requisitioning supplies, imposing fixed prices, making special provision for the elderly and the infirm and issuing ration cards. By late 1917, there was one single 'national loaf' per person per day and a 6 p.m. curfew with blacked-out windows was in operation, which not only saved energy but hopefully offered some protection against German bombers. Not that it prevented a night-time attack by twenty-eight bombers in January 1918, which left sixty-five dead and hundreds wounded, or a daytime raid which caused seventy-one deaths. Overall, there were 266 deaths and 633 wounded from the bombing, on top of which was the havoc wrought by the giant German cannon with an 80-mile range, christened Big Bertha in honour of the wife of the arms manufacturer Krupp – a compliment of a kind – which killed eighty-eight people in the Saint-Gervais church during a Good Friday service. Despite the difficult living conditions, and because the opposing political parties had agreed on a 'Sacred Union' to defend the homeland, political protest was relatively muted at this time. However, there were demands for an 'English five-day week' for women workers and there was heavy criticism both from *Le Petit Journal* on the right or from *La Bataille* on the left of wealthy profiteers – a theme that would recur.[4]

Although the war ended in victory, it was quite a hollow one. Germany would remain unreconciled and would attack at another time. The solidarity between the victors would weaken as Britain drifted away and the US did not even ratify the Treaty of Versailles. France had lost 898,000 men killed in action, or 1,327,000 when those missing in action or dead from wounds or disease were included. Being at a demographic disadvantage to Germany, it had needed to call up more men per thousand and had proportionately lost more. Unlike Britain or Germany or the US, it had also suffered much physical destruction on its territory. Ironically, the war also spread far and wide the great flu epidemic of 1918, which killed far more people in Paris than the bombing had done and proceeded, as though mocking the number of deaths caused by the war, to kill an estimated 50 million people worldwide. Not that any of this troubled the enormous crowds gathered to watch the spectacular Bastille Day Victory Parade of 14 July 1919, which saw the generals and regiments of the victorious allied armies, along with naval and colonial detachments, march triumphantly to martial music down the Champs-Élysées – although at the traditional local street dancing in the evening, there were those who reflected sadly on the shortage of younger men.

* * *

The post-war years in Paris were difficult. The value of the franc fell sharply, and the country felt increasingly left on its own as its wartime allies drifted away. The Russian revolution had given a strong impetus to the Communist Party and the existing political divisions became more fractious. There was the awkward problem of ensuring that the millions of demobilised soldiers were placed back in work while at the same time converting war industries back to civilian production. The city set up an employment bureau, while the Senate confirmed a law bringing in the forty-eight-hour week and the eight-hour day in April 1919. However, this did not prevent violence breaking out in several places during the trade unions' annual May Day procession, which in turn set off a whole series of strikes over rising prices and forced the authorities to bring in the army to keep the Métro running. Since the Germans had flooded the coalmines in the north, fuel was in short supply during what became a hard winter and electricity had to be restricted, to the point that half of the factories had to operate at night if they were to operate at all. However, the trade unions had rather overplayed their hand and at the election of December 1919 it was the conservative National Block that won, emboldening the employers to sack strikers, including twenty thousand railwaymen, which weakened the power of the unions over the next decade.

Beneath the political surface of events, there was increasing disillusionment and a questioning of the society that had produced this war. For who, apart from some profiteers and possibly the United States, which was comfortably far away, had gained from this war? It was not just that the north had been laid waste, that there was not enough money to deal with Paris's housing needs, or that people who had bought government bonds to pay for the war were going to be reimbursed in a devaluated currency and be left impoverished. It was that lives had been lost on all sides and that, ironically, all the much-vaunted progress of the past forty years had been turned to deadly ends – the automobile industry had been converted to producing tanks, just as the exciting new aeroplanes and balloons had been dropping bombs. And even more ironically, the progress had proved almost irrelevant as the war settled down to become a three-year battle in the trenches, a static semi-underground struggle in the mud. The idea of the glory of war had disappeared along with the dashing red uniforms of the infantry, which had simply set men up to be mown down anonymously by the new heavy machine guns. Where had all that progress got anybody? And how could French, Germans and Americans, as they buried their dead, all claim that the same God approved their sacrifice: *Dieu avec nous, Gott mit uns,* God is on our side?

Of course, there were already so many voices, some previously in the background but now rendered topical by events, that were offering stark interpretations. There was Friedrich Nietzsche, saying that Western man had killed God and was now faced with the problem that the only finality left was Death. This was carried forward by André Malraux in *D'une Jeunesse Européenne* and *La Tentation de l'Occident,* who went on to say that since humans retained their Christian sensibility and values even though God was dead, their situation was absurd. There was Oswald Spengler's *The Decline of the West,* already anticipated by the poet Paul Valéry in his influential article of 1919 on the European crisis, beginning with the words: 'we civilisations now know that we are mortal'. There was Albert Einstein with his theory of relativity, which nobody may have quite understood but that did not stop everybody saying that everything was relative. There was Henri Bergson, elevating intuition over intelligence, and André Gide telling people to go and do something 'gratuitous' and shocking, regardless of the consequences. Most significantly, there was Sigmund Freud, with his emphasis on the unconscious and the significance of dreams. Although the dream cycle was only discovered long after his *Interpretation of Dreams* of 1900 and dreaming today is largely seen as akin to computer clearing, Freud encouraged the view that almost every dream was libido-driven and significant. This led to the Surrealists' belief that there was a real self, or a true self in the unconscious, which had to be liberated by new techniques.

Add these background elements together – that life has become a journey to nowhere, that the human situation is therefore absurd, that rationalism and its progress have led to destruction, and that the only way forward is through the unconscious – and you get a rather explosive mixture, especially when they are combined with the desire to be free and rejoice at the ending of a disastrous world war. For a start you get Dada, which in French means 'hobby horse' but which was apparently picked at random from a dictionary and, since it implies the rejection of conceptual definition, it strictly does not matter what it meant, or whether it meant anything. It began in Switzerland during the war, travelled as far as New York and flourished in Paris after the armistice. It saw itself as fighting the values, the logic and indeed the aesthetic practices of a self-destructive capitalist society, which it regarded as merely reinforcing those false values. So its art was anti-art made up of collage, photomontage or ready-mades such as Marcel Duchamp's *Fountain*, consisting of a standard porcelain receptacle from a gentlemen's urinal signed 'R. Mutt'. Those associated with Dada included the future communist writers Louis Aragon and Paul Éluard, as well as Philippe Soupault, who was said to have actualised his lack of identity by picking an apartment block at random and asking the concierge if Philippe Soupault lived there.[5] This gave rise to a student prank whereby you rang a bell at random and, if the door opened, announced smilingly 'C'est moi!' and tried to see how long you could last – as the putative son of some distant cousin or whatever – before they threw you out or sent for the police.

When the Romanian-born Tristan Tzara declared that the true Dadaists were against Dada, the movement was obviously beginning to bite its own tail.[6] It turned into the more organised Surrealism, although initially there were two competing strands, one led by Yvan Goll and the other by the imperious André Breton. They clashed over the right to the term 'Surrealism' and although

Breton won the battle, the movement remained a fractious one, leading him to operate like a kind of cultural pope, defining its tenets and solemnly excommunicating dissenters. Nevertheless, it had an intellectual basis drawing on Hegel's dialectic, on Marx and on Freud, and it saw itself as trying to resolve the societal and personal contradictions that it deemed to have led to the war. So the task, an immensely ambitious one, was to liberate the unconscious in order to connect it properly to consciousness and thus release the real self from the prison of the cardboard 'rational man' assumed by a ruinous bourgeois society. The prime means used were unthinking automatism, whether in writing or painting, or the deliberate juxtaposition of unrelated or conflicting elements in order, as it were, to force meaning from contradiction.

The problem with this approach, of course, is that uncontrolled automatic writing is not really possible, that too much importance was attached to dreams and to the unconscious, and that there may be no such latent 'real self' to liberate. Yet what is doubtless more important than the underlying philosophy of the movement is the favourable climate it created for so many artists and writers at one stage or another of their careers. There is also, obviously, the quality and suggestiveness of many of the works themselves, for a wide range of talented performers was involved – from Breton or Aragon in literature, to Luis Buñuel or René Clair in film, to a whole procession of painters and sculptors such as Klee, Chagall, Giacometti, Magritte, Ernst, Dalí or de Chirico. It should be recognised also that for many, often impoverished artists, pursuing a difficult career in a disturbed time, this was a serious business, to the point that several committed suicide. Nevertheless, the Surrealists certainly added to the gaiety of 'Gay Paris' with their various provocations. There were the letters to the directors of lunatic asylums telling them that it was they rather than the inmates who were insane, or to the heads of universities blasting them for presuming to think that they had any knowledge to dispense. There were surreal suggestions for improving public monuments and of course,

among other stunts, there was the outraged Salvador Dalí protest-
ing bitterly at the scandalous expulsion of a perfectly honourable
gentleman from the Métro for the 'pure and generous act' of expos-
ing himself to a pretty female passenger. It was called *épater le bourgeois*; shock the respectable. And it worked.

There were already surreal things happening in the real world,
like the elderly gentleman in pyjamas walking along the railroad
track south of Paris on a cold February morning in 1920 claiming
to be the president of the French Republic, who turned out – and
why ever not? – to be the president of the French Republic. And it
was a rather surreal coincidence that the centre of artistic and
intellectual life in Paris, at the time it could claim to be the cultural
capital of the world, should have been called Montparnasse, after
Mount Parnassus, the home of the Muses in ancient Greek
mythology. The name was conferred ironically in the eighteenth
century upon a large mound of rocks, excavated in the creation of
the catacombs, by students who came here to declaim verse and
direct it towards the distant city. For the area was quite rustic
before the twentieth century, as the name of the church Notre-
Dame-des-Champs suggests. The only developed areas were the
bourgeois section close to the Latin Quarter towards the north,
and the rather disreputable strip centring on the well-named Rue
de la Gaîté, which along with the Montparnasse Cemetery had
been left outside the old tariff wall surrounding the city and was
therefore exempt from taxes on alcohol and other desirables. This
led to the creation of cheap taverns, comic theatres, the famous
Bobino music hall and brothels – today replaced by sex shops. But
it was only after 1900 that the artists began to move in, searching
for somewhere cheaper than the increasingly fashionable
Montmartre, a move that was eased by the creation in 1905 by the
sculptor and benefactor Alfred Boucher of La Ruche, or the
beehive, to provide accommodation and studios at cheap or even
optional rates.[7]

La Ruche was a curious structure, built on a piece of wasteland adjoining the slaughterhouses of Vaugirard and assembled partly from materials left over from the World Fair. It had no heating and only a single water tap on the ground floor, while its 140 studio-residences were too narrow for comfort, but for struggling artists it provided a home from home. Of the small number whose names still linger, it is noteworthy that several were of eastern European or Russian origin. There was Constantin Brancusi, the influential Romanian abstract sculptor, and the Belarussian-born Ossip Zadkine, seen as a Cubist sculptor, who now has a museum devoted to him in Paris. Of painters, there was Marc Chagall, of Jewish and Russian background, who created his own world of colour, was given the honour of painting anew the ceiling of the Opéra and who also has a dedicated museum. Another of Jewish and Russian background was the Expressionist painter Chaïm Soutine, whom the others tended to avoid since he was unpredictable, more than usually unkempt and always on the scrounge – although his exasperated neighbour did cut him down when he found him hanging from a rope. They even called the police in protest at the blood and stench from a rotting beef carcass, which he got from the slaughterhouse and insisted on painting over and over again under the title *Le Boeuf*. When he finally got money from a dealer, he hailed a taxi and told the driver to take him to Nice, almost 700 kilometres away. He had to live in hiding, often in the forest, during the German Occupation and died of an untreated stomach ulcer in 1943. What would he have thought of the sale of one version of *Le Boeuf* at Christie's in 2015 for $28 million? Those penniless young artists who tended to see themselves as being against Western values rarely realised that they were operating at the lottery end of the capitalist market system.

With the completion of the Boulevard Raspail in 1911, the centre of interest of Montparnasse for writers and artists moved to the point at which the new boulevard crossed the Boulevard du

Montparnasse, the Place Vavin, which later featured Auguste Rodin's powerful statue of Balzac and which is now called the Place Pablo-Picasso. To the longstanding café-restaurant La Closerie des Lilas, which had been frequented among others by Monet, Renoir, Zola and Baudelaire, was now added a clutch of large brasseries where artists and writers – who would often write there – would congregate. There was the Dôme, where Lenin would conspire with Trotsky; the Rotonde, where the owner Lipion would accept a drawing from a poor artist as a temporary payment and contrive not to notice the theft of the odd croissant; Le Select, one of the favourite haunts of F. Scott Fitzgerald and Ernest Hemingway; the lavishly decorated La Coupole, which had music and dancing in the basement, not to forget the very American Dingo Bar in the Rue Delambre around the corner. It was this fusion of an artistic and intellectual hub at one end with the popular pleasure hub of the Rue de la Gaîté at the other end that constituted the compelling charm and sense of freedom of Montparnasse. This is 'where it was at'.

In addition to the French writers, it has been calculated that there were over three hundred known foreign writers in Paris during the inter-war period, although that figure would include refugees from Nazi Germany in the 1930s.[8] While they included Japanese, Scandinavian and Argentinian figures, they divided broadly into two fairly distinct groups, the first being Jews fleeing oppression in eastern Europe and Russians who were either expelled or had voluntarily left the new Soviet Union. Quite apart from Russian aristocrats now earning a living as lordly head waiters or whatever in grand establishments on the Right Bank, or musicians such as Diaghilev, Stravinsky or Prokofiev, there was a surprising number of writers from this background, such as Tristan Tzara, Henri Troyat and Nathalie Sarraute. The other group was what Gertrude Stein labelled the 'lost generation' of American writers and artists, including Hemingway, Man Ray and Fitzgerald. Apart from Paris's reputation as a cultural centre, some had discovered the city in the course of the war, there were older figures already there to help them, living in Paris was surprisingly cheap, you could be yourself, drink freely and generally have a wonderful time. In fact, with the exception of Hemingway and Fitzgerald, they found it almost as hard to make a living as their eastern European and Russian counterparts but, while it lasted, they did have a wonderful time.

Although they frequented the cafés in Montparnasse, the more established writers and artists such as Braque and Breton did not live there. Nor indeed did Picasso, who had moved up in the world since his marriage in 1918 to Olga, a ballerina with Sergei Diaghilev's Ballets Russes, and now lived in a grand apartment close to the premises of his dealer Paul Rosenberg in the Rue La Boétie off the Champs-Élysées. Through the very proper Olga, with whom he had not slept before the marriage, he entered high society, distanced himself from his old friends and acquired a luxurious Hispano-Suiza motor car complete with chauffeur. However, the marriage never really came alive and by 1927 he had met the seventeen-year-old Marie-Thérèse and installed her in a flat across the street, close enough to Rosenberg's place so that his secret visits would not attract attention. Since he could not contemplate divorce, which would have meant losing half of the pictures he was storing in a bank vault, he was condemned to a double life and indeed this was reflected in his living arrangements. The official flat was furnished in the orthodox good taste of the *beaux quartiers*, with cool twin beds and a Cézanne and a Renoir or two, while the flat directly above, which he had acquired as a studio and which had some blistering treatments of Olga, was cluttered with everything imaginable, down to the broken pens and empty cigarette packets that Picasso, notoriously, could never let go.[9]

Meanwhile, the upper-class salons where ideas and the arts were traditionally discussed had largely been taken over by wealthy modernist, sexually liberated English or American ladies. One who had been long established in Paris was the dignified Singer sewing machine heiress Winnaretta Singer, who had a mutually respectful if unconsummated marriage with the homosexual Prince de Polignac, which left her free to pursue her affairs with women, including the painter Romaine Brooks and the conductor Ethel Smyth. Although an accomplished painter, her main interest was in promoting avant-garde music and she was heavily support-ive of Diaghilev and his Ballets Russes. She commissioned work by a wide range of composers, from Igor Stravinsky and Darius Milhaud to Kurt Weill and Germaine Tailleferre, the only female member of 'Les Six'. Works by Debussy, Fauré and Chabrier, as well as Ravel's *Pavane pour une infante défunte*, which he dedicated to her, were premiered in her salon. It was frequented over the years by other prominent figures such as Monet, Colette, Le Corbusier and Jean Cocteau, and it was a rich source for Proust's evocation of the aristocratic world in his *In Search of Lost Time*.

Another longstanding resident who held a regular salon was the wealthy American Natalie Barney, so longstanding indeed that the refreshments still consisted of tea and cakes. She rode every day in the Bois de Boulogne in masculine attire, with black tie and bowler hat, and claimed to have been the lover of over forty women, including the painter Romaine Brooks and Dolly Wilde, the niece of Oscar Wilde.[10] As well as offering support to several male writers, she set up an informal Women's Academy in oppo-sition to the then all-male Académie Française. Invited to her salons in the 1920s were French writers such as André Gide, Max Jacob and Jean Cocteau, as well as English-language authors such as Ford Madox Ford, F. Scott Fitzgerald and Thornton Wilder. An equally spectacular, if heterosexual, heiress in the avant-garde scene was Nancy Cunard, of the British Cunard shipping family. She was flamboyantly heterosexual, drank freely and dressed extravagantly in Bohemian style with short skirt, heavy African wooden or bone adornments and a row of bangles on each arm.

She became involved with the Dadaists and Surrealists after 1920, had a two-year affair with Aragon and would later have one, shockingly for the period, with the black American jazz musician Henry Crowder. She later became strongly anti-fascist. Her own poetry was regarded as indifferent, but she started a printing press and among other things published *Whoroscope*, the first dedicated publication of a Samuel Beckett work.

Two salons of particular interest for English-language writers and artists were those of Sylvia Beach and Gertrude Stein. The daughter of a Presbyterian minister in Baltimore who was appointed as assistant to the American Church in Paris, Beach had already spent several teenage years in the city before returning after the war to pursue research in French literature. She discovered the bookshop-cum-lending library run by Adrienne Monnier, became a friend and eventually her long-time lover, and set up an equivalent shop for English-language books called Shakespeare and Company across the street in the Rue de l'Odéon. She ran regular sessions for members, while American writers also used it as a mailbox, and it acted as an informal meeting place for many French and American authors. When she ran into difficulty during the Depression in the 1930s, André Gide organised financial support and although her shop was closed down and she was interned for six months during the German Occupation, she helped in sheltering Allied airmen shot down in France.

One day she found a slightly withdrawn, obviously short-sighted man peering at the titles on the shelves and guessed that he was James Joyce. He had been teaching English in Zurich but had now come with his family to Paris and, as she soon discovered, he was not short of problems. He had persistent money concerns, despite regular financial help from Ezra Pound and the wealthy English leftist Harriet Weaver, who had serialised his *Portrait of the Artist as a Young Man*. He had such strong self-belief that he took it for granted that others would support him financially or act as unpaid secretaries – and they did. However, he also had the problem that the serialisation in the American *Little Review* of his newly completed novel *Ulysses* had just been stopped and the editors convicted of obscenity. So when she asked if he would like her to publish *Ulysses*, he simply answered 'yes' and, though it would later put her in some financial difficulty, it enhanced the reputation of the bookshop. However, the other problem, with which she could not help, was the painful situation that arose from his disturbed daughter Lucia's belief that the young Samuel Beckett, who was constantly helping Joyce in various ways, was basically coming to see her. When she had a breakdown, Joyce was innocently surprised. When he later had her analysed, Carl Jung decided that she was schizophrenic – and, having afterwards read *Ulysses*, decided that Joyce too was schizophrenic.

A contrast to the cheerful, very feminine Sylvia Beach was the studiously mannish Gertrude Stein. She had come to Paris in 1903 and now lived with the wifely and attentive Alice B. Toklas, who achieved reflected fame through the *Autobiography of Alice B. Toklas* – written by Gertrude Stein. From a wealthy Pennsylvanian Jewish family but orphaned in her teenage years, she was influenced by the 'stream of consciousness' theory when she studied under the psychologist William James and this, along with the activities of the Surrealists, influenced her own experimental writing. This included such famous examples as 'Rose is a rose is a rose is a rose', and 'there is no there there'. Since she regarded herself as being primarily an author – and indeed saw herself as a genius – she was aggrieved when her work was often turned down. However, she had accumulated with her brother a wonderful collection of paintings by such artists as Cézanne, Daumier, Renoir and Matisse and had her portrait painted by Picasso – who, when he heard that she thought she did not look like her portrait, said grimly, 'Don't worry, she will!' Her very successful Saturday salon brought together Anglophone writers and well-known artists such as Braque and Apollinaire, while Alice dealt separately with the wives in another room.

For the young Ernest Hemingway, arriving in 1920 as a press correspondent after being wounded as a volunteer ambulance driver in Italy, she acted initially as a mentor and did indeed help him to perfect a direct, uncluttered style. A tall handsome action man, he continued to box, enjoyed bull fighting, and was colourfully dismissive of the Dadaist and Surrealist tendencies. He was supported initially by monthly payments from his first wife Hadley's family – he rather romanticised poverty thirty years later in *A Moveable Feast* – and gradually became one of the few financially successful writers.[11] The Paris years produced two notable novels, the first being *The Sun Also Rises*, about the activities in Paris and in Spain of a group of disillusioned, hard-drinking English and Americans of the 'lost generation' – based on his acquaintances, who were not uniformly pleased. He followed this with his first bestseller, *A Farewell to Arms*, about a love affair set against the background of the Italian campaign in the world war. He was back in Paris in an army jeep in 1944, when he formally 'liberated' Sylvia Beach and presented the startled Picasso, whom he saw as a comrade-in-arms, with the unwelcome present of a box of grenades.

But what about the women who became famous without having fortunes to fall back on, who did it the hard way? Some, such as Jeanne Hébuterne, whose face – elongated – is so familiar from the Modigliani portraits, acquired fame through tragedy. A shy, attractive salesgirl at the Bon Marché, she had a flair for drawing and dreamt of becoming a painter. She studied at the Académie Colarossi, where in 1917 at the age of nineteen she met and fell in love with the charismatic Modigliani. Despite objections from her devout Catholic family, she moved in with him and became his main model, while she painted him in her turn. Not only was he poor, but he suffered from tuberculosis, which he tried to mask with alcohol and hashish. They moved to Nice in the hope of making money from the wealthy art lovers who wintered in the

Midi and their daughter Jeanne was born there. They returned to Paris the following year, she became pregnant again and they were preparing to marry when, in January 1920, he died and on the following day she leapt backwards to her death from a fifth-floor window. He was also destitute when he died, but then, like many another artist, he would be worth more dead than alive.

A contrasting figure was Kiki de Montparnasse, a model, painter, singer and actress whose bouncy vitality and range of activity would have her hailed as the 'Queen of Montparnasse'. Illegitimate and brought up in extreme poverty as Alice Prin, she graduated from working in a bakery to becoming a nude model in her teens, despite her mother's objections, and then a runaway helped by Soutine until she became a favourite model for a score of artists including the Japanese Tsuguharu Foujita, Alexander Calder and the ubiquitous Jean Cocteau. For most of the 1920s she lived with Man Ray, the American photographic artist and painter influenced by African art, and was the subject of many of his creations including the famous Surrealist nude picture *Le Violon d'Ingres.* She was a popular music hall performer, singing and dancing in her black stockings and garters. She had a very successful showing of her characteristically life-enhancing Expressionist paintings and drawings in 1927, and she published her autobiography with introductions by Foujita and Hemingway in 1929. Unfortunately, she too would suffer later in life from the alcohol and drug dependency that went with the territory.

Josephine Baker, variously dubbed the 'Black Venus' or the 'Bronze Venus', always caused a sensation at the Folies-Bergère when she emerged from a large feathery ball wearing only her string of bananas and a necklace and performed a dance of savagely sensual intensity, which had the audience gasping with delight. Born of a black mother and an unknown white father, she came from the direst poverty in St Louis, was married twice in her teens but left for New York and fought her way to success in vaudeville. Jumping at an opportunity at the age of nineteen to come to Paris, she first performed her erotic *danse sauvage* in the *Revue Nègre* at the Thèâtre des Champs-Élysées in 1925, before moving on to the Folies-Bergère. She certainly lived up to her prestigious image with her gold-painted fingernails, her pet cheetah and her pet snake as a necklace, and was much admired by Hemingway, Cocteau, Picasso and others. Beyond the jazz age, she went on to act as an agent for the Resistance during the German Occupation, was honoured for her service by General de Gaulle and became a vocal supporter of civil rights in the US in the 1950s. She received the ultimate honour as a national heroine by having her remains transferred to the Panthéon in November 2021.

If Kiki and Josephine Baker taught women how to dance without restraint, the designer Coco Chanel, yet another who rose from harsh poverty, freed them from the cumbersome corseted clothing that made it less than easy. Brought up in an orphanage, where at least she learnt to sew, she was getting nowhere as a café singer when she was picked up by a wealthy textile heir, Étienne Balsan, and lived the high life with him for three years before becoming the mistress of the wealthy upper-class Englishman Captain Arthur 'Boy' Capel. She grieved when he left her after nine years to marry Lady Diana Wyndham in 1918, but he died in a car crash a year later. By that time, with his financial backing, she had set up highly successful fashion and perfume boutiques in Paris, Deauville and Biarritz – where she had a fling with the Russian expatriate the Grand Duke Dmitri Pavlovich. In between creating Chanel No. Five and the little black dress, she supported Stravinsky and designed costumes for Diaghilev's Ballets Russes. Having begun a ten-year affair with the wealthy and anti-Semitic Duke of Westminster, she found herself translated into the higher reaches of British society, met Winston Churchill among others and is presumed to have had a rich encounter with the Prince of Wales. During the German Occupation in the Second World War, she became involved with the German diplomat and spy Freiherr von Dincklage and would have been tried for collaboration had it not been for the discreet intervention of Churchill.

The great Wall Street crash at the end of 1929 saw the departure of many American writers and pleasure-seekers who had been living on remittances from home – several, such as Harry Crosby and indeed Hemingway, decades later after he had won the Nobel Prize, committed suicide. Painters would also suffer from the drop in prices, several galleries would close down and not all were comforted by the view of the Cubist and influential art teacher André Lhote that this was to be welcomed since it saved painting from the tyranny of the market.[12] Yet if it left a drop in customers in the Montparnasse cafés, everything else seemed normal. Since the French still tended to hold their wealth in gold rather than subject it to market speculation, they were not significantly affected by the Wall Street collapse. In fact, considering that the country had been recovering from the disaster of the First World War, both 1929 and 1930 were turning out to be remarkably good years.

For by the end of the decade, France had recovered its poise remarkably well. It had been a difficult start due not only to the high cost of reconstruction but to the difficulty of obtaining the financial reparations from Germany owed under the terms of the Treaty of Versailles. This drove the then prime minister Raymond Poincaré to occupy the Ruhr with French forces in 1923 in order to seize raw materials. However, the move caused a general strike there and he was getting no support from the British or Americans – who were afraid of bringing about a communist revolution – so he was driven to withdraw and accept arbitration. This humiliating setback caused a collapse of the franc, which helped to bring down not only the National Block but its successor, the Cartel of the Left government of 1924. Fortunately, the experienced and far-seeing Aristide Briand had taken over as prime minister and established a rapport with the German foreign minister Gustav Stresemann, which led to the Locarno Pact of 1925, including

Britain, Belgium and Italy. This guaranteed the frontiers as defined at Versailles, provided for the entry of Germany to the League of Nations and brought both men the Nobel Peace Prize. He followed that up with the Kellogg–Briand Pact of 1928, which brought the United States into a fifteen-nation pact to outlaw war – and now, in 1930, he was setting out a proposal for a European Union. France was leading the way.

Naturally there was some political agitation in the margin, with the Communists competing with the Socialists on the left and with the setting up of the Croix de Feu and the new pro-fascist, anti-Semitic weekly *Gringoire*, on the right, but that was hardly unusual and was not preventing the country from moving forward. And Paris itself reflected this national success, whether through the holding of the Olympic Games in 1924, the Exhibition of Modern Decorative and Industrial Arts in 1925 or the First International Nautical Salon in 1927. It had seen France win the Davis Cup, seen the Tour de France become an international event and had welcomed the arrival of Charles Lindbergh at Le Bourget after the first successful non-stop transatlantic flight. At the domestic level, it had demolished the old ring of fortifications around the city and begun to use the space for an ambitious programme of public housing and the creation of a Cité Universitaire. It was the home of advanced research in science, with the Joliot-Curies at the Institut du Radium and Nobel Prizes in Physics in separate years for Jean Perrin and Louis de Broglie. It had maintained its high reputation as a centre of art and culture. Unfortunately, the Wall Street crash would set off reverberations beyond France's control and the thirties would not be easy.

Paris in the Thirties and under German Occupation

....

'Today capitalism triumphs in the world,' declared the minister of finance Paul Reynaud in 1930, 'and we see its benefits rain down upon the working masses.'[1] If Reynaud may seem in retrospect to have been oddly deluded, it is fair to say that the Great Depression following the Wall Street crash of the previous year, which would have such dire political as well as economic consequences, baffled many economists and national leaders. Again, the crisis came late to France and was initially less damaging to industry and employment than in the United States, Britain and Germany, a fact that appeared to vindicate the cautiously traditional and protectionist national policy. The truth, however, was that France was hit later because it was less developed as a capitalist economy, was less integrated in the world economy, had a more traditional banking system and, due to its disproportionately heavy losses during the war, had less of an unemployment problem. The irony was that when it was eventually hit in its turn it was hit all the harder and took longer to recover so that, although there was a general recovery across the West from 1935 onwards, the French economy had not returned to its 1929 level when it was overtaken ten years later by the Second World War.[2]

France had of course had a strong protectionist tradition going back to Colbert in the time of Louis XIV and to a large degree its problem was that it was pursuing an outdated, narrowly nationalist approach to the new and much changed post-war global economic situation. Budgets had to be strictly balanced and national wealth was measured in gold, of which France had the highest reserves of any country in the world in 1927. Indeed, there was much suspicion of the adventurousness and risk taking of the American economy in particular, which the collapse of Wall Street in 1929 appeared amply to justify. Again, since it had taken so long to get the country back on an even keel after that draining 1914–18 war, there was a strong aversion to taking risks. So when Britain left the gold standard in 1931, followed by the United States in 1933, letting their currencies float freely, France stood firm, only to see its trade suffer as its goods became less competitive, its services become comparatively expensive, and its important tourist sector languish miserably. By the time it devalued belatedly in 1936, the whole economic situation had been angrily politicised, the country had been sharply divided, the European situation was becoming ominous and the outlook was bleak.

As the most modern and most rapidly developing part of the country, the Paris area was the region that suffered most from the general stagnation of the economy and from the ill-considered determination of successive governments to play it safe and avoid investment risk. This combination of ignorance and Malthusianism, as one economic historian terms it, was also reflected in the housing sector.[3] Since co-ownership barely existed at this time, the ownership of properties was largely in the hands of rich individuals or large private companies which, since the government controlled rents, had little interest in regular maintenance once the franc began to lose value. There had been an attempt in 1928 to ease the housing problem with the so-called Loucheur law, which did see some 40,000 apartments created, but this lapsed under the economic pressure. Whereas Britain had recovered economically on the back of a housing boom, the restrictive French approach meant that while, in the years leading up to the Second World War, Britain and Germany were each building an average of around two hundred thousand dwellings a year, France was only building some ninety thousand.[4] In Paris itself, construction had declined from 6,470 storeys a year in 1914 to merely four hundred storeys in

1938–9.[5] Which meant that around two hundred thousand people in Paris lived in lodgings, with many of the poor occupying only a single room, without running water and with no sanitation other than a chamber pot.

If this situation in Paris still seems surprising, it may be remarked that it cohered with a traditional sense of the potentially dangerous tension between Paris and the country at large, the view that 'Paris n'est pas la France'. This was reflected in the 'Prost plan' for the reorganisation of the Paris region, named after the architect who drew it up, which appeared in 1934 but which only began to be implemented, by the Vichy regime significantly enough, during the German Occupation. By advocating the preservation and greening of the outer suburbs, it was in effect aiming at restricting the growth of the city. Yet this attitude combined with the restrictive economic approach to create a permanent housing crisis, increase social segregation between the bourgeoisie in the centre and the working class in the growing 'red belt' in the suburbs, and damage the health of many of the citizens. Diseases such as tuberculosis, diphtheria and syphilis were rife, alcoholism was rampant and the number of deaths, stillbirths and miscarriages increased markedly while the number of births declined.[6] As a result, the British were outliving the French by three years and the Dutch by seven while, more alarmingly, the birth rate was falling behind that of Germany and Italy.

With the Landry law of 1932 a first, limited, step was taken towards providing a family allowance for those with two children who were working in industry or in trade, but it was only in November 1938 that the allowances began to be paid without regard to the place of work. It also established the broad principles of what would become standard features of the system, notably allowances increasing progressively along with the increase in the size of the family and payment independent of the amount of income. This was firmed up in a decree of 1939, which established very explicitly a new national plan to support the family – which had always been a central value in a traditionally Catholic country – and increase the birth rate. Yet in view of France's demographic deficit and in the shadow of the disquieting developments in Europe at this time, it was very late. The war deaths had left a shortage of men in the appropriate age group, the economic outlook was poor, the restricted living conditions did not encourage people to have children, the political outlook both at home and abroad had become concerning, and altogether it did not look like a world into which people were tempted to bring children. So the reason the family allowances had to be increased by the end of the thirties was basically that they had not so far worked.

Whereas in 1913 there had been six hundred and sixty thousand young men aged twenty and available for military service, by 1938 the number had fallen to four hundred thousand. With around a quarter of couples being childless and a third having only one child, the creation of a family was becoming a minority activity. When the government finally reacted to the seriousness of the crisis, it had little time for feminist demands for sex education and birth control. It took strong measures against abortion, which for want of contraception had been the main method of birth control, by introducing terms of imprisonment ranging from one to five years – a law that was not revoked until 1974. As for its treatment of a feminist propagandist such as Madeleine Pelletier, a specialist in mental health conditions who argued for the right to contraception and abortion, she was arrested and confined to a mental clinic, where she died.[7] Yet punitive measures did not solve the problem any more than the family allowances and other financial inducements. There were too many contrary factors: the hangover from the war, the economic uncertainty, the poor living conditions, the internal political conflict and the growing sense as the decade moved on that the same European catastrophe could happen all over again. Parisians were not just suffering from an economic crisis, but from a lack of self-belief, from what had become a national crisis of confidence.

*   *   *

Meanwhile, the world had seen yet another Paris spectacular in the form of the Colonial Exhibition of 1931, which brought some 8 million visitors from across the world to the enormous site in the Bois de Vincennes on the eastern edge of the city, organised around a triumphal 'grand avenue of the French colonies', lined with palm trees. In the now familiar manner, it brought together exhibits along with their attendants not only from all the twenty-eight French colonies and protectorates, but from a number of other colonial powers including the Netherlands, Portugal, the United States and Japan. As before, in addition to the pavilions in which the various territories displayed their arts, crafts and characteristic exports, there were the scaled recreations of native monuments, with the star of the show being the remarkable recreation of the great Angkor Wat temple in Cambodia – which some joked sourly was in better shape than its neglected original. There were also around two hundred pavilions let out to private businesses with an interest in this area, which enabled colonial writers and artists to present their work and restaurants to create a market for North African, Vietnamese and other ethnic cuisines. The exhibition also introduced a permanent colonial museum, known today as the Cité Nationale de l'Histoire de l'Immigration.

There was some internal opposition to the exhibition, with the Communist Party organising its own small exhibition entitled *The Truth about the Colonies*, but it did not attract much attention, any more than did a critical statement from a group of Surrealists. Anti-colonialist feeling was not widespread on the left of the political spectrum, and not simply because people paid little detailed attention to this faraway 'greater France' of the France d'Outre-mer, with all its colonies and protectorates and its 80 million inhabitants. There was general sympathy, influenced by history teaching at school, for the idea that France was carrying out a noble 'civilising mission' in bringing forward these peoples into the developed world. Indeed, there was a belief that imperialism was a way for mature societies to avoid sinking into a comfortable decadence.[8] Of course, given that the French economy was aligned with a traditional imperial preference, the empire was a valuable source of raw materials, whether tea, coffee, bananas, rubber or anthracite, and it could also provide troops to supplement the declining national forces. However, it is somewhat ironical that such a triumphalist display as the Paris Colonial Exhibition should take place just as the world economic crisis was beginning to hit – and to hit parts of the empire even more than the metropolis. If the situation was stable for the moment, it would not be for very long.

Within three years Paris was going to treat itself to another *grand spectacle* of a very different kind in the form of the battle on the Place de la Concorde in 1934, which became known as the 'Sixth of February'. The growing disquiet over the international situation and the economy had not been lessened by a series of financial-cum-political scandals going back to that of the *Gazette de France*, which had seen the arrest of the fraudster Marthe Hanau in December 1928. The apparent inability of either the left or the right to achieve unity and continuity combined with the rise of Nazism and anti-Semitism in Germany to provide a perfect background to the Stavisky affair. An embezzler with a Russian Jewish background, Alexandre Stavisky specialised, among other imaginative activities, in selling worthless bonds on the supposed surety of royal emeralds, which were no more than glass. He protected himself through political connections and by buying off police and critics to the extent that his trial in 1927 was repeatedly postponed and he was granted bail nineteen times. While a judge involved in his case was murdered, he himself was assumed to have been murdered to contain the scandal in January 1934, although he was officially declared to have committed suicide.

Events moved swiftly. The Radical prime minister Camille Chautemps resigned, to be replaced by the Radical-Socialist Édouard Daladier, whose failure to persuade the Socialists to join him left the impression that nothing had changed. The influential Federation of Taxpayers threatened to clear out the deputies with whips and batons, the minister of the interior unwisely sacked the prefect of police, Jean Chiappe who, being right-wing himself, had been able to contain the anger of the Paris branch of the National Union of Ex-Servicemen, and the scene was set for the rioting that would begin on the Tuesday evening of 6 February 1934. A vast crowd of at least forty thousand people – of various political persuasions, although the most threatening to the regime were the far-right and pro-fascist leagues – gathered on the Place de la Concorde, the Tuileries, the Cours-la-Reine and part of the Champs-Elysées, and attempted to cross the bridge to get at the deputies in the Palais-Bourbon. Twice the police had to resort to gunfire to avoid being overcome by the mob, who were armed only with stones, sticks or whatever was to hand. It took until midnight, even with reinforcement by mounted guards, for them to turn the tide and begin an elaborate pursuit of fleeing rioters all across the city centre. The end result was sixteen rioters killed and 655 wounded, while the police suffered many injuries from non-lethal weapons and missiles.

In the course of the night, the cabinet met at the Ministry of Foreign Affairs, was dissuaded by party leaders from declaring a state of emergency and arresting leading figures on both right and left, but decided that Daladier would be replaced as prime minister by Gaston Doumergue. So how significant was this revolt? Although in its combination of anger and confusion it could just conceivably have ended in a fascist takeover, that was never likely. In fact, the Sixth of February was even less organised than the parallel attack on the Capitol in Washington on 6 January 2021. Not only were the rioters unarmed, but there was no planned takeover of the key ministries, Préfecture de Police or communication centres, and no unity of viewpoint or purpose between the right-leaning and left-leaning parties involved – the Communists turned up but did not take part in the fighting. Yet, even if there was in fact no plot, the event signalled that the country felt vulnerable and unsure of itself in the face of a rising Nazi Germany, a feeling which would split the nation further between the left and the right. In practice, the Sixth of February prepared the way for the Popular Front of 1936.

Of course, there was a number of peaceful developments in Paris over these years, such as the creation of Air France, the start of the National Lottery and the creation of the Vincennes Zoo, but with the city's air-raid protection measures being tested in May 1935, there was clearly no escape from bad news. The mineral-rich Saar was voting by plebiscite to return to Germany, Mussolini was invading Ethiopia, the right-wing Nationalist General Francisco Franco was starting an insurrection against the Popular Front government in Spain and refugees were coming in from Germany. With the population now split into two bitterly opposed camps, each aligned with one or other side in the European conflict between fascism and democracy, Paris was becoming a city of demonstrations and marches. The Communists, under guidance from the Comintern, were switching from their opposition to the Socialists, with whom they had been competing for control of the left, to a policy of non-aggression in the interests of a more unified defence against fascism. This enabled the creation of the Popular Front, which was celebrated by the inevitable march through Paris of up to half a million people on Bastille Day 1935, followed by its victory in the national election of May 1936.

However, its path would hardly be smooth. Even before the Socialist prime minister Léon Blum had finished setting up his cabinet, he was held to ransom by the trade unions by means of a widespread and novel sit-in strike, which began in the metalworks and aircraft factories before spreading beyond Paris to other parts of the country. It was a highly disciplined affair, with the workers forbidden to damage the machinery, practise violence or indulge in drunken behaviour. As it spread beyond the factories to department stores, insurance companies, railway stations and even cafés, it became one great carnival, with the strikers camping on site, fed by family and friends, playing cards or listening to music and revelling in their power. This enabled Blum to force through an agreement whereby the working week would be reduced to forty hours and there would be an entitlement to a paid holiday of two weeks. On the strength of this quite transformative, if economically risky agreement, he was able to ban a scattering of extreme right-wing organisations. However, the unity of the left, already fragile since the Communists had not actually joined the government, was soon broken due to different attitudes towards the civil war in Spain among other issues – and Blum would find himself held to ransom once again.

The government had been keen to promote the long-planned International Exhibition of Modern Arts and Techniques of 1937, which was intended to encourage a still traditionalist French industry to see the interdependence of art and technology and the gain from integrating them in modern commercial production. Once again, it was a vast enterprise, involving fifty-four countries and extending over a large area including the Champs de Mars, the Trocadéro Gardens and the Esplanade des Invalides. France's own pavilions included one on Solidarity, one on Hygiene – both designed to advertise the values of the Popular Front – and a striking one on Electricity. However, the most eye-catching pavilions were the triumphalist towers of the Soviet Union and Nazi Germany confronting each other across the Trocadéro Gardens, both completed early, unlike so much of the exhibition. For the unions had struck for extra wages, then struck for more money for the extra hours engendered, so that the failure by almost a month to open the exhibition on 1 May was a national humiliation which drew much mockery from the right.

Blum's social reforms would transform the lives of a large number of Parisians after the war, enabling many for the first time to see the sea, but in the immediate economic context, with the country so uncompetitive, they were unhelpful. As for the political damage, it was there for the world to see, especially since the medals for the best buildings at the exhibition were awarded to those of the Soviet Union and Nazi Germany, a point rammed home by the medal for the best documentary being awarded to Leni Riefenstahl for her celebration of Hitler's new Germany in *The Triumph of the Will*. An incidental feature of the exhibition was that, since the Spanish Republican pavilion opened far behind schedule due to wartime difficulties, Picasso's mural *Guernica*, inspired by a Nazi atrocity in Spain, was almost ignored and the little comment it attracted was unfavourable. It would only be later and in the larger context of the Second World War, since his then mistress (the Surrealist photographer and painter Dora Maar) had arranged for it to be sent to the United States, that it would achieve its reputation.

This uneasy atmosphere did not prevent the Parisians from amusing themselves in the 1930s. Sport developed strongly, though women were scarcely involved except in the upper-class area of ladies' tennis. Soccer and cycling were the most widely practised, especially as big money gradually came into the game and professionalised both. Rugby developed in the universities and only became popular in the south, since it entered the country via the wine trade through Bordeaux – and developed a faster, more stylish game on firm dry ground than the laborious version slogged out on muddy pitches in Britain. The wider significance of sport was emphasised by the poor performance of the French athletes in the Berlin Olympics of 1936.

The thirties represented a golden age of French *chanson*, which was becoming increasingly available to a wider audience through recordings, the radio and indeed the cinema. Jazz came on to the scene, reinforced by the Paris visits of Louis Armstrong in 1933 and Duke Ellington in 1934. A move away from the old smooth stage style is well represented by two renderings of 'Y'a d'la Joie', a song created at the Casino de Paris in 1937. While

Maurice Chevalier in his evening dress and white scarf is suave and controlled, the 'singing madman' Charles Trenet begins smoothly but ends up jumping around feverishly and enacting the joy. However, the realist mode was still dominant, whether for lyrical or comic purposes, and the gravelly popular Parisian accent is built into the singing of the 'little sparrow' Édith Piaf, who was found singing in the street and never did less than sing her heart out. The crooning style came in with the 'French Bing Crosby' Jean Sablon in 'Vous qui passez sans me voir', which has a melancholy female counterpart in Rita Ketty's 'J'attendrai', which would doubtless be sung by lonely women in wartime. However, a much livelier ironic comment on the political situation by Ray Ventura in swing mode was 'Tout va très bien, madame la marquise' – which would be adapted for anti-German propaganda by the BBC during the war.[9]

René Clair's happy picture of the life of ordinary Parisians in his 1930 film *Sous les toits de Paris* of 1930, since it is partly a silent and partly a sound film, marks conveniently the transition to modern cinema. However, the new genre demanded far higher production costs and since the country failed to compete in investment, it was not until the promise of state assistance in 1936 that high-quality French cinema could properly emerge – and tend, incidentally, to popularise the modes and mannerisms of Paris.[10] There were excellent actors available, such as Louis Jouvet, Michèle Morgan, Charles Boyer, Danielle Darrieux or Jean Gabin. And there was the usual range of genres, from broad comedy with the clownish Fernandel to black comedy as in Marcel Carné's *Drôle de drame*, to adaptations of Hugo's *Les Misérables* and Georges Simenon's Maigret crime novels, or to the engaging Provençal trilogy of Marcel Pagnol. Inevitably, however, the films that stand out, whether in the poetic realist or the naturalistic style, are those that reflect the uneasy situation in the country. This is evident in the work of the two outstanding directors of the period, Jean Renoir and Marcel Carné. In *La Grande Illusion*, dealing directly with war in the form of two prisoners from totally different social backgrounds escaping together, Renoir is criticising the class system while expressing the hope that differences can be overcome, but in *La Règle du Jeu*, following the collapse of the Popular Front, the satire is the more savage for being so polished. In Marcel Carné's powerful *Quai des Brumes* and *Hôtel du Nord*, with their brooding titles and uncertain characters, the pessimism is the more telling for permeating dark corners of the everyday world.

The novel also played a significant role in the 1930s and here too there was a range of genres, extending from crime fiction to the *roman-fleuve* or sweeping historically based series such as the Nobel Prize-winner Roger Martin du Gard's twelve-volume *Les Thibault*, or Jules Romains' twenty-seven-volume *Les Hommes de bonne volonté* (*Men of Good Will*). There were two major Catholic authors, François Mauriac, another Nobel Prize-winner, and Georges Bernanos, both of whom incidentally went against majority Catholic opinion in criticising the actions of Franco in Spain. Both were fine writers, even if their often troubled novels demonstrated the difficulty of inserting God and the Devil (disguised as a travelling horse dealer in Bernanos) into the dominant realist mode in fiction. Inevitably, however, the most striking were those who projected the central anxieties of the time, starting with the nihilistic, anti-Semitic and future collaborator Louis-Ferdinand Céline, whose semi-autobiographical *Voyage au bout de la nuit* gives a harrowing account of the absurdities of war and of humanity in general. But perhaps the most interesting figure is André Malraux, seen as a man of action since he had an early venture in the East and was a volunteer rear air-gunner for the Republican side in Spain, but whose central preoccupation in *La Condition humaine* is less the Chinese revolution than the tragic division within the self in a world that has become absurd. This theme will become hallucinatory in the early novel *La Nausée* by Jean-Paul Sartre, where Roquentin's distance from the world leads him to start to doubt his own existence. The writing on the wall was becoming disturbing.

With Hitler moving systematically forward, the war was not long in coming. In March 1938, he absorbed Austria. In September of that year, he absorbed the Sudetenland part of Czechoslovakia through the Munich Agreement, hailed by the innocent British prime minister Neville Chamberlain (and by his less innocent but resigned French counterpart Édouard Daladier) as guaranteeing 'peace in our time'. On 15 March 1939, Hitler absorbed the rest of Czechoslovakia. On 23 August, he concluded a non-aggression pact with the Soviet Union – warmly welcomed in Paris on the 25th by the communist daily *L'Humanité* as a 'considerable contribution to maintaining the peace by the great leader Stalin'[11] – and at the end of the week, on 1 September, he attacked Poland. There followed the eerie *drôle de guerre*, or phoney war, before Hitler turned to France the following May, ignoring the outdated, expensive Maginot Line and attacking with armoured divisions through the supposedly impassable Ardennes forest. There was no adequate answer to this *Blitzkrieg* and by 14 June 1940, while the British had managed to scramble troops back to England in small boats, there was a swastika flag fluttering on top of the Arc de Triomphe as German troops paraded in immaculate order down the largely empty Champs-Élysées.

If Paris seemed oddly silent, it was mainly because the bombing raid of 3 June had led to an enormous flight from the city, not only of Parisians but of refugees from the north who had been blocking the traffic with their trucks and country carts, transporting women and children along with hastily bundled necessities or even farm animals. There had been organised evacuations from schools and other institutions, but the railway stations were finding it difficult to cope and once the news came out on 10 June that the government itself was leaving the city, the situation got completely out of hand. People were jostling and fighting one another at the Gare de Lyon and the Gare d'Austerlitz to get on to the last available trains, others were struggling towards the Porte d'Orléans to get out of the city by road, and over the next few days there developed an exodus of biblical proportions. There were people of all kinds, including soldiers who had jettisoned their weapons, and vehicles of every description – cars, lorries, vans, buses, bicycles, ambulances, hearses, a wheelbarrow transporting a grandmother – all caught up in a miles-long snail-like procession through the countryside that, to underline the humiliation, was being dive-bombed at intervals by German planes.

Paris was declared an open city on 13 June, so at least it largely escaped damage. The government moved on to Bordeaux, where power was assumed by the eighty-four-year-old Marshal Philippe Pétain, who agreed an armistice on 22 June, whereby Germany would occupy most of the country north of the Loire plus the whole Atlantic seaboard, leaving a 'free zone' run from the southern spa town of Vichy, which Pétain would call the French State but which would in practice be known as Vichy. In reality, since Germany kept 1.5 million prisoners of war as hostages, using them as forced labour in the service of its war machine, it was in effect turning France into a colony, from which it would also drain half of the country's public sector revenue and many of its treasures. Vichy was less of a free zone than a reservation, which would unceremoniously be reoccupied in November 1942 following the Allied landings in North Africa. The immediate reality for Paris was that it was now entirely subject to rulings from the German military command. Which enabled Hitler to visit an apparently empty city along with his architect Albert Speer on the morning of 23 June, perform a triumphant little jig on the esplanade of the Trocadéro and meditate gravely before the tomb of Napoleon.

The situation in which Paris now found itself was a paradoxical one. In the first place, the city council had been dissolved, replaced by a new body of direct appointees which, since it met only once a year and then only in private session, was merely an arm of Occupation control. Yet if Paris had been dethroned, it still had the ministries and civil service offices, it was still the largest city in the country and the key prize for the Germans. In the second place, it was becoming clear that Paris had a second enemy, in the form of Vichy itself. Marshal Pétain, now offering himself, though childless, as the 'father of the nation' like Louis XVI, or perhaps as its benevolent grandfather, had in fact been opportunist in abolishing the apparatus of representative government in order to create his French state. The 'national revolution' he advocated arose from the fusion of two influences. One was the right-wing monarchist and anti-Semitic Action Française, which had been so active in the Dreyfus affair, while the other was the Christian personalist movement, which saw itself as defending the family against the state. The dream was to 'get back to the land', to the 'true France', the 'eternal France', the old traditional provincial organisation of society that all those revolutions had destroyed – let Germany be the modern industrial driver in Europe, but let France get back to being itself.[12]

In effect this meant getting away from what was seen as the empty modern cosmopolitanism, the dangerous social mixing and the pursuit of pleasure exemplified by Paris itself. The unreal, sentimental nature of the Vichy project, from a position of dependency, would lead it inexorably as the war developed from passive to active collaboration with the Germans and bring it to disgrace and disaster. In the meantime, however, Parisians were trying to get used to life in this strange city that had become a garrison town for the German army and a sexy recreation centre for its soldiers on leave. The streets were empty of civilian traffic, there were large street directions in German and large signs in German on commandeered hotels, restaurants and cinemas. The German High Command, with its red-and-black swastika flag, was in the Hôtel Majestic in the Avenue Kléber, the local command with the identical flag was in the Hôtel Meurice in the Rue de Rivoli and the Gestapo, it was whispered, was in the Rue Lauriston in the fashionable 16th arrondissement. And there were Germans, Germans everywhere; Germans looking at maps on street corners, Germans looking in shop windows, Germans sitting on café terraces reading the new German-language Paris newspaper, Germans that you were pretending not to notice sitting opposite you in the now constantly crowded Métro. Time itself was now German, since the clocks had been set to Berlin time and it was a strange, almost comical feeling to be so completely dispossessed of your own city.

Then there was the hunger. Paris was particularly hard hit, since such a large share of the normal supplies was being shipped to Germany and since it had less direct access to agricultural produce than provincial centres. Ration cards were introduced, with allowances varying according to age and available on a strictly dated weekly basis. However, as the war progressed and supplies became more difficult, the rations were gradually reduced and people were often left queuing for hours for food that was late or simply unavailable. The other great problem was the cold, especially since the winter of 1940–1 was one of the longest and harshest on record. With the mines in the north now being controlled by the German authorities in Brussels, coal supplies were scarcer than before and destined essentially for industry, driving people to look for warmth in cafés or public libraries. Inevitably, for the better off or the desperate, there was a flourishing black market and for the *beau monde* dining at vast expense at Fouquet's, the Chapon Fin or the Pré Catalan, there was never a shortage of beef or butter. However, the end result would be an increase in the annual death rate by a half, an increase in tuberculosis by a third, and a marked lack of normal growth in children.[13]

Even so, the most shocking and shameful feature of the Occupation was the persecution of the Jews. Not that Vichy's anti-Semitism was the same as that of Hitler, whose fantasy was rather of the need to annihilate the Jews in order to destroy the 'Jewish-Bolshevisation' that was threatening his dream of a racially pure

Nordic civilisation. The lesser aim of Vichy's National Revolution was to expel foreign Jews and to marginalise severely those remaining so that they would have no influence in the True France. However, its contribution to their elimination was decisive, and not just by scrapping anti-racist laws and unleashing a torrent of virulent anti-Semitic propaganda. For it was Vichy itself which, in March 1941, established the heavily staffed Commissariat Général aux Questions Juives, which the Germans without local knowledge and with their overstretched resources could hardly have contemplated. The elaborate database that it drew up was a free gift for the Germans and left the Jews nowhere to hide. In addition, of course, it was the Vichy administration and police force – even before the move to open collaboration with Prime Minister Pierre Laval in 1942 – that was conducting the operation and making the arrests. And it was important to the Germans that the process should look like a bureaucratic French operation, since the smooth running of the Final Solution programme relied on the victims not realising that they were to be exterminated until the cyanide granules were dropping from the ceiling.

Certainly, the operation in Paris was well planned and carefully phased. It was supported by a propaganda blitz with the showing of the fiercely anti-Semitic film *Süss the Jew* promoted by Joseph Goebbels, and by a large 'educational and scientific' exhibition on 'the Jews in France', while local fascist groups were prompted to wreck Jewish shops on the Champs-Élysées. Meanwhile, step by step, from the autumn of 1940 onwards, the pressure was applied, starting with the requirement for Jews to present themselves at the police station for compulsory registration. Those defined as foreign could be forbidden to leave their apartment or assigned to an internment camp, and in May 1941 some three thousand seven hundred were deported – to end up in Auschwitz. Jewish shops and businesses now had to have prominent signs identifying them as such, Jews had to wear the yellow star (which cost them one clothing coupon), they were excluded from the liberal professions and public services jobs, their assets were frozen, they could not use the telephone or possess a radio, they could only travel in the last carriage in the Métro, were kept under curfew and were only permitted to shop – a refined touch – between 3 and 4 p.m., when the shops were normally shut. This culminated in the great raid of July 1942, conducted as usual by the French police, which saw some thirteen thousand deported to Auschwitz – 'to general public indifference', as one writer puts it.[14] The process continued at intervals until mid-1944, by which time almost eighty thousand had been deported.

Blindly or not, what Pétain's regime did in effect was to take advantage of its own subjection to the Germans, and the consequent stifling of parliamentary and public opposition, to try to get rid of the Jews – and not ask questions about what might happen to them. And its reputation was further darkened by the activities of the French wing of the Gestapo, active at several addresses and ironically dubbed the *carlingue*, or cockpit. In order to make use of local knowledge in detecting and dealing with any opposition, the more important as the Resistance developed, the Gestapo released from prison a number of hardened criminals, including pimps, blackmailers, thieves and fraudsters. They equipped them with identity cards assimilating them to the German police to protect them from the French authorities, gave them a free hand to chase up opponents and, in particular, gave them the dirty work of carrying out interrogation under torture, whether by repeated plunging in a bath or by the use of surgical instruments. They also gave them a free hand to pursue their own criminal activities, one notorious example being a certain Lafont, who made a fortune in the process, moved freely in high society and was said to be addressed by Pierre Laval by the familiar form of '*tu*'.[15] The Occupation was corrupting in many ways, to the point that there were Parisians reporting their neighbours to the authorities for purely personal reasons.

In addition to their anti-Semitic and anti-Bolshevik propaganda, the Germans tried to win over the population to their culture with visits from the Berlin Philharmonic and the Schiller Theatre, not to mention an embarrassing exhibition of the giant, naked, glaringly homo-erotic male figures of Hitler's favourite artist Arno Breker. Jean Cocteau did himself few favours by making a vague, windy speech to a large invited audience, many of whom knew not only that the Germans were oppressing homosexuals but that Breker had been one of Cocteau's many lovers when he was studying in Paris under Aristide Maillol.[16] There was also the invitation for artists to tour Germany, taken up among others by André Derain, Kees van Dongen and Maurice de Vlaminck – who also made a savage public attack on Picasso's Cubism.[17] Meanwhile, Paris went on being 'Gay Paree', for the benefit of German soldiers. Singers such as Édith Piaf, Charles Trenet and Maurice Chevalier – who had a Jewish wife to protect – went on singing. Actors, who also had to make a living, went on acting, although Jean Gabin was off fighting with the Free French. Serious authors had largely stopped contributing to the distinguished *Nouvelle Revue Française*, which tended to isolate collaborationist writers such as its new editor Pierre Drieu la Rochelle and Robert Brasillach, but as the overall situation brightened Camus felt free to publish his novel *L'Étranger* and Sartre could stage his play *Les Mouches*.

Resistance to the Germans began in a scattered, spontaneous fashion, an early episode being a student riot in the Latin Quarter in November 1940. The first real network was formed at the anthropological museum the Musée de l'Homme by a group of intellectuals led by Paul Rivet and its underground newsletter *Résistance*, the first issue of which appeared in December, would give its name to the whole movement. However, they were soon betrayed, individuals were picked off and, following a trial, seven male members were shot and three women deported – the hard lesson being that resistance needed to go further underground and be more highly organised. This did not necessarily mean the shooting of single German soldiers initiated by the Communists in August 1941. The Party had been uncomfortably facing in different directions, since it had welcomed the Hitler–Stalin pact and had sought to have *L'Humanité* continue publishing under Vichy, only to swing the other way after Hitler attacked the Soviet Union and try both to adjust to the new Comintern line and to establish itself politically within the Resistance.[18] Since for every soldier shot the Germans executed up to fifty innocent hostages, the tactic was criticised by other branches of the Resistance and, from London, General de Gaulle argued that such random killings were both too costly and would have no effect on the outcome of the war.[19]

There was considerable variation in the Resistance groups both in Paris and across the country, involving people of different social levels, political persuasion and religious affiliation. There were professional or ex-military groups, those set up by the British Special Operations Executive and the more political groups such as the Gaullists or the Communists. But in May 1943, as the war went on and victory became conceivable, Jean Moulin, a martyred hero of the Resistance, chaired a secret meeting in Paris which brought together the main Resistance groups through the National Council of the Resistance. In September, the Council intervened to prevent the Communists anticipating the creation of a Paris Liberation Committee by creating one of their own and instituted a politically balanced committee that led on to the agreement of February 1944, whereby all the Resistance organisations agreed to accept the authority of the Free French government based in Algiers. Now called the French Forces of the Interior or FFI, the Resistance was geared up with a hundred thousand men to sabotage and harry the Germans following the Allied landings in Normandy on 6 June and in the Midi on 15 August.

However, de Gaulle had a problem. He had already had difficulty in getting the Americans, who had earlier dealt with Vichy, to recognise his France Libre as the authentic Provisional Government of the country, but he had resolved that issue with a recent visit to President Franklin D. Roosevelt. He now had the problem of establishing that status within the country itself and he was all too aware, as the Allied armies surged forward, of the symbolical significance of Paris. The American command intended to bypass the city rather than be delayed by street fighting, but when the insurrection broke out on 19 August, de Gaulle rushed to see General Dwight D. Eisenhower, explained the political context, and persuaded him to detach General Philippe Leclerc's Second French Armoured Division. So Leclerc entered Paris on 25 August, the German commander ignored Hitler's screaming phone calls to destroy the city and surrendered, so, on 26 August, de Gaulle could walk in triumph down the Champs-Élysées to the traditional service in Notre-Dame. Having ensured that the French could appear to the world to have been freed by the French, the lofty general could go on to insist that the country be treated as one of the victorious Allies, with a share in the occupation of Germany. It was a remarkable achievement.

The 'Thirty Glorious Years', 1946–75

The war was over, France had been accepted as one of the victorious Allied powers, the Resistance had played an important part, and the martyrs who had died an honourable death during the Liberation of Paris would have their deeds recorded in neat grey plaques on the city's walls. In comparison with other major European centres such as London or Rotterdam, or indeed with French towns such as Caen or Brest, the city had suffered relatively little damage, but the Allied bombing had still left in ruins vehicle factories, metal foundries and other enterprises that had worked for the German war machine. This combined with the relative neglect of shops and other businesses to create a difficult period of adjustment as regards jobs, especially since Paris suffered indirectly from the considerable war damage elsewhere in the country. So there was rationing of basic foodstuffs until May 1949 and, indeed, a grey air of deprivation about the city into the early fifties – one notorious index being the sheets torn from an old *bottin*, or telephone directory, cut into squares and held together by a wire ring, which served as toilet paper in the city's cafés. That the economist Jean Fourastié could famously describe the years from the end of the Second World War to the start of the oil crisis in 1973 as the 'thirty glorious years' is the more remarkable in that they started from a very low base.

For there was also the general dismay at the revelation of the horrors of the concentration camps, which further darkened the reputation of Vichy for having aligned itself with Germany. Over seven hundred people were executed, including Laval and the writer Robert Brasillach, while there were unofficial killings of collaborators, and women who had slept with enemy soldiers were being paraded with shorn heads through the streets. In the area of entertainment, prominent figures such as Arletty, Sacha Guitry and Maurice Chevalier saw their careers suffer. Yet the wound to the nation's self-image was too deep, and the political cost of healing it too high, so de Gaulle commuted Pétain's death sentence to life imprisonment on the Île d'Yeu and maintained officially that, since Vichy had been an irregular regime, the real France had not collaborated. This convenient fiction began to be questioned in the 1970s, notably by the documentary film *Le Chagrin et la Pitié*, which demonstrated the ordinariness of collaboration. However, it was only in the 1990s that justice caught up with three leading collaborators: René Bousquet, the police chief responsible for the round-up of 1942 who had since served as a minister; Paul Touvier, the leader of the Vichy Militia responsible for civilian murders and who had been hidden by a wing of the Church; and Maurice Papon, also responsible for deportations, who had since become prefect of police. President Chirac would apologise in 1995 for the deportation of the Jews, while the Church would apologise for its support of Vichy, but it would not be until 2009 that the direct responsibility of the state would be officially recognised by the leading court in the land, the Conseil d'État.

The resulting animosities did not make for an easy transition, especially since the country's politics would soon become entangled in the larger Cold War antagonisms. Three main parties emerged from the immediate post-war elections, in which women had for the first time been given the vote: the Communist Party with around 30 per cent and an enforced combination of the new centrist Catholic Mouvement Républicain Populaire (MRP) and the Socialists, with around 45 per cent between them. And since both de Gaulle and the Communists at least agreed on nationalisation, significant measures were put in train. Much of the economy, whether transport, banking, coal, gas or electricity, was brought under state control and the École Nationale d'Administration was founded to create a new class of properly professional, supposedly omnicompetent administrators. However, following a row over a new constitution, de Gaulle, who viewed political parties as representing merely sectional interests and wanted a strong presidential system, resigned in January 1946. Despite his continued opposition, the proposal to return to the familiar two-chamber constitution was carried by referendum in October of that year and the Fourth Republic – the sixteenth regime since 1789, no less[1] – was born.

The year 1947 – which appropriately had the hottest summer on record – was a turning point in this politically heated situation. Having miscalculated in gambling that the shock of his resignation would bring the parties to their senses, de Gaulle now set up his own 'rally', the Rassemblement du Peuple Français (RPF), and proceeded to attack the Communist Party as being in the service of Moscow. For this was also the year that the Cold War became real with the declaration of the Truman Doctrine and the proclamation of the Marshall Plan to aid the European recovery. In the municipal elections in October, de Gaulle's new RPF won absolute majorities in the thirteen largest towns including Paris, where his brother Pierre became the new leader of the city council. It was now the turn of the Communists to overplay their hand by encouraging a general strike, which created the fear of a takeover, but the government took firm defensive measures, the trumpeted general strike did not happen, the socialist wing of the Confédération Générale du Travail (CGT) broke away to become the separate Force Ouvrière (FO), and the Communists, having gambled on a calculated resignation when refusing to follow the government's line on wage restraint, found themselves out of power. Which left a shaky centrist government in charge in a still bitterly divided Paris, where even students from the prestigious École Normale Supérieure could be seen at night putting up Communist posters and engaging with the police who were bent on tearing them down.

*   *   *

To add to the strains of life in Paris at this time there was the housing crisis. Of course, the city had suffered from serious deficiencies in this area before the war and had failed consistently to build enough accommodation to deal with the problem, so that the housing density, with 340 people to the hectare, was unique in Europe and associated with higher rates of alcoholism and infant mortality. The situation was now further complicated by the sharp rise in the number of births brought by the peace, so that the population was growing by fifty thousand a year, to produce three hundred and eighty thousand extra over the years 1946–54.[2] The exceptionally cold winter of 1953–4 and the campaign on homelessness of the Abbé Pierre would reveal the extent of the problem. Not only were so many apartments old, neglected and lacking in modern facilities, but there was also the shortage, which left half of young married couples living with their parents and a further 15 per cent living in lodgings. With an official report describing conditions in some of the poorer areas as 'atrocious', something clearly had to be done.[3]

However, there were two impediments. The first was the ingrained practice of rent control, which meant that the return on the investment was not sufficient to tempt owners either to maintain the accommodation properly or to build further apartments to rent – the percentage of income spent on rent had fallen to 5.5 per cent in 1939. Since it was politically difficult to raise controlled rents beyond the long-outdated idea of a 'fair rent', it could only be done gradually and would take too long to have any immediate effect. The other problem was that there was no consensus as to what the nature and functions of a future Paris should be. On the one hand, there were those who were still worried about the political balance between Paris and the rest of the country, a concern that chimed with the practical question of whether it could realistically continue to be both the self-consciously beautiful capital and a major industrial centre.[4] The trend would be towards moving industry out of the city, beginning in 1955 with regulations requiring special permission for the construction of industrial and even of official buildings over a certain size. Meanwhile, the approach to housing in Paris did not suggest much coherence or control.

Obviously, materials were in short supply immediately after the war and it was understandable that priority should be given to restoring the infrastructure. Nevertheless, France was devoting comparatively little to housing at only 4 per cent of its GNP, with the emphasis being heavily on private ownership. In the case of the Paris area, this combined with the uncertainty about the industrial future of the city to produce a serious shortage of rented apartments for the working class, since up to the end of 1953 only 14 per cent of the 57,800 dwellings completed were for rent.[5] An attempt was now made to increase the stock by using prefabri-cated materials to construct large blocks of *logements économiques*, or cheap flats, in the suburbs where land was both available and much cheaper. However, these blocks were far from public trans-port, jobs and shops, to the point that a development of thirteen thousand units in the northern suburb of Sarcelles gave rise to the condition ironically termed '*sarcellitis*', and they were largely abandoned by workers when the situation began to improve after 1960, to provide something of a ghetto for immigrants.

Paris had now lost its standing as the world's art market, partly because of inactivity during the war and partly because there was more money in New York, but it still led in the *haute couture* and luxury trades, a key area of business that would also bring in much-needed hard currency for the struggling post-war economy. And if 1947 was a key year in political terms, it was also the year in which Christian Dior introduced the New Look. Many other familiar names would soon be in play – Schiaparelli, Balenciaga, Givenchy, Pierre Cardin and Balmain among others – but it was the plump, shy Christian Dior who began the parade in February 1947 with this expensive creation, which of itself seemed to abolish all memories of war, rationing and characterless utility clothing. The New Look was a womanly hourglass figure, with a tiny waist, full hips, generous bust and natural rather than squared shoulders, with elegant, well-cut jacket, mid-calf full flowing skirt over layers of petticoats – with shoes, gloves and other accessories to match, not to forget the fetching broad-brimmed Chinese-style hat. It was new, it was revolutionary, and it was wildly successful – if not quite with everybody. For though it seemed like a smart publicity idea to film the new style in the typical Parisian setting of the Rue Lepic in Montmartre, the lead-ing model was stared at in astonishment, then in resentment and finally attacked by a stall holder and another woman, who slapped her, tore at her hair and tried to pull the New Look costume off her, until she was rescued and taken back to the *beaux quartiers*. As usual in Paris, there were conflicting versions of reality.[6]

For various reasons the centre of entertainment had now moved from Montparnasse to Saint-Germain-des-Prés. Before the war, Picasso had to come to the Left Bank to find a studio large enough to accommodate his mural *Guernica* and was regularly to be seen with a Vittel water in front of him – since he did not drink alcohol – in conversation with Paul Éluard and other supporters of the Popular Front at the Deux Magots. During the war Sartre could be seen huddled near the stove in the Café de Flore, scrib-bling away for six hours a day, with Simone de Beauvoir working less frenetically nearby. Since for intellectuals it was vulgarly bourgeois to own an apartment, and since the students' accom-modation was so limited, the obvious meeting places were the cafés. Also, it was now the age of jazz, and the advantage of Saint-Germain was that there were cellars available, able to limit the sound of late-night performances – and if they were dank and disreputable, that just added to the charm. So there was now a series of famous *caves*, or cellars, such as Le Tabou or La Rose Rouge, with such stars as the American jazz saxophonist Sidney Bechet and the widely talented trumpet player Boris Vian. The fun lasted until the early sixties, when New Orleans jazz would give way to rock 'n' roll.

Needless to say, the traditional *chanson*, which carried so much of the popular French sensibility, was going along merrily in parallel. There were the music halls Bobino in Montparnasse and the Olympia on the Boulevard des Capucines, which between them featured every singer worth mentioning. But there were also the cabarets, ranging from the Trois Baudets, where you could listen to Georges Brassens or Serge Gainsbourg, to the Échelle de Jacob, where you could find Jacques Brel, Charles Aznavour or Léo Ferré. The audience was being increased by exposure on the radio and at the cinema, if not yet on television, and the persona of the singer was becoming as important as the song. Several figures stand out in this context, one being the colourful Charles Trenet, who was twice absurdly denounced in collaborationist newspapers in 1944, firstly for suspiciously resembling Harpo Marx and secondly because the name Trenet was suspected to be an anagram of the known Jewish name of Netter. He fled from the Gestapo, was shot in the leg and only later managed to demonstrate that he had no Jewish ancestry whatsoever – ironically, he was excluded for some months after the war for having performed in Germany. Then there was Édith Piaf, whose desperate intensity in living her own myth won over all who heard her. Not to forget Yves Montand, whose social sympathies were encased in a warm fraternal delivery.

Although Juliette Gréco in fact gained her great success as a singer on the more fashionable Right Bank, she is always associated with Saint-Germain and indeed illustrates the mixture of entertainers and intellectuals that made it so extraordinary. After seeing her mother and her sister carted off to a concentration camp, she was beaten up by the Vichy Militia and thrown on to the street at the age of fifteen. She started in acting, but Sartre set her up in a hotel and encouraged her to move into singing, providing her with the chilling little number 'Dans la Rue des

Blancs-Manteaux' and then arranging for Raymond Queneau's 'Si tu t'imagines', a lively if disillusioned poem, to be put to music for her. So Juliette Gréco, dressed funereally in black sweater and slacks, along with the pipe-smoking Sartre writing busily close to the stove and with the jazz at night, came to symbolise the moment. It was a curious conjunction, a kind of enjoyable despair, but it reflected the sense – even beyond the concentration camps, the atomic bombs and the rising Cold War – that the vaunted European institutions of democracy, justice and religion had collapsed like cobwebs under pressure from a murderous madman named Adolf Hitler. So it was back to ground zero. Not just the civilisation but Man himself had to be reinvented.

So it was the time of the existentialists, led by Sartre and Simone de Beauvoir with such figures as Kierkegaard, Nietzsche and Heidegger, with his tormented terminology, in the background. 'Existence precedes essence' was the message, so there were no ready-made definitions. Individuals were seen as free but *condemned* to be free in an absurd and meaningless world in which they had to forge their own values – although Sartre would have difficulty making the jump from this extremely subjectivist position to a collective political viewpoint. Needless to say, the Parisians were not all suddenly reading existentialist texts, with the possible exception of Simone de Beauvoir's ground-breaking feminist study *Le Deuxième Sexe*. However, this was an attempt to give philosophical form to a new perspective that was infiltrating the arts in general, to which the existentialists themselves contributed with novels and plays. There were Sartre's novels *La Nausée* and *Les Chemins de la Liberté* or the plays *Les Mouches* and *Huis-Clos*, Camus's novels *L'Étranger* and *La Peste* or the plays *Le Malentendu* and *Les Justes*, and Simone de Beauvoir's novels *L'Invitée* and *Les Mandarins* or the play *Les Bouches inutiles*.

The climate of pessimism and scepticism – fashionable to a degree but encouraged by the failure of the country to solve its problems – had brought about a 'theatre of the Absurd' with Eugène

Ionesco's long-running *La Cantatrice chauve*, first performed in English as *The Bald Primadonna*, which shows a Mr and Mrs Smith threshing around helplessly in a wilderness of increasingly meaningless language. There was also Samuel Beckett's *Waiting for Godot*, with its two tramp-like characters in bowler hats churning around aimlessly while nervously at intervals awaiting the arrival of a doubtless non-existent Godot – which the scriptural allusions also suggest is a mocking reference to God. This pessimism and sense of estrangement are if anything more sharply conveyed by the *Nouveau Roman* (New Novel) as practised by such as Alain Robbe-Grillet, Marguerite Duras and Michel Butor. The basic technique here is to decontextualise, to present a human action without indicating its intention, or simply to state the dimensions of an object without indicating its purpose. So the world of the novel is now a mystery and the narrator, who may be merely implied, is also a mystery, as though a consciousness is encountering life on planet earth for the first time – it can be a disquieting exercise. In the cinema also, the New Wave of directors such as François Truffaut or Jean-Luc Godard were similarly treating film not just as telling a story, but as the search for a structure of meaning. Among the most successful films of the period were Godard's *À Bout de Souffle* and Alain Resnais's haunting *Hiroshima, mon amour*.

Beneath the confused political surface of the ill-fated Fourth Republic, there was one visionary figure in the form of the extraordinary Jean Monnet. A much-travelled cognac producer and strategist, he had among other things created a pooling system for Allied shipping from London to the United States in the First World War, been assistant general secretary of the League of Nations, worked closely with Churchill in 1940 and represented Roosevelt to the Free French from 1943 in Algiers – all of which leads one major historian to say that 'he succeeded more than anyone in the world ever had in becoming the intimate of a prodigious number of heads of state and of government'.[7] Although de

Gaulle and he were totally different types, the general had put him in charge of a national recovery plan after the Liberation, and Monnet had worked discreetly in a technocratic fashion, giving priority to basic industries and infrastructure. He then incorporated the Marshall Plan funds into his own plans. Since these credits were conditional on France balancing its budget and opening up its markets to American goods – Hollywood films, Coca-Cola and all – this was a rude shock to an over-protected economy, but it was a salutary one. By 1953 France was on the road to the expansion that would be dubbed the 'thirty glorious years'.

Yet that was only the lesser part of the achievement of this man who had the gift of seeing matters in realistic non-ideological terms, and who realised that the sequence of three increasingly destructive wars between France and Germany in eighty years – ending in industrialised genocide and many millions of deaths in combat – could not sensibly continue. So when a dispute arose over control of iron and steel production in the Saar and the Ruhr, he combined with the French foreign minister Robert Schuman to create the European Coal and Steel Community, involving Italy, the Netherlands, Belgium and Luxembourg as well as France and Germany. When the United States, otherwise occupied by war in Korea, put pressure on Europe to do more for its own defence, he proposed a European Defence Community. There was fierce opposition in France itself to ratifying the treaty over the issue of German rearmament, but this whole question was bypassed by the admission of West Germany to NATO in 1955, while the Coal and Steel Community was expanded into the European Economic Community by the Treaty of Rome in 1957. Jean Monnet's dream – which had also been that of Victor Hugo one hundred years before – was beginning to take shape.

As it happened, this coincided with a momentary relaxation of internal tension following Nikita Khrushchev's speech about the crimes of Stalin and the crushing of the Hungarian uprising. The awkward reaction of the Communist leader Maurice Thorez lacked credibility and the drift of intellectuals away from the Party increased.

However, this was more than balanced by an Anglo-French disaster over the Suez Canal and by rebellions in the colonies, prompted by broader changes wrought by the war and by a drop in France's prestige due to the defeat in 1940. The immediate problem was Vietnam, where an uprising by the Viet Minh, now supported by China in answer to American support for the French, was merging with a new and broader Cold War. In May 1954, Paris was shocked to hear that the French army had suffered a humiliating defeat at the hands of a largely peasant army at Dien Bien Phu – and further shocked when the long list of French captives published in *Le Monde* was seen to include an embarrassingly large number of Foreign Legionaries with German names. The situation was so serious as to call for Pierre Mendès France – who, as one commentator said, was too clever normally to be made prime minister[8] – and he negotiated the partition of the country. Just in time for the greater Algerian drama to attract the attention.

Algeria had been formally, if rather ambiguously, part of France since 1881, with three Departments under the jurisdiction of the minister of the interior, and around 1 million out of the population of 10 million were French Algerians, who saw themselves as equal to those on the mainland. The official policy of assimilation was never likely to be implemented, since the Muslim majority feared that normal French citizenship would deprive them of their Islamic laws and identity, while the French Algerians feared that equal status would leave them swamped by Muslims. However, in a changing world following the French defeat and the arrival of American troops in Algeria in 1942, there was a demand for full internal independence culminating in an uprising in 1945, which left over eighty European Algerians dead. This was savagely repressed, but the National Liberation Front (Front de Libération Nationale, FLN) had now launched a guerrilla war, which confronted the government with a stark situation. Since it was deemed to be politically impossible to grant independence to Algeria, the only alternative was to treat the rebellion as a civil war. This meant using the conscript army for repression, which in turn divided the nation politically and indeed, since the FLN clearly enjoyed the support of the Algerian population, drove the army in its search for intelligence to the excess of using 'clean' electrical torture on both men and women.[9] Since this further alienated the local population, the situation worsened to the point that the Fourth Republic itself collapsed in May 1958, when the poisoned chalice was handed to de Gaulle.

Some idea of the depth of the wound to France's self-esteem inflicted by the bitter struggle over Algeria's independence was conveyed in October 2021 by President Emmanuel Macron's ceremonial laying of a wreath at the Pont Saint-Michel to mark the sixtieth anniversary of the massacre of Algerian demonstrators on 17 October 1961. The affair was officially hushed up, so that no accurate estimate of the number of victims was ever made available, but it is calculated that well over a hundred bodies turned up along the river. Since the prefect of Paris at the time was the collaborationist Maurice Papon, the affair connects with equally divisive memories of the Occupation. Certainly it was noted that, while he described the event as 'an unforgivable crime', the president refrained – perhaps with an eye to the upcoming 2022 election – from offering an official apology. This was still delicate terrain.

It is probable that only de Gaulle had the stature to prevent the country from being plunged into a full-scale civil war over Algeria. Even then, with his own ministers being divided on the issue, it was close. Initially, since he saw no clear solution, he played for time with a visit to Algeria where he calmed the settlers with a few soothing ambiguities. He then sought to situate the problem in the larger context of a new French Community, one akin to the British Commonwealth. Since all the French African colonies, apart from Guinea, opted to remain within the Community rather than choose independence, this provided the structure for a possible compromise solution. With this in mind, he granted the

Algerians French citizenship and accelerated plans to improve services and employment, but since the repressive measures had alienated the population further and the FLN was now mounting terrorist attacks in Paris, it was all too late. With the war dividing the nation and damaging France's reputation abroad, he was forced to recognise Algerian independence as a possible outcome.

Although he obtained a 76 per cent majority for this position in a national referendum in January 1961, he still had to deal with an attempted coup d'état in Algiers in April, led by four army generals. He was already using commanding television appearances as a weapon and, with Paris now under the imminent threat of a parachute attack from its own forces, he made a dramatic appeal to the people for help, saying 'Françaises, Français, aidez-moi!' The coup did collapse, but peace negotiations would drag on for another year, during which Paris would suffer riots and intermittent bomb attempts from the FLN on one side and a new anti-independence Secret Army Organisation (Organisation de l'Armée Secrète, OAS) on the other. It is some indication of the depth of the problem that the OAS, which would kill some two thousand people in bomb outrages, should mimic ironically the Resistance organisation of the same name and be led by men such as Georges Bidault and Jacques Soustelle, old wartime comrades of de Gaulle who had walked with him down the Champs-Élysées on Liberation day in 1944. Even after the peace treaty was signed in March 1962, the OAS attempted to assassinate the president and his wife by machine-gunning his car at the Petit-Clamart roundabout just south of Paris. Happily they survived – along with the four live chickens they were transporting for the cook – and de Gaulle was more than ready to take command.

It was suddenly as though the country had been released from the weight of history and, instead of suffering it, was making it. Plans that had been on hold were being implemented and affecting life in all directions. An independent foreign policy was being pursued with the backing of a nuclear deterrent and de Gaulle was holding the country separate from both East and West. The state-directed economy was being modernised at pace and growing at an enviable 5 per cent a year, which gave France a GDP twice as high as that of Britain, with a new 'strong franc', worth 100 old francs, making the point clear. During Fourastié's 'thirty glorious years' the population would increase by some 30 per cent to 56 million, infant mortality would come down dramatically and the length of life increase markedly. With improved medical facilities and increased family allowances, there was a new young generation that was taller, healthier, more self-confident and sometimes, with the growing Americanisation of popular culture, disconcertingly different. If young French people travelling abroad had previously tended not to broadcast their nationality, they could now look self-confident to the point of seeming arrogant. France was back.

And Paris was looking like a building site. An overall plan of 1959 had decreed that no less than 20 per cent of the built-up area of the city needed to be renovated, which meant the elimination of slums and the provision of modern housing for a population that was increasing not just because of natural growth but because of an influx of loyalist refugees from Indochina and Algeria. However, the price of land had doubled in ten years and sites were now worth more that the buildings sitting on them, while the welcome economic expansion was underlining the inadequacy of office provision in the city and emphasising the fact that Paris was too small for its ambitions. The overall answer to these interrelated problems was to create a modern business centre, to build housing units high within the city, but also to develop the suburbs and incorporate them properly within a new greater Paris by means of an up-to-date commuter network, while also improving the road connections with the rest of the country and, indeed, creating a new major hub airport – to be called, inevitably, Charles de Gaulle – at Roissy. It amounted to a major recasting of the city.

Work now began on the new and very large business district La

Défense on the western edge of the city, a Paris 'Manhattan' of skyscrapers, which would also have a social and cultural dimension for permanent residents. It would acquire over time not only office buildings, but the Léonard-de-Vinci university and no fewer than five business schools. As regards housing, whole neighbourhoods in the poorer, more marginal neighbourhoods were redesigned during the 1960s, notably in the 13th, 15th, 19th and 20th arrondissements, with the tower blocks replacing the dilapidated buildings. The potential residents, especially older ones, were often repelled by the height of the towers – the twenty known as the Front de Seine in the 15th arrondissement were thirty storeys high – and they served in part as 'Chinatowns' for refugees from Indochina. The middle classes were now being drawn towards living in the suburbs, partly because apartments could be larger and better appointed for the same rental or purchase price, and partly because of the considerable improvements now being made in the suburban housing developments as regards commuter travel, shopping and social facilities. Over the thirty years up to 1975, the population of the old inner city fell by over half a million.

The longstanding problem of what to do about the traffic congestion and other problems caused by the central market of Les Halles was finally resolved by moving it out to the suburb of Rungis and replacing it with the elaborate underground shopping centre Le Forum des Halles. Some of the old Haussmann residential buildings in the centre were transformed into offices and the traditional business centre in the area of the Opéra was connected to La Défense by a new fast line that took no more than fifteen minutes. Five new satellite towns were created in the new greater Paris area, at Évry, Cergy, Saint-Quentin, Marne-la-Vallée and Melun-Sénart, each carefully planned and provided with shopping, social and sports facilities. And the public was generally accepting of all these changes, although there was the familiar story of the dismay at the building of the Montparnasse Tower, which, like the Eiffel Tower, seemed to get alarmingly taller by the day as it grew from the planned 150 metres high to a modified 170 metres high and finally 200 metres high. Will Parisians end up by becoming as proud of the Montparnasse tower as they became of the Eiffel Tower? Perhaps – and perhaps not.

Despite all this modernising activity, there was still a concern for preserving the elements of major historical and aesthetic interest in the city, and much of the work in this area was taken up by the novelist and art historian André Malraux. 'On my right I have, and shall always have, André Malraux,' wrote de Gaulle in his description of Fifth Republic cabinet meetings. 'The presence at my side of this friend of genius and devotee of high destinies gives me the sense of being protected against the commonplace.'[10] Certainly Malraux, in his splendid office in the Palais-Royal, enjoyed a special, symbolical position within the government since he was both unelected and had not even joined the Gaullist party – although active as the first minister for culture, he also represented a kind of guarantee to the left. Indeed he borrowed the idea of Maisons de la Culture, or cultural centres, from a left-wing example in Paris in the 1930s in order to promote a score of such centres in the new satellite towns and more widely in the provinces with a view to extending Parisian cultural standards throughout the country. Described by him as 'modern cathedrals, without the religion', they were sometimes criticised as elitist, but they did stimulate theatrical and other activities, especially since he took steps to make access to them affordable.

He took a keen interest in the appearance of Paris and laid down new rules regarding the cleaning of public buildings, the effect of which would be to transform the Place de la Concorde from a grim grey to the original pleasant ochre and Notre-Dame from a blackish to a white cathedral. He also saw the interest of preserving not only certain buildings of particular significance but the *quartiers* that provided the context for that significance. So the 'Malraux Law' introducing *secteurs sauvegardés*, or protected areas, provided not just for the preservation but for the restoration of the buildings and streets involved, a lengthy and expensive undertaking. The first district to be treated as of 1964 was the Marais, which suffers a little from its own success by becoming a rather expensive and self-conscious tourist attraction, while the second, begun in 1972, was the old aristocratic area of the 7th arrondissement. Malraux also gave state commissions to major artists such as Braque, Chagall and André Masson, and as cultural representative travelled widely abroad. As the guarantee to the left in de Gaulle's exceptional regime, he was walking something of a tightrope, but he was sufficiently independent to go further than any minister of the Fourth Republic by condemning torture, to the great irritation of French Algerian extremists, who attempted to assassinate him in 1962.

The 'Events' of May 1968 – so called because nobody quite knew what else to call them – started modestly at a new university campus built close to the shanty town in the suburb of Nanterre in order to cater for an overflow of students from the Sorbonne. The male students, feeling that they were not being treated as grownups when they were refused permission to visit their girlfriends in their rooms, began to defy the authorities. When the university reacted strongly, the students defiantly extended their occupation and the authorities closed down the Nanterre campus, only to see the occupation migrate to the Sorbonne and then to other universities and even *lycées* across the country. The Sorbonne was being partly trashed, Surrealist slogans such as 'it is forbidden to forbid', or 'the dream is the reality', were being painted on walls, and organised anarchist elements were moving in. The authorities unwisely sent in the Compagnies républicaines de sécurité (CRS) police force, whose brutal tactics only increased sympathy for the students as a battle royal with barricades and paving stones was fought out in the streets around the university for the edification of television audiences throughout the country and beyond. With hundreds of students now injured, the Socialist and Communist parties and the trade unions were dragged in, 10 million employees were soon on strike, factories were occupied, and this youthful middle-class carnival had somehow left the country in a state of paralysis and shock.

So what was it all about? Was it some sort of Surrealist psychodrama or more grandly, as André Malraux put it, a 'crisis of civilisation'? For the Socialists, Communists and trade unions showed no desire to own it politically – there would be lasting generational conflicts within left-wing families because of it. Yet 'how could it be,' as Raymond Aron asked, 'that a localised student protest turned into a national crisis which caused the regime to tremble, when no political party and no leader of a mass movement had any real intention of taking power?'[11] Certainly, although Prime Minister Georges Pompidou was trying to play off the unions against the students with large wage increases, the situation was getting dramatically out of hand, de Gaulle had disappeared and the Socialist François Mitterrand was appearing on television offering nervously to replace him. For once in his life de Gaulle, as he later told Pompidou, had completely lost his nerve, but he recovered it and had actually been on a secret trip to assure himself of the loyalty of the army and returned in commanding form.[12] He announced fresh elections, the country relaxed, there was a mass demonstration in support of him on the Champs-Élysées and he romped home triumphantly in the elections. France had turned a complete somersault.

So what in fact *was* it all about? There were various factors involved, the most obvious of which was that, with the development of television in particular, students were more directly aware of such events in the wider world as the divisions over war in Vietnam, Mao in China and Castro in Cuba, as well as of the student protests and the developing counterculture in America. The traditional hierarchies and values were now relatively discredited in this new consumer society of sexual freedom, the contraceptive pill and the miniskirt, yet the materialist individualism of this new order was itself suspect. The background culture at this time was itself confusing since the structuralist tendency in the New Wave in cinema as in philosophy and history was to question language itself. At a more down-to-earth level, the large increase in student population, at a time when the economic boom was running out of steam, suggested that jobs could be harder to find. It was in this perspective that the existing university system could be seen as traditionalist and paternalist, with a poor staff–student ratio and little or no staff–student interaction for the majority of students outside the privileged *grandes écoles*. Like the state monopoly of television, it was out of date.

De Gaulle, unlike many of his followers, took the point. He spoke of the need to reform 'narrow and outdated structures' and establish a policy of 'participation' – which became particularly noticeable in the area of television. He set the very competent Edgar Faure to decentralise and democratise education, which resulted in the five faculties of the University of Paris being broken up into thirteen independent campuses. However, de Gaulle himself was almost beginning to look a little out of place in this evolving Gaullist regime and he may well have felt that he had done enough. He took an unnecessary risk by insisting on a national referendum for a measure on greater autonomy for the regions, lost it as he probably half-expected, retired to Colombey in 1969 and died the following year.

De Gaulle's successor as president, with the resounding name of Pompidou, was the son of a primary schoolteacher and a graduate of the École Normale Supérieure who had been a banker before becoming prime minister. His tenure as president coincided with the oil crisis of 1973, which signalled the ending of the 'thirty glorious years' reliant on cheap energy, but which also demonstrated the wisdom of having developed an independent nuclear programme. His name is kept alive today by two features that in their different ways are illustrative of this period of change. The first is the Pompidou Centre in the area vacated by the Halles, which reflects André Malraux's vision of a multi-cultural centre available to everyone. It contains a very large information library, a centre for music and associated research and the National Museum of Modern Art, the largest such museum in Europe. It resulted from a large international competition – the first time non-French entrants had been invited to take part in this type of tender – and the winning submission by Richard Rogers and Renzo Piano was startlingly revolutionary. As though influenced not just by the Structuralists of the period but by the Situationists, who regarded modern society as oppressive, it was a playful inside-out building with all its working parts on the outside and painted in bright colours. It became almost too successful as a tourist attraction, has had to be closed at intervals for renovation and, indeed, is scheduled to close in 2023 for four years.

Pompidou is also associated with the inevitable traffic problem presenting itself in a developing city. Not only did the number of cars grew fivefold between 1950 and 1972, but the industry kept producing increasingly sophisticated models starting with the Citroën 1955 DS – sounding like *déesse*, or goddess – that were viewed at the annual Salon de l'Automobile almost as objects of veneration. Pompidou was persuaded that 'Paris must give up an outdated aesthetic and adapt itself to the automobile'.[13] This approach had already led to the Right Bank expressway, which deprived pedestrians of part of the one side of the Seine, and it was proposed not just to do the same to the Left Bank, but to drive a north–south autoroute through the city. Although there was as yet little broader concern about the environment, there were those who felt that the character of the city had to be preserved and President Valéry Giscard d'Estaing cancelled these plans when he took over following Pompidou's death in 1974.

Contemporary Paris

The development of Paris since the death of Pompidou has naturally been affected by the view taken of its role as capital city, which posed a longstanding problem. On the one hand, it had for centuries been not just the seat of government, but to an unusual degree the economic, judicial, cultural and educational capital of the country. On the other hand, it had seen anti-government insurrections at regular intervals, leading to the view that it was not only too powerful but that it was becoming different from the rest of the country and that its influence must be curtailed – which is why it still came under the control of a government-appointed prefect rather than an elected mayor. And this mirrored another anomaly in that France, though a multi-party democracy, had been left by de Gaulle with a powerful presidency not accountable to parliament or to the law and with the power to appoint to hundreds of posts. So how was Paris to resolve these contradictions within a situation where France was having to redefine itself in a world undergoing rapid change due to oil crises, Middle Eastern wars, the collapse of the Soviet Union, the rise of the European Union, globalisation and indeed, as demonstrated at the Paris conference of 2015, the threat of climate change?

Pompidou, although he was seen as having yielded too much to the cult of the motor car as to 'Americanisation' in the building of skyscrapers, had at least attempted to rationalise the Gaullist hybrid part-presidential, part-parliamentary constitution but had got no farther with this 'Gordian knot' than arguing that it might be a more flexible system for a people as notoriously difficult to govern as the French.[1] However, he did take steps to give more freedom to his prime minister and to improve the link with the parliament.

This approach was carried on by his successor Giscard d'Estaing, an independent conservative who tried to humanise the presidency by having an open day at the Élysée Palace on the *Quatorze Juillet* and by visiting citizens in their homes as part of his drive to bring about a more relaxed 'advanced liberal society'. Coming to power in 1974, the year which saw the emergence of an ecologist Green candidate, he came out strongly against the Pompidou 'era of concrete' and by cancelling both a Left Bank expressway and a proposed international business centre on the site of the old Halles markets, he infuriated the Gaullists, whose backers had heavy investments in these projects.[2] Although he had tried to keep them sweet by appointing Jacques Chirac, otherwise known as 'le Bulldozer', as his prime minister, he had not seriously involved him in decision-making and this caused further animosity.

It was in this tense atmosphere that Giscard set out to increase local democracy by re-establishing the elected office of mayor of Paris. Chirac opposed this openly, was sacked, but then stood in the election himself and became mayor of Paris in 1977, which meant that Giscard had in effect innocently institutionalised the conflict between the capital and the state. Although the open warfare that ensued made it difficult to get agreement on further major projects, Giscard was responsible for several notable achievements, beginning with the vast underground central train hub of Châtelet–Les Halles, which opened in 1977. Taking the view that it might be better to adapt than to replace, he decided to transform the old but quite elegant Gare d'Orsay station into a museum of nineteenth-century art. The original plan needed some adaptation and the whole project was widely criticised, but it has proved to be both successful and enormously popular. Giscard also decided to use the site of the abattoirs at La Villette, on the north-eastern edge of Paris, to create a Cité des Sciences et de l'Industrie, by now the largest science museum in Europe, which has since been surrounded by further attractions in what has become known as the Parc de la Villette.

This ambitious venture, now a prime tourist attraction, is of particular interest in that it combined several of the distinctive features of the presidential *grandes oeuvres*, or major projects, of the period. In the first place, it showed that the 'era of concrete' was to be followed by the era of glass and steel – indeed one study of Paris architecture of this time is entitled *The Glass State* – and this was exemplified in the architect Adrien Fainsilber's creation of the science museum itself.[3] Secondly, it echoed both Malraux's aim to democratise culture and the less solemn and even playful approach seen in the Pompidou Centre by providing a range of attractions from high culture to simple entertainment that would both be unifying and provide something of interest for everyone. Whence the enormously wide collection of additional attractions, ranging from an IMAX cinema inside a large geodesic dome to several concert venues for all sorts of music, conference centres, a theatre, an equestrian centre, a circus tent, an outdoor cinema, which also presents an annual film festival, and a decommissioned military submarine named the *Argonaute*. Thirdly, this being Paris, the Swiss architect Bernard Tschumi, who was responsible for the enormous park itself, sought the advice of the Deconstructionist philosopher Jacques Derrida. This led to a large expanse of garden full of 'follies' and surprises, which does not play to the visitor's expectations but is designed to offer the opportunity for personal discovery.

The year 1981, the point at which Giscard's seven-year tenure was due to end, proved to be a significant, if unexpected, turning point. Despite his modernising efforts the economy, which had been so buoyant in the 'thirty glorious years' up to the middle of the decade, had run into problems, which the second oil crisis arising out of the Iranian Revolution merely emphasised. Although the dirigiste approach was successful in building up the nuclear industry, the attempt to introduce neo-liberal measures to create a more competitive modern economy and reduce the deficit had its own problems. The removal of subsidies to lame-duck industries was resulting in failures among a number of enterprises, unemployment was increasing, inflation was approaching 14 per cent and there were complaints, as expressed by one commentator, that France still had an 'archaic, artificial, semi-developed political system suffering from excessive centralisation' that was unfit for an advanced industrial society.[4] Nevertheless, with the left divided as usual, it was assumed that Giscard would comfortably win a second term in the forthcoming election.

That assumption was clearly shared by the 'Bulldozer' Jacques Chirac, who stood against Giscard in the first round and, having obtained only 18 per cent of the vote, decided to get rid of him by pointedly refraining from urging his Gaullist voters to support him in the second round. The shock result was that he split the right-wing vote, gifted the presidency to the Socialist candidate and caused a run on the stock exchange, only to find himself for the next fourteen years re-enacting the tension between the mayor of Paris and the president by wrestling not with the straightforward Giscard but with the cannier, smoothly impenetrable François Mitterrand.

Mitterrand, whose two seven-year terms as president meant that he would serve in that office for longer even than de Gaulle, was in his own way a dominant figure who would leave an abiding mark on Paris in particular. If he was also seen as something of a mystery man and even a Machiavellian, this was initially because his personal history and loyalties were not always clear. From a provincial Catholic family of traditionalist views, he had been captured in the war and escaped to begin working for Vichy, but switched in 1943 to work for the Resistance, a development which may have been perfectly natural but which some would later consider opportunist – the more so since his unconvincing claim in 1959 to have escaped a political assassination attempt was dismissed as a publicity stunt. There was also the mystery surrounding his private life, not just that he kept a mistress as well as his wife, or that he concealed the existence of his daughter

Mazarine, but that, as only recently revealed, he also had a secret amorous relationship with a young law student called Claire fifty years his junior for some eight years up to his death in 1996.[5] More damagingly, he maintained his friendship with the collaborationist René Bousquet, who had been responsible for deporting Jews to Auschwitz, and was seen as ambivalent by distancing himself only when Bousquet was publicly accused of crimes against humanity.

If Mitterrand was hardly your traditional Socialist – he had no obvious interest in left-wing theory or economics – he did sympathise with the need for a fairer society and he took a political risk by coming out strongly in favour of abolishing the death penalty. He was a cultivated individual but also an ambitious one, drawn to the exercise and mystique of power, and a determined one who plotted his way coolly and deliberately towards it. Having succeeded in becoming leader of the Socialist Party, he had manoeuvred towards bringing the Communist Party – to its ultimate disadvantage – into the left-wing electoral pact that would end the Gaullist domination. Having succeeded, with that little bit of help from his opponent Jacques Chirac, he was determined not only to hang on to power but to exercise it in the grand manner. The real 'mystery' of Mitterrand was that, like some inscrutable Renaissance prince playing several tactical games simultaneously, he exercised power through a complex network of dependants, often unknown to one another, playing them off one against the other as required – even concealing his cancer towards the end of his tenure because he believed that the exercise of power was keeping him alive. Meanwhile, in 1981 he had created what one of his ministers called a 'Copernican revolution', banished the right wing and opened a highway towards socialism – especially since he coolly dissolved the Assembly and increased his majority.

The next fourteen years saw him surfing the waves of economic and political change. Paris itself, with the racy Jack Lang enlivening the streets with his festival of music and setting a popular cultural tone, was more than enthusiastic as Mitterrand set about 'changing people's lives' by nationalising firms, raising family allowances, increasing the annual holiday to five weeks, and beginning the move towards the goal of a thirty-five-hour working week and a pensionable age of sixty. When the unhappy result, given that France was now firmly embedded in the global economy, was inflation, devaluation and rising unemployment, he switched briskly towards a neo-liberal free-market approach. However, unemployment continued to be a problem and, although he had limited the damage in advance by switching to proportional representation, the left still lost its parliamentary majority in the Assembly election of 1986. Even if the constitution did not formally require it, he was expected to resign, but instead he appointed Chirac as prime minister and brought the country into the cloudy era of 'cohabitation'. Over the next two years he outplayed him smoothly, suggesting that Chirac's runaway policy of privatisation was irresponsible in view of the stock market crash of 1987, prior to defeating him comfortably in the presidential election of 1988 to secure his second seven-year term.

Once again Mitterrand dissolved the Assembly to improve his position, but this election only produced a minority Socialist government. With an ongoing battle even among the Socialists between traditionalists and modernists in relation to the economy, there followed a succession of prime ministers up to the parliamentary elections of 1993, by which time the unemployment rate had risen to 12 per cent. The Socialists duly suffered a heavy defeat, obtaining under 20 per cent of the votes, so that for the last two years of his presidency Mitterrand found himself with a non-Gaullist centre-right government under Prime Minister Édouard Balladur. A calm and shrewd individual, Balladur balanced the privatising of the Banque Nationale de Paris and the Elf Aquitaine oil company with gestures towards the unions, and was the obvious right-wing candidate for the presidential election of 1995 – if one discounted Jacques Chirac. Meanwhile, Mitterrand's interest had switched not only towards binding France and Germany together for permanent peace and prosperity within the new European Union, but towards following the royal and latterly presidential practice of leaving his personal imprint on the historic city of Paris.

Immediately on taking office, Mitterrand picked up and modified Giscard's proposal for an Institut du Monde Arabe. He switched the site to the Quai Bernard in the 5th arrondissement and instead of retaining the chosen architect decided to have an open competition, which was won by Jean Nouvel. Intended to showcase Arabic civilisation, it contains a museum, a library, a lecture theatre and exhibition halls within a large and splendid steel and glass structure with the particular feature on the south façade of delicate automatic metal shutters, or Islamic mashrabiyas, to control and filter the sunlight. It was intended that it should be jointly funded by France and by eighteen often oil-rich Arab states, but these did not always meet the commitment and others, such as Iraq, Syria or Libya, wanted to use the institute for propagandist exhibitions that were less than welcome. In these circumstances, construction was delayed, the building was rather neglected, and the general cultural and political aim underlying the project was not quite achieved.[6]

Mitterrand also shared the longstanding view of many art lovers that the Ministry of Finance should be transferred from the wing it occupied in the Louvre, so that the whole of the old palace could be devoted to the collections. It was moved upriver to Bercy in the 12th arrondissement to a new, long, seven-storey structure standing at right angles to the Seine, likened by some wags, in view of its line of arcades, to a motorway tollbooth. This now left the daunting problem of how to proceed with the new enlarged Louvre and Mitterrand was acutely aware of the iconic status of this monument, set in the centre of Paris at the beginning of the

Voie Triomphale stretching along the Champs-Élysées and through the Arc de Triomphe towards the distant Grande Arche de la Défense. It signified the grandeur and continuity of the state to the point that his minister of works Émile Biasini could claim that it occupied 'the subconscious of France'.[7] Mitterrand, already incurring criticism of his monarchist tendencies for dismissing any idea of a competition, appointed the Chinese American architect I. M. Pei and worked with him in great secrecy for months before the design was revealed to the public. When it was finally revealed, he was seen by some as acting less like a Bourbon monarch than as a pharaoh.

It was accepted that the enlarged museum might need a different entrance and the large new underground complex of ticket offices, shops, cafeteria, auditorium and tourist bus depot was certainly helpful. However, this new entrance in the middle of the courtyard covered by a large glass pyramid surrounded by three small pyramids was so controversial that it provoked almost daily argument in *Le Figaro* for over a year in 1984–5. For some, the intrusion of this glass structure into the very centre of old Paris was a monstrous attack by the Socialist Mitterrand on monarchist sensibilities; for more thoughtful others the pyramid might be functionally acceptable but its stark novelty was at odds with the incremental way the palace had developed over centuries; while for fastidious others, it was turning the nation's greatest cultural monument into a supermarket for the international tourist trade. It is fair to add, after so much controversy, that public opinion has become accustomed to it and now views it favourably, and that the enlarged Louvre for good reasons is now the most visited museum in the world.

It was already clear that Mitterrand was pursuing the aim of making culture democratically available, as already advocated by André Malraux and implemented in the Pompidou Centre and the Parc de la Villette. If he was interested in the use of glass in construction, it is not simply because he saw it as an exciting new

medium, but because he viewed its transparency – often, in practice, its translucence – as a metaphor for that availability. A previously elitist French culture was being made accessible to the
public at large and the siting of a new opera house on the Place de
la Bastille, inaugurated on the bicentenary of the Revolution in
1989, made the point clear. A massive round glass and marble
building, it is one of the largest opera houses in the world, with a
2,700-seat auditorium and various other facilities, and while an
attempt was made to fit it plausibly into the old square, it has been
described among other things as a 'rhinoceros in a bathtub'.[8] For
all that, it attracts almost a million spectators a year to operas,
concerts and ballets presented by distinguished conductors and
performers.

Much of the criticism of these new buildings related to
conflicting ideas of the character and function of Paris. For one
historian, Paris was already a splendid large open-air museum,
which could only be destroyed by grandiose modernist presidential projects.[9] For others, who saw the city as having to live in the
modern world, all this was on the contrary turning Paris into a
museum when it should be concerned with developing the
suburbs and improving the living conditions of industrial workers. The issue was complicated politically by the rather ill-defined
and competitive relationship between the presidency, the mayor
of Paris, the departments and the Île-de-France region. Despite
these considerations, it is clear that, if not welcomed so warmly as
the business district of La Défense or the Parc de la Villette, the
enlarged Louvre and the new Opéra Bastille have certainly fulfilled
their primary function successfully. And it only requires a routine
trip in a *bateau-bus* on the river to see that Paris still retains its
grace and cohesion.

It is in this context that it was unfortunate for Mitterrand that
his name should remain associated primarily with the new
Bibliothèque Nationale de France, now referred to simply as the
Bibliothèque François Mitterrand. In the same spirit as before,

this was designed not just to replace the old national library in the Rue Richelieu, whose accumulated contents had long outgrown its capacity, but was intended to be available not only to recognised scholars but to the public at large – indeed, the original competition brief included provisions for exhibitions halls, restaurants, ten cinemas and even a Turkish bath.[10] Explicitly designed to be one of the largest and most modern libraries in the world and to represent the literary and intellectual riches of France as the Louvre represented its artistic riches, it would be the last of his *grands projets* and he needed to get it secured before his second term came to an end in 1995. This led to undue haste, to the architect Dominique Perrault yielding too much to Mitterrand's insistence on transparency and to the failure to consult librarians, so that the volumes stored in the four glass corner towers, themselves suggestive of open books, soon had to be protected from the sunlight. The rather daunting monumentalism of the high plinth on which the towers stand, which leaves users in a semi-underground reading room working by artificial light, incurred much criticism, as indeed did the unduly large heavy internal doors and the dangerously slippery Brazilian hardwood on the perimeter steps. Nevertheless, as some modifications have been made, the building has been accepted as part of the scene.

While the Eiffel Tower was gloriously lit up to celebrate the start of the new millennium on the eve of 2000, the feelings of Parisians may well have been mixed. They had seen the inauguration of the Channel Tunnel and the glorious gain on home soil of the 1998 World Cup title. However, they had also seen the dramatic death of Princess Diana in the Pont de l'Alma tunnel, which had led to so many spontaneous tokens of sympathy on the nearby Flame of Liberty monument, and they had seen the arguments over the introduction of the euro. What would this new century bring?

It brought the continuance of the presidency of Jacques Chirac. The opposite in some sense of François Mitterrand, the 'Bulldozer' was a populist opportunist with no deep political convictions, a warm, backslapping man with a preference for beer over fine wines. Not untypically, he had won the election in 1995 by promising to lower taxes, only to find that to meet the convergence criteria for the euro he had to practise austerity, so to increase his majority he dissolved the Assembly, only to end up with a Socialist prime minister. To improve his chances of winning the presidential election of 2002, since by the end of a second seven-year term he might look too old at seventy-seven, he reduced the term by referendum to five years. However, he was rather discredited by this time and he only won so easily because his opponent was the National Front candidate Jean-Marie Le Pen. Yet Chirac had his moments. Although he had difficulty in an increasingly integrated Europe in maintaining the Gaullist sense of France as a separate great power, he was the first president to recognise officially the nation's responsibility for the deportation of Jews and he showed some independence and foresight, by way of the memorable speech at the Security Council in 2003 by his foreign minister Dominique de Villepin, in resisting the call for the invasion of Iraq.

Meanwhile Paris, as though to emphasise the structural tension between the presidency and the capital city, had moved to the left by electing the openly gay Bertrand Delanoë as its first Socialist mayor since 1871. He would be followed in 2014 by the Socialist Anne Hidalgo, the first female mayor of Paris, who would be re-elected in 2020. Their tenure over twenty years would shift the emphasis in the improvement of the city more towards everyday living conditions. Of course, there would still be notable new museums, such as the striking Musée du Quai Branly designed by Jean Nouvel, which opened in 2006. Promoted by Chirac himself, in answer to the long-canvassed need for a museum that would do justice to the indigenous arts and cultures of Africa, Asia and the Americas, it has a rich collection of exhibits that also serve for research. There would also be in 2014 the Fondation Louis Vuitton, a highly original flamboyant glass structure by Frank Gehry, which hosts contemporary art exhibitions. Suggestive of the white wings of a gigantic swan, it is the more startling for being situated in the middle of the Bois de Boulogne, with peacocks prancing precisely around and inspecting the visitors.

However, the prime concern now was with making living conditions in the city as pleasant as possible and one aim, as indeed it had been an aim for Haussmann, was to provide green spaces for the enjoyment of Parisians, particularly in the outer arrondissements. Mitterrand himself, of course, had set this in train with new parks on old industrial sites such as the Parc André Citroën or the Parc de Bercy, but the principle now adopted was that any new housing development, or indeed any existing free space, should be used to provide garden facilities as appropriate.[11] Delanoë also brought in a whole series of outdoor festive events, notably the extraordinary Paris-Plages, for which each summer thousands of tons of sand are ferried in to create an artificial beach resort on the bank of the Seine, with deckchairs, parasols and even palm trees, as well as the all-night Nuit Blanche festival in the autumn. All of this obviously went hand in hand with the need to tackle the combined problem of traffic and urban pollution. The river itself, which had long been heavily polluted, was now cleaned up by a process of systematic oxygenation and restocked so that today there are over thirty species of fish swimming within the city limits.[12]

Delanoë's main focus was on the problems caused by the congested Paris road traffic. He pioneered a non-polluting tramway system on the Boulevards des Maréchaux, increased the number of cycle lanes, brought in bus and taxi lanes, increased parking charges while also reducing the number of parking spaces and generally took what steps he could to discourage the private motorist – who could be seen unkempt in dressing gown in the early morning moving their car to the other side of the street to comply with alternate day parking regulations. He brought in the Vélib' system of self-service rental bikes – later copied by London – and pioneered the Autolib', a parallel electric car scheme. Against the background of the 2015 Paris Agreement on climate change, Anne Hidalgo – who has also increased social housing in the city – has continued on the same path by further increasing parking charges and by banning cars from key areas while making public transport free on the first Sunday of each month. She aims to remove half of the parking spaces in the course of her current term of office (due to run to 2026), to extend protected cycle lanes, to have diesel cars banned, to green and pedestrianise much of the Champs-Élysées and, as far as possible, to replace private car usage with a 24/7 Métro service – in short, to make the city healthier and safer for Parisians.

For Chirac's successors as president – Nicolas Sarkozy until 2012, François Hollande until 2017, followed by Emmanuel Macron, whose second term runs until 2027 – a persistent problem has been that of Islamist terrorism. Not that the problem was new since there had been sporadic incidents since the 1980s. Nor indeed that it was entirely surprising. France had been an imperial power with a strong presence in Muslim countries in Africa in particular, as a result of which it had a large Muslim minority of around 8 per cent, although at least half were by now non-practising, especially among the young. As part of the Schengen free movement area, the country was also easy to access. And France seemed to incarnate what was most offensive about Western civilisation to those radicalised Muslims who went to join the Islamic State of Iraq and the Levant (ISIS) when it arose in 2014 – and who might have been inclined to return after its collapse in 2019. Not only had France engaged militarily against ISIS in Syria and Iraq, but it was an officially secular country which, even if religions were allowed, was opposed to any open display of religious symbols. It had no law against blasphemy, it tolerated mockery of religious practices in the name of freedom of expression and it allowed gay marriage. More even than the United States or Britain, in crystalised in the Jihadist mind all that was evil about Western civilisation.

Sarkozy, when minister of the interior under Chirac, had handled clumsily the riots that arose spontaneously in the suburbs in 2005 after two teenagers were accidentally electrocuted in attempting to flee from the police. The outer suburbs, or *banlieues*, that ring Paris proper with their functional housing blocks, were a separate world from which people travelling to work found their days reduced to *Métro, boulot, dodo*; Métro, work, sleep. Indeed, the alienation was such that the rioters were setting fire to the very schools and youth centres set up for their benefit. Fortunately, Chirac himself saw that the way to deal with this 'identity crisis' was to seek to abolish discrimination and ensure equal access for Muslims to employment. The religious motivation only really became dominant after the setting-up of the caliphate with the attack on the satirical weekly *Charlie Hebdo* in January 2015, which killed twelve people and was clearly prompted by some provocative caricatures of the Prophet Mohammad.[13] This was met with defiance, both on the part of President Hollande, who organised freedom marches involving major international figures, and on the part of the magazine itself, which immediately prepared a special number extolling freedom of speech.

A more sophisticated, coordinated and militarised attack took place in November of that same year, combining an attempted bomb outrage at the Stade de France, the indiscriminate shooting of people at a café terrace and, in particular, a systematic assault on customers at the popular concert hall Le Bataclan, leaving 130 dead and 352 wounded overall. Claimed by ISIS, or Daesh, this truly shocked the nation. The perpetrators made it clear by their exchanges with the 'idolaters' at the Bataclan that they saw themselves as punishing this Paris of 'abominations and perversions', the capital of the 'filthy French'. This seemed rather incongruous since many of them turned out to have a history of drug use and petty crime, and were seeking absolution in sanctified violence or suicide. At all events, they were widely condemned by high Muslim authorities not only in France but around the world, as well as by Iran, Iraq, Turkey and other Middle Eastern Arab states. It also alarmed many of the Muslims in Paris, who collaborated with the discreet preventive measures introduced by the authorities to the extent of tipping off the police – in over five thousand cases in two years – that a relative was in danger of being radicalised.

Nevertheless, with the trial of the Bataclan perpetrators not beginning until November 2021 and with the rise of populist nationalist movements in the Western world encouraging an extreme-right pundit such as Éric Zemmour to stand for the presidency in 2022, the political consequences lingered on.

Paris today is the shining face of a highly developed country, which was ranked in 2020 as the world's seventh largest economy and the largest recipient of foreign direct investment in Europe.[14] The city itself, which contains the Organisation for Economic Co-operation and Development (OECD) headquarters, was also seen as having the leading business district on the continent as well as being the most attractive global city in the world. Indeed, the French government itself, at the time of the United Kingdom's Brexit vote in 2016, was not shy of listing twenty reasons why the greater Paris-Île-de-France area had all the advantages required to take over Europe's economic leadership. These included as factors that, with nearly 12 million inhabitants including the 2 million in central Paris, this was the most populated urban complex in Europe, that it was a globally connected city, that in Euronext it had the leading technology exchange, that it had more than five hundred international businesses operating there, that it was number one in Europe for the number of head-quarters of Fortune Global 500 companies and that it had the leading research-and-development clusters in Europe.[15] In short, Paris was not just the world leader in tourism, fashion and luxury goods, it was the capital of an important and independent power in the globalised economy.

So if a well-remembered café or two on the good old 'Boul' Mich', or Boulevard Saint-Michel, is today called Big Mac or Burger King, are we to conclude that Paris has allowed itself to be 'Americanised'? Not quite, for although recent history and the process of globalisation have forced France to measure itself against an American standard, it has sought by a selective and critical approach to adjust to modernity within a continuing sense of its own identity. For there has long been the mythical belief, running from Saint Louis in the thirteenth century onwards, in the 'French exception'. For Louis XIV, the union of throne and state that he personified, in that it was seen as the successor of ancient Rome and sanctified by the only true universal religion, had the special responsibility of creating the perfect society, which implied a centralist organisation not only of politics or the economy, but of architecture, manners and even the language. Of course, the Enlightenment and the Revolution threw up other universalisms, but the idea was still alive by 2007, when we find Chirac in his swansong presidential address declaring that 'France is not like other countries. It has special responsibilities, inherited from its history and from the universal values which it has contributed to forging.'

Although it may seem rather odd to the outsider, there is therefore a continuity from the mercantilism of a Colbert to the economic and cultural dirigisme that, with differing emphases, French governments have been pursuing since the Second World War. As Kuisel points out, they have successfully adapted to the market economy and globalisation while maintaining the republican social contract, a mixed economy, a vigorous state and a distinctive cultural identity.[16] They have also maintained France's cultural as well as its political distinctiveness, as far as it is possible to do so in a globalised world. They took steps to preserve the language against imports, competed with Paris Disneyland by building their own theme parks, and brought in quotas to protect French cinema and TV. They took steps to limit the expansion of Coca-Cola, which in any case spawned French imitators in the soft drinks industry, and although McDonald's and Burger King made some inroads, they found it necessary to adjust to the established taste of the natives, so that the Boul' Mich has not been lost to the more traditional idea of civilisation.

Naturally, it has been a delicate balancing act to keep up with a rapidly changing global capitalist economy while directly managing key industries and sustaining one of the largest welfare states in Europe. It involves a high tax burden and a level of bureaucracy for both companies and individuals that invites regular complaints.[17] Clearly, as the economy becomes ever more sophisticated, there are those who are left behind and there are indeed pockets of poverty in the Paris *banlieues*. More visibly, there have been the populist Gilets Jaunes, with their yellow high-visibility vests, a largely provincial group of protesters, who brought their manifestations to the capital in 2018. The initial complaint, understandable given greater travel distances for those living in the rural areas, was about the high cost of car fuel, but even after President Macron lowered the fuel tax, the movement expanded on social media and only subsided when the COVID-19 pandemic arrived. The sense of being neglected was real, as underlined by the high percentage of women taking part in the protest.[18] However, it illustrates a running problem that arises from the very virtues of the French approach in that, since it is in practice still operating within the global competitive economy, there is a necessary trade-off between high welfare costs and jobs. To sustain a retirement age of sixty-two at a time when the length of life is increasing, or a formal thirty-five-hour working week along with high welfare allowances, requires the highest tax burden in Europe, which in a vicious circle may deter investment, limit job creation and thereby require even more taxation. As the Nobel Prize-winning economist Jean Tirole put it sharply, 'you may be protecting them so heavily that you are not protecting them at all'.[19] At a time of rising populism in France as elsewhere, it was not an easy balancing act to manage.

Meanwhile, the capital's Socialist mayors had taken further steps to improve and level up Paris, to 'put an end to the division between the Eastern and Western parts of the city and create a more dynamic, cohesive Paris', as Delanoë put it.[20] Clearly, the difference in the cost of housing had much to do with the increasing gentrification of the working-class arrondissements in the east, but there were two other factors. One was a deliberate social housing policy that was extended to lower middle-class applicants in the belief that this would unify districts and improve schooling and other services. The other was simply that the younger generation of professionals, often engaged in the new high-tech industries, tended to find the bourgeois areas in the west rather boring. These were the trendy new '*bobos*', or *bourgeois bohémiens*, who were drawn to the idea of living in the village atmosphere of a more socially and often racially varied community, who combined a comfortable lifestyle with a social conscience and had mostly voted for a Socialist mayor in the first place.

This levelling-up endeavour slotted into the broader, ambitious decision to create a *Grand Paris*, or Greater Paris, by combining the city with its nearest surrounding suburbs to make a unified, homogeneous conurbation, or metropolis. The idea was first mooted by Sarkozy in 2007 and the new Métropole formally came into existence in 2016, though it was recognised as a long-term project with two related aims. The first is to confirm the status of Greater Paris as a global economic powerhouse which, once completed, will have a population of 7.5 million and account for a quarter of the country's wealth. The second is to improve the quality of life in the suburbs by improving housing and transport, while also in an age of climate change making it a showcase for sustainable urban development. The success of the plan obviously depends on that of the officially separate project dubbed the Grand Paris Express, which is intended to rationalise traffic over the whole area. The aim is to create a new rapid transit system with four automated lines circling the capital to connect the suburbs directly with one another, improving mobility and work opportunities for immigrants in particular. It will join up with the existing Métro and RER network, connect employment areas with seven regional business hubs, and see the creation of sixty-eight new stations by 2035. All this, apart from demonstrating that Paris is not just an open-air museum, is also designed to reduce car usage and thereby energy consumption, pollution and traffic congestion.

So Paris was marching boldly into the future, Yet, as the reaction to the devastating fire in Notre-Dame Cathedral in April 2019 demonstrated, it had not lost a sense of its own past. Time had not spared the twelfth-century structure, stonework had suffered erosion, the spire was weakened by water ingress and the roof timbers had been left brittle by age. The fire arose in the course of restoration work and since it started in the early evening it provided a grim night-time spectacle on television for the whole world. People in Paris were to be seen standing staring in dismay, some weeping, far into the night as the fire crackled and the flames lit up the sky. Even for non-believers this was an iconic building, which signified a thousand years and more of Western civilisation, which symbolised their city and their historical cultural identity. And this was recognised far and wide as the messages of sympathy came from religious and political leaders across the world, soon followed by pledges of financial help towards the restoration, which President Macron immediately declared would be completed within five years. The rose windows and the altar had fortunately been little affected, but it still took two years to make the building safe before the restoration could begin in 2021. With the pandemic further complicating the timing, it was doubtful whether the restoration could be completed by 2024, when the city would be hosting the Olympic Games, but with the famous façade untouched and still perfectly visible, Paris could move into the future while retaining a firm hold on its past.

Notes and References

....

INTRODUCTION.

1. Patrice Higonnet, *Paris: Capital of the World* (Cambridge, MA and London: Belknap Press of Harvard University Press, 2002), p. 235.
2. Elaine Sciolino, *The Seine: The River that Made Paris* (New York: Norton, 2020), p. 138.

CHAPTER 1. THE EMERGENCE OF PARIS

1. Alfred Fierro, *Histoire et Dictionnaire de Paris* (Paris : Laffont, 1996), pp. 849–60.
2. Barry Cunliffe, *The Ancient Celts* (Oxford: Oxford University Press, 1997), or Jean-Louis Brunaux, *Les Gaulois* (Paris: Les Belles Lettres, 2005).
3. Julian, *Works*, ed. W. C. Wright (Cambridge, MA: Harvard University Press, 1998), vol. II, pp. 429–31.
4. Maurice Druon, *The History of Paris: From Caesar to Saint Louis* (London: Hart-Davis, 1969), p. 20.
5. Donald Attwater, *A Dictionary of Saints* (London: Burns Oates & Washbourne, 1938), p. 119.
6. Gregory of Tours, *History of the Franks*, trans. L. Thorpe (Harmondsworth: Penguin, 1974), p. 158.
7. Cited in Edward James, *The Origins of Paris: From Clovis to the Capetians, 500–1000* (London: Macmillan, 1982), p. 29.
8. Druon, *History of Paris*, p. 28.
9. Cited in David Schoenbrun, *The Three Lives of Charles de Gaulle* (London: Hamish Hamilton, 1966), p. 37.
10. R.H. Bautier, cited in Alfred Fierro, *Histoire et Dictionnaire*, p. 16.
11. Abbon, *Le siège de Paris par les Normands, 885–892*, ed. H. Waquet (Paris: Droz, 1942), p. 15.

CHAPTER 2. MEDIEVAL PARIS: CULTURAL CAPITAL OF EUROPE

1. Jean Favier, *Paris, deux mille ans d'histoire* (Paris: Fayard, 1997), p. 228.
2. J. W. Baldwin, *The Government of Philip Augustus* (Berkeley: University of California Press, 1986), chapter 11.
3. See Roland H. Bainton, *Christian Attitudes Towards War and Peace, a Historical Survey and Critical Re-evaluation* (New York: Abingdon Press, 1960).
4. On the colourful Aliénor, see Jean Flori, *Aliénor d'Aquitaine, La Reine insoumise* (Paris: Payot, 2004), and Robert Fripp, *Power of a Woman, Memoirs of a Turbulent Life: Eleanor of Aquitaine* (Toronto: Shillington Press, 2006). She has frequently been represented in literature: in theatre as in Shakespeare's *The Life and Death of King John*, and in cinema in *The Lion in Winter*.
5. Alfred Fierro, *Histoire et Dictionnaire*, p. 980.
6. Cited in Stephen C. Ferruolo, *The Origins of the University: The Schools of Paris and their Critics* (Redwood City, CA: Stanford University Press, 1985), p. 73.
7. Roger Lloyd, *Peter Abelard: The Orthodox Rebel* (London: Latimer House, 1947).
8. Alistair Horne, *Seven Ages of Paris* (London: Pan Boks, 2017), p. 9.
9. Roselyne de Ayala, ed., *Dictionnaire Historique de Paris* (Paris: La Pochothèque, 2013), p. 692.

CHAPTER 3. PARIS IN TURMOIL: FOURTEENTH AND FIFTEENTH CENTURIES

1. J. R. Strayer, *The Reign of Philip the Fair* (Princeton, NJ: Princeton University Press, 1980), p. 13.
2. Bronislaw Geremek, *The Margins of Society in Late Medieval Paris* (Cambridge: Cambridge University Press, 1987), p. 53.
3. Helen Nicholson, *The Knights Templar: A New History* (Stroud: Sutton, 2001), p. 4.
4. Strayer, *Reign of Philip the Fair*, p. 291.
5. Raymond Cazelles, *Nouvelle Histoire de Paris: De la Fin du Règne de Philippe Auguste à la Mort de Charles V, 1223–1380* (Paris: Hachette, 1972), p. 148.
6. Michel Vovelle, *La Mort à l'Occident, de 1300 à nos jours* (Paris: Gallimard, 1983), pp. 119–20.

7. Jacques Castelnau, *Étienne Marcel, un révolutionnaire au XIVe siècle* (Paris: Perrin, 1973), p. 298.

8. Guy Fourquin, *The Anatomy of Popular Rebellion in the Middle Ages* (Amsterdam, New York, Oxford: North-Holland, 1979), p. 124.

9. Colin Jones, *Paris: Biography of a City* (London: Penguin, 2004), p. 97.

10. Alfred Fierro, *Histoire et Dictionnaire*, p. 56.

Chapter 4. Paris in the Renaissance: Humanism and Holy War

1. See *The Relationship of Francis I's entry into Paris in 1515*, Bibliothèque d'Humanisme et Renaissance, Work & Documents, Tome lxxvi (Geneva: Droz, 2014).

2. Franck Ferrand, *François Ier; Roi de Chimères* (Paris: Flammarion, 2014), p. 219.

3. Ferrand, *François Ier*, p. 39.

4. Jean-Pierre Babelon, *Paris au XVI Siècle* (Paris: Hachette, 1986), p. 286.

5. Babelon, *Paris*, pp. 148–9.

6. Mireille Huchon, *Rabelais* (Paris: Gallimard, 2011), p. 18.

7. George Huppert, *The Style of Paris: Renaissance Origins of the French Enlightenment* (Bloomington, Indianapolis: Indiana University Press, 1999), p. 38.

8. Babelon, *Paris*, p. 92.

9. Huppert, *Style of Paris*, p. 41.

10. Alfred Fierro, *Histoire et Dictionnaire*, p. 772.

11. Babelon, *Paris*, p. 200.

12. Pierre Champion, *Paris au temps des Guerres de Religion* (Paris: Calmann-Lévy, 1938), p. 52.

13. Michel de Montaigne, 'Des Cannibales', in *Les Essais*, Book I (1580), chapter XXXI.

14. Thierry Wanegffelen, *Catherine de Médicis* (Paris: Payot, 2005), p. 403.

15. Barbara Diefendorf, *Beneath the Cross* (New York, Oxford: Oxford University Press, 1991), pp. 102–3.

16. Denis Crouzet, *La Nuit de la Saint-Barthélemy* (Paris: Fayard, 1994), p. 525.

17. Babelon, *Paris*, p. 31.

Chapter 5. The Seventeenth Century: Towards the New Rome

1. M. Gaillard, *Paris de place en place, Guide historique* (Paris: Martelle Éditions, 1997), p. 4.
2. Jones, *Paris*, p. 58.
3. For this view see Philippe Erlanger, *L'Étrange Mort de Henri IV* (Paris: Perrin, 1999); for the opposing view see Roland Mousnier, *L'Assassinat d'Henri IV* (Paris: Gallimard, 1964).
4. See R. Xavier, D. Philippe and L. G. Geoffrey, 'Discussion surrounding the identification of Henry IV's alleged skull', *Journal of Forensic Science*, no. 5 (January 2014).
5. Simone Bertière, *Louis XIII et Richelieu, La Malentente* (Paris: Éditions de Fallois, 2016), p. 428.
6. Roland Mousnier, *Paris Capitale au Temps de Richelieu et de Mazarin* (Paris: Éditions Pedone, 1978), p. 131.
7. Pierre Mélèse, *Le Théâtre et le Public, à Paris sous Louis XIV* (Paris: Droz, 1984), p. 6.
8. René Pillorget, *Paris sous les Premiers Bourbons, 1594–1661* (Paris: Hachette. 1988), p. 446.
9. John Lough, *Seventeenth-Century French Drama: The Background* (Oxford: Clarendon Press, 1979), pp. 30–1.
10. Lough, *Seventeenth-Century French Drama*, p. 73.
11. Lough, *Seventeenth-Century French Drama*, p. 54.
12. Thierry Sarmant, *Louis XIV, Homme et roi* (Paris: Tallandier, 2012), p. 137.
13. Sarmant, *Louis XIV*, p. 61.
14. Sarmant, *Louis XIV*, p. 113.
15. Alfred Fierro, *Histoire et Dictionnaire*, p. 753.

Chapter 6. Paris versus Versailles

1. Sarmant, *Louis XIV*, p. 552.
2. Sarmant, *Louis XIV*, p. 553.
3. Georges Dethan, *Paris au temps de Louis XIV* (Paris: Hachette, 1990), p. 98.
4. Sarmant, *Louis XIV*, p. 238.
5. Sarmant, *Louis XIV*, p. 238.

6. Maurice Bardèche, *Histoire des Femmes* (Paris: Stock, 1968), p. 220.

7. Bernard Rouleau, *Paris; Histoire d'un espace* (Paris: Seuil, 1997), p. 241.

8. Alfred Fierro, *Histoire et Dictionnaire*, p. 75.

9. Dethan, *Paris au temps de Louis XIV*, p. 164.

10. Alfred Fierro, *Histoire et Dictionnaire*, p. 78.

11. Daniel Roche, *La France des Lumières* (Paris: Fayard, 1993), p. 401.

12. Alfred Fierro, *Histoire et Dictionnaire*, p. 104.

13. Alfred Fierro, *Histoire et Dictionnaire*, p. 195.

14. Valerie Steele, *Paris Fashion: A Cultural History* (London: Bloomsbury, 2017), p. 27.

15. Joan Dejean, *How Paris Became Paris: The Invention of the Modern City* (London: Bloomsbury, 2014), p. 168.

16. Tobias Smollett, *Travels Through France and Italy* (London: Folio, 1979), p. 52.

17. Louis-Sébastien Mercier, *Tableau de Paris, édition abrégée* (Paris: Louis-Michaud, 1907), pp. 194–6.

18. Bardèche, *Histoire des Femmes*, p. 244.

CHAPTER 7 PARIS IN THE REVOLUTION

1. David Garrioch, *The Making of Revolutionary Paris* (Berkeley: University of California Press, 2002), p. 289.

2. Jean-Pierre Poirier, *Turgot: Laissez-faire et progrès social* (Paris: Perrin, 1999), p. 343.

3. Marcel Reinhard, *Nouvelle Histoire de Paris; La Révolution 1789–1799* (Paris: Hachette, 1971), p. 115.

4. Georges Lefebvre, *La Révolution française* (Paris: Presses Universitaires de France, 1951), p. 134.

5. Cited in Laurence L. Bongie, *La Bastille des Pauvres Diables* (Paris: Presses de l'Université de Paris-Sorbonne, 2010), p. 69.

6. Simon Schama, *Citizens; A Chronicle of the French Revolution* (London: Penguin, 2004), p. 332.

7. Reay Tannahill, *Paris in the Revolution* (London: Folio Society, 1966), p. 44.

8. Jacques Godeschot, *Les Révolutions (1770–1799)* (Paris: Presses Universitaires de France, 1963), pp. 371–3.

9. J. M. Thompson, *English Witnesses of the French Revolution* (Oxford: Blackwell, 1938), p. 231.

10. G. Lenôtre, *La Vie à Paris pendant la Révolution* (Paris: Calmann-Lévy, 1936), p. 223.

11. Evelyne Lever, *Paris Sous la Terreur* (Paris: Fayard, 2019), pp. 279–82.

12. Eugène Pottet, *Histoire de la Conciergerie* (Paris: Société Française d'Éditions d'Art, 1901), pp. 160–1.

13. See Dominique Godineau, *Citoyennes Tricoteuses* (Aix-en-Provence: Alinéa, 1988).

CHAPTER 8. PARIS UNDER NAPOLEON

1. Lefebvre, *La Révolution française*, p. 637.

2. Reinhard, *La Révolution*, p. 402.

3. René Héron de Villefosse, *Histoire de Paris* (Paris: Union Bibliophile de France, 1948), p. 269.

4. Garrioch, *Making of Revolutionary Paris*, p. 298.

5. Bardèche, *Histoire des Femmes*, p. 294.

6. Tim Clayton, *This Dark Business: The Secret War against Napoleon* (London: Little, Brown, 2018), p. 9.

7. Stuart Semmel, *Napoleon and the British* (New Haven and London: Yale University Press, 2000), p. 7.

8. Norman Hampson, *The Perfidy of Albion: French Perceptions of England during the French Revolution* (London: Macmillan, 1998), p. 139.

9. Clayton, *This Dark Business*, p. 118.

10. An excellent film by Édouard Molinaro, *Le Souper*, depicting a confrontation between Fouché and Talleyrand after Waterloo at the end of the regime, is available online.

11. Alfred Fierro, *Histoire et Dictionnaire*, p. 145.

12. Clayton, *This Dark Business*, p. 349.

CHAPTER 9. THE IMAGE OF PARIS DARKENS, 1815–48

1. Philip Mansel, *Paris Between Empires: 1814–1852* (London: John Murray, 2001), p. 100.

2. Bernard Marchand, *Paris, histoire d'une ville; XIXe–XXe siècle* (Paris: Éditions du Seuil, 1993), p. 8.

3. Alfred Fierro, *Histoire et Dictionnaire*, p. 1178.

4. Christopher Prendergast, *Paris and the Nineteenth Century* (Oxford: Blackwell, 1992), p. 6.

5. Guillaume de Bertier de Sauvigny, *Nouvelle Histoire de Paris: La Restauration 1815–1830* (Paris: Hachette, 1995), p. 277.

6. De Bertier de Sauvigny, *La Restauration*, p. 359.

7. Alfred Fierro, *Histoire et Dictionnaire*, p. 613.

8. Henri d'Almeras, *La Vie Parisienne sous la Restauration* (Paris: Albin Michel, 1910), p. 411.

9. Joanna Richardson, *The Bohemians: La Vie de Bohème in Paris 1830–1914* (London: Macmillan, 1969), p. 27.

10. Mansel, *Paris Between Empires*, p. 307.

11. Mansel, *Paris Between Empires*, p. 309.

12. Mansel, *Paris Between Empires*, p. 286.

13. Alfred Fierro, *Histoire et Dictionnaire*, p. 526.

14. Mansel, *Paris Between Empires*, p. 386.

15. Mansel, *Paris Between Empires*, p. 383.

16. Marchand, *Paris*, p.65.

17. Frank. E. Manuel and Fritzie P. Manuel, *Utopian Thought in the Western World* (Oxford: Blackwell, 1979), p. 645.

18. Marchand, *Paris*, p. 66.

CHAPTER 10. THE NEW PARIS OF NAPOLEON III

1. Mansel, *Paris Between Empires*, p. 406.

2. Louis Girard, *Nouvelle Histoire de Paris; La Deuxième République et le Second Empire, 1848–1870* (Paris: Hachette, 1981), p. 19.

3. Mansel, *Paris Between Empires*, p. 410.

4. Gaston Bouniols, *Histoire de la Révolution de 1848* (Paris: Delagrave, 1918), p. 425.

5. Éric Anceau, *Napoléon III* (Paris: Tallandier, 2008), p. 31.

6. Michel Carmona, *Haussmann* (Paris: Fayard, 2000), p. 15.

7. Carmona, *Haussmann*, p. 166.

8. Hervé Maneglier, *Paris Impérial; La Vie Quotidienne sous le Second Empire* (Paris: Armand Colin, 2009), p. 29.

9. Patrice de Moncan, *Le Paris d'Haussmann* (Paris: Éditions du Mécène, 2007), p. 199.

10. Pierre Milza, *Napoléon III* (Paris: Perrin, 2004), p. 454.

11. Girard, *Deuxième République*, p. 311.

12. Milza, *Napoléon III*, p. 440.

13. Milza, *Napoléon III*, p. 299.

14. Patricia Mainardi, *Art and Politics of the Second Empire: The Universal Expositions of 1855 and 1867* (New Haven and London: Yale University Press, 1987), p. 197.

15. T. J. Clark, *The Painting of Modern Life: Paris in the Art of Manet and his Followers* (London: Thames & Hudson, 1985), pp. 85–6.

16. Milza, *Napoléon III*, p. 476.

CHAPTER 11. THE PARIS COMMUNE AND THE 'GOOD OLD DAYS', 1870–1914

1. De Ayala, *Dictionnaire Historique*, p. 176.

2. Cited in Eugene Schulkind, ed., *The Paris Commune of 1871: The View from the Left* (London: Jonathan Cape, 1972), p. 27.

3. Karl Marx and Friedrich Engels, *Selected Works* (London: Lawrence and Wishart, 1968), pp. 307, 259.

4. Jacques Rougerie, *Procès des Communards* (Paris: Julliard, 1964), pp. 240–1.

5. Robert Tombs, *The Paris Commune, 1871* (London: Longman, 1999), p. 215.

6. Tombs, *Paris Commune*, p. 187.

7. Christophe Charle, *Paris Fin de Siècle; Culture et Politique* (Paris: Éditions du Seuil, 1998), p. 13.

8. De Ayala, *Dictionnaire Historique*, p. 258.

9. Roger Shattuck, *The Banquet Years: The Arts in France 1885–1918* (London: Faber and Faber, 1955), p. 9.

10. These last two Degas canvases are from the large number donated by the distinguished Jewish Camondo family, the last members of which were dispatched to Auschwitz under the wartime Pétain regime. Their house in the Rue de Monceau is now a fine museum.

11. Clark, *Painting of Modern Life*, p. 267.

12. Bernard Dorival, *Les Étapes de la Peinture Française contemporaine* (Paris: Gallimard, 1948), vol. 1, pp. 22 ff.

13. Nigel Gosling, *Paris 1900–1914: The Miraculous Years* (London: Weidenfeld and Nicolson, 1978), p. 117.

14. Brian Moynahan, *The French Century* (Paris: Flammarion, 2007), p. 80.

CHAPTER 12. THE FIRST WORLD WAR AND THE 'CRAZY TWENTIES'

1. De Ayala, *Dictionnaire Historique*, p. 609.
2. Charles Rearick, *The French in Love and War: Popular Culture in the Era of the World Wars* (New Haven and London: Yale University Press, 1997), p. 20.
3. Jean-Pierre Rioux and Jean-François Sirenelli (eds), *La Culture de Masse en France de la Belle Époque à aujourd'hui* (Paris: Fayard, 2002), p. 176.
4. Jay Winter and Jean-Louis Roberts (eds), *Capital Cities in War: Paris, London, Berlin, 1914–1919* (Cambridge: Cambridge University Press, 1997), pp. 106–7.
5. André Breton, *Les Manifestes du Surréalisme* (Paris: Sagittaire, 1946), p. 72.
6. William Wiser, *The Crazy Years: Paris in the Twenties* (London: Thames & Hudson, 1983), p. 40.
7. Wiser, *Crazy Years*, p. 95.
8. Ralph Schor, *Écrire en Exil; Les écrivains étrangers en France, 1910–1939* (Paris: CNRS Éditions, 2013), p. 12.
9. Arianna Stassinopoulos Huffington, *Picasso, Creator and Destroyer* (London: Pan Books, 1989), pp. 161–2.
10. Wiser, *Crazy Years*, pp. 111, 114.
11. Jean-Christophe Sarrot, *Balades Littéraires dans Paris, du XVIIe au XXe siècle* (Paris: Nouveau Monde, 2019,) p. 458.
12. Wiser, *Crazy Years*, p. 230.

CHAPTER 13. PARIS IN THE THIRTIES AND UNDER GERMAN OCCUPATION

1. Eugen Weber, *The Hollow Years: France in the 1930s* (London, Sinclair-Stevenson, 1995), p. 30.
2. Henri Dubief, *Le Déclin de la Troisième République, 1929–1938* (Paris: Éditions du Seuil, 1976), p. 19.
3. Alfred Sauvy, *Histoire Économique de la France entre les deux Guerres* (Paris: Fayard, 1965), vol. 2, p. 470.
4. Marchand, *Paris*, p. 251.
5. Weber, *Hollow Years*, p. 48.
6. Moynahan, *French Century*, p. 213.

7. Weber, *Hollow Years*, p. 78.

8. Dubief, *Déclin de la Troisième République*, p. 39.

9. Jean-Claude Klein, *Florilège de la Chanson française* (Paris: Bordas, 1990), p. 185.

10. Dubief, *Déclin de la Troisième République*, p. 133.

11. Alfred Fierro, *Histoire et Dictionnaire*, p. 234.

12. Herman Lebovics, *True France: The Wars over Cultural Identity, 1900–1945* (Ithaca, London: Cornell University Press, 1992), pp. 171–7.

13. Robert Aron, cited in Marchand, *Paris*, p. 264.

14. Gilles Perrault, *Paris Under the Occupation* (London: André Deutsch, 1989), p. 31.

15. Perrault, *Paris Under the Occupation*, pp. 38–40; also Henri Michel, *Paris Allemand* (Paris: Albin Michel, 1981), pp. 300–5.

16. Frederic Spotts, *The Shameful Peace: How French Artists and Intellectuals Survived the Nazi Occupation* (New Haven, London: Yale University Press, 2008), p. 44.

17. Spotts, *Shameful Peace*, p. 153.

18. Stéphane Courtois, *Le PCF dans la Guerre* (Paris: Éditions Ramsay, 1980), p. 222.

19. Henri Michel, *Paris Résistant* (Paris: Albin Michel, 1982), p. 165.

CHAPTER 14. THE 'THIRTY GLORIOUS YEARS', 1946–75

1. Moynahan, *French Century*, p. 325.

2. Marchand, *Paris*, p. 270.

3. Jean Bastié, *La Croissance de la Banlieue Parisienne* (Paris: Presses Universitaires de France, 1964) p. 343.

4. Simon Texier, *Paris Contemporain* (Paris: Parigramme, 2005), p. 140.

5. Bastié, *Croissance*, p. 356.

6. Antony Beevor and Artemis Cooper, *Paris after the Liberation: 1944–1949* (London: Hamish Hamilton, 1994), p. 315.

7. Jean-Baptiste Duroselle, *Deux Types de Grands Hommes; le Général de Gaulle et Jean Monnet* (Geneva: Institut Universitaire de Hautes Études Internationales, 1977), p. 16.

8. Raymond Aron, in Éric Roussel, *Pierre Mendès France* (Paris: Gallimard, 2007), p. 525.

9. See Raphaëlle Branche, *La Torture et l'Armée pendant la guerre d'Algérie, 1954–6* (Paris: Gallimard, 2001).

10. Charles de Gaulle, *Mémoires d'Espoir, I, Le Renouveau, 1958–1962* (Paris: Plon, 1970), p. 285.
11. Raymond Aron, *La Révolution introuvable* (Paris: Arthème Fayard, 1968), p. 141.
12. Éric Roussel, *Charles de Gaulle* (Paris: Gallimard, 2002), p. 877.
13. Pierre Lavedan, *Histoire de l'Urbanisme à Paris* (Paris: Hachette, 1975), p. 536.

Chapter 15. Contemporary Paris

1. In Georges Pompidou, *Le Noeud gordien* (Paris: Plon, 1974).
2. Alfred Fierro, *Histoire de Paris illustrée* (Paris: Le Pérégrinateur, 2010), p. 1195.
3. Annette Fierro, *The Glass State: The Technology of the Spectacle, Paris 1981–1998*, (Cambridge, MA: MIT Press), 2003.
4. Alain Duhamel, *La République giscardienne* (Paris: Grasset, 1980), p. 11.
5. See Solenn de Royet, *Le Dernier Secret* (Paris: Grasset, 1921).
6. Marchand, *Paris*, p. 351.
7. Carter Wiseman, *I. M. Pei: A Profile in American Architecture* (New York: Abrams, 1990), p. 235.
8. De Ayala, *Dictionnaire Historique*, p. 310.
9. Thierry Sarmant, *Histoire de Paris* (Paris: Gisserot, 2010), p. 63.
10. Annette Fierro, *Glass State*, p. 227.
11. Texier, *Paris Contemporain*, p. 211.
12. Sciolino, *Seine*, p. 118.
13. For the effect on one survivor of the attack, see Philippe Lançon, *Disturbance, surviving Charlie Hebdo* (New York: Europa, 2019).
14. 'GDP European Countries', *Statista*, 2020; Ernst and Young Report, May 2020.
15. French government publication, *Business France*, 6 July 2016 (online).
16. Richard F. Kuisel, *The French Way* (Princeton, NJ, Oxford: Princeton University Press, 2012), pp. 388–9.
17. See *L'Express*, 10–17 November 2021, pp. 18–25, for various authors on the burdens of bureaucracy.
18. Emmanuel Todd, *Les luttes de classes en France au XXIe siècle* (Paris: Éditions du Seuil, 2020), p. 359.
19. *Le Monde*, 23 January 2014, online.
20. In Sophie Corbillé, *Paris bourgeoise, Paris bohème: La ruée vers l'Est* (Paris: Presses Universitaires de France, 2013), p. 242.

Select Bibliography

....

Apart from general studies, which are listed alphabetically, the bibliography follows the historical chronology.

GENERAL SOURCES

French Language

Roselyne de Ayala (ed.), *Dictionnaire Historique de Paris* (Paris: Librairie Générale Française, 2013).

Gilles Durieux, *Le Roman de Paris, à travers les siècles et la litterature* (Paris: Albin Michel, 2000).

Jean Favier, *Paris, deux mille ans d'histoire* (Paris: Fayard, 1997).

Alfred Fierro, *Histoire et Dictionnaire de Paris* (Paris: Laffont, 1996).

M. Gaillard, *Paris de place en place, Guide historique* (Paris: Martelle Éditions, 1997).

Éric Hazan, *L'Invention de Paris, il n'y a pas de de pas perdus* (Paris: Seuil, 2002).

Pierre Lavedan, *Histoire de l'Urbanisme à Paris* (Paris: Hachette, 1975).

Pierre Pinon, *Paris, Biographie d'une capitale* (Paris: Hazan, 1999).

Jean-Robert Pitte, *Paris, Histoire d'une ville* (Paris: Hachette, 1993).

Bernard Rouleau, *Paris; Histoire d'un espace* (Paris: Seuil, 1997).

Jean-Christophe Sarrot, *Balades Littéraires dans Paris, du XVIIe au XXe siècle* (Paris: Nouveau Monde, 2019).

René Héron de Villefosse, *Histoire de Paris* (Paris: Union Bibliophile de France, 1948).

English Language

Susan Cahill, *The Streets of Paris: A Guide to the City of Light* (London: St Martin's Press, 2017).

Gregor Dallas, *Metrostop Paris: History from the City's Heart* (London: John Murray, 2008).

Joan Dejean, *How Paris Became Paris: The Invention of the Modern City* (London: Bloomsbury, 2014).

Patrice Higonnet, *Paris: Capital of the World* (Cambridge, MA, London: Belknap Press of Harvard University Press, 2002).

Alistair Horne, *Seven Ages of Paris* (London: Pan Boks, 2017).

Andrew Hussey, *Paris: The Secret History* (London: Viking, 2006).

Colin Jones, *Paris: Biography of a City* (London: Penguin, 2004).

Richard F. Kuisel, *The French Way* (Princeton, NJ, Oxford: Princeton University Press, 2012).

Graham Robb, *Parisians: An Adventure History of Paris* (New York: Norton, 2011).

Elaine Sciolino, *The Seine: The River that Made Paris* (New York: Norton, 2020).

Anthony Sutcliffe, *Paris: An Architectural History* (New Haven and London: Yale University Press, 1996).

Edmund White, *The Flâneur: A Stroll through the Streets of Paris* (New York: Bloomsbury, 2015).

SOURCES BY PERIOD

From Celtic River Fort to the 'New Rome' (Chapters 1–5)

Barry Cunliffe, *The Ancient Celts* (Oxford: Oxford University Press, 1997).

Maurice Druon, *The History of Paris: From Caesar to Saint Louis* (London: Hart-Davis, 1969).

Donald Attwater, *A Dictionary of Saints* (London: Burns Oates & Washbourne, 1938).

Gregory of Tours, *History of the Franks*, trans. L. Thorpe (Harmondsworth, Penguin Books, 1974).

Abbon, *Le siège de Paris par les Normands, 885–892*, ed. H. Waquet (Paris: Droz, 1942).

J. W. Baldwin, *The Government of Philip Augustus* (Berkeley: University of California Press, 1986).

Roland H. Bainton, *Christian Attitudes Towards War and Peace, a Historical Survey and Critical Re-evaluation* (New York: Abingdon Press, 1960).

Jean Flori, *Aliénor d'Aquitaine, La Reine insoumise* (Paris: Payot, 2004).

Stephen C. Ferruolo, *The Origins of the University: The Schools of Paris and their Critics* (Redwood City, CA: Stanford University Press, 1985).

Roger Lloyd, *Peter Abelard: The Orthodox Rebel* (London: Latimer House, 1947).

J. R. Strayer, *The Reign of Philip the Fair* (Princeton, NJ: Princeton University Press, 1980).

Bronislaw Geremek, *The Margins of Society in Late Medieval Paris* (Cambridge: Cambridge University Press, 1987).

Helen Nicholson, *The Knights Templar: A New History* (Stroud: Sutton, 2001).

Raymond Cazelles, *Nouvelle Histoire de Paris: De la Fin du Règne de Philippe Auguste à la Mort de Charles V, 1223–1380* (Paris: Hachette, 1972).

Michel Vovelle, *La Mort à l'Occident, de 1300 à nos jours* (Paris: Gallimard, 1983).

Jacques Castelnau, *Étienne Marcel, un révolutionnaire au XIVe siècle* (Paris: Perrin, 1973).

Guy Fourquin, *The Anatomy of Popular Rebellion in the Middle Ages* (Amsterdam, New York, Oxford: North-Holland, 1979).

Franck Ferrand, *François Ier; Roi de Chimères* (Paris: Flammarion, 2014).

Jean-Pierre Babelon, *Paris au XVI Siècle* (Paris: Hachette, 1986).

Mireille Huchon, *Rabelais* (Paris: Gallimard, 2011).

George Huppert, *The Style of Paris: Renaissance Origins of the French Enlightenment* (Bloomington, Indianapolis: Indiana University Press, 1999).

Pierre Champion, *Paris au temps des Guerres de Religion* (Paris: Calmann-Lévy, 1938).

Thierry Wanegffelen, *Catherine de Médicis* (Paris: Payot, 2005).

Barbara Diefendorf, *Beneath the Cross* (New York, Oxford: Oxford University Press, 1991).

Denis Crouzet, *La Nuit de la Saint-Barthélemy* (Paris: Fayard, 1994).

Pierre Champion, *Paris au temps des Guerres de Religion* (Paris: Calmann-Lévy, 1938).

Michel de Montaigne, 'Des Cannibales', in *Les Essais*, Book 1, 1580, Chapter XXXI.

Philippe Erlanger, *L'Étrange Mort de Henri IV* (Paris: Perrin, 1999).

Simone Bertière, *Louis XIII et Richelieu, La Malentente* (Paris: Éditions de Fallois, 2016).

Roland Mousnier, *Paris Capitale au Temps de Richelieu et de Mazarin* (Paris: Éditions Pedone, 1978).

Pierre Mélèse, *Le Théâtre et le Public, à Paris sous Louis XIV* (Paris: Droz, 1984).

René Pillorget, *Paris sous les Premiers Bourbons, 1594–1661* (Paris: Hachette, 1988).

John Lough, *Seventeenth-Century French Drama: The Background* (Oxford: Clarendon Press, 1979).

Thierry Sarmant, *Louis XIV, Homme et roi* (Paris: Tallandier, 2012).

From Louis Le Grand to Napoleon III (Chapters 6–10)

Georges Dethan, *Paris au temps de Louis XIV* (Paris: Hachette, 1990).

Daniel Roche, *La France des Lumières* (Paris: Fayard, 1993).

Valerie Steele, *Paris Fashion: A Cultural History* (London: Bloomsbury, 2017).

Tobias Smollett, *Travels Through France and Italy* (London: Folio, 1979).

Louis-Sébastien Mercier, *Tableau de Paris, édition abrégée* (Paris: Louis-Michaud, 1907).

Maurice Bardèche, *Histoire des Femmes* (Paris: Stock, 1968).

David Garrioch, *The Making of Revolutionary Paris* (Berkeley: University of California Press, 2002).

Jean-Pierre Poirier, *Turgot: Laissez-faire et progrès social* (Paris: Perrin, 1999).

Marcel Reinhard, *Nouvelle Histoire de Paris: La Révolution, 1789–1799* (Paris: Hachette, 1971).

Georges Lefebvre, *La Révolution française* (Paris: Presses Universitaires de France, 1951).

Laurence L. Bongie, *La Bastille des Pauvres Diables* (Paris: Presses de l'Université de Paris-Sorbonne, 2010).

Simon Schama, *Citizens; A Chronicle of the French Revolution* (London: Penguin, 2004).

Reay Tannahill, *Paris in the Revolution* (London: Folio Society, 1966).

Jacques Godeschot, *Les Révolutions (1770–1799)* (Paris: Presses Universitaires de France, 1963).

J. M. Thompson, *English Witnesses of the French Revolution* (Oxford: Blackwell, 1938).

G. Lenôtre, *La Vie à Paris pendant la Révolution* (Paris: Calmann-Lévy, 1936).

Evelyne Lever, *Paris Sous la Terreur* (Paris: Fayard, 2019).

Eugène Pottet, *Histoire de la Conciergerie* (Paris: Société Française d'Éditions d'Art, 1901).

Dominique Godineau, *Citoyennes Tricoteuses* (Aix-en-Provence: Alinéa, 1988).

Tim Clayton, *This Dark Business: The Secret War against Napoleon* (London: Little, Brown, 2018).

Stuart Semmel, *Napoleon and the British* (New Haven: Yale University Press, 2000).

Norman Hampson, *The Perfidy of Albion: French Perceptions of England during the French Revolution* (London: Macmillan, 1998).

Jean Tulard, *Le Grand Empire, 1805–1815* (Paris: Albin Michel, 1982).

Philip Mansel, *Paris Between Empires: 1814–1852* (London: John Murray, 2001).

Bernard Marchand, *Paris, histoire d'une ville; XIXe–XXe siècle* (Paris: Éditions du Seuil, 1993).

Christopher Prendergast, *Paris and the Nineteenth Century* (Oxford: Blackwell, 1992).

Guillaume de Bertier de Sauvigny, *Nouvelle Histoire de Paris: La Restauration 1815–1830* (Paris: Hachette, 1995).

Henri d'Almeras, *La Vie Parisienne sous la Restauration* (Paris: Albin Michel, 1910).

Joanna Richardson, *The Bohemians: La Vie de Bohème in Paris 1830–1914* (London: Macmillan, 1969).

Frank. E. Manuel and Fritzie P. Manuel, *Utopian Thought in the Western World* (Oxford: Blackwell, 1979).

Louis Girard, *Nouvelle Histoire de Paris: La Deuxième République et le Second Empire, 1848–1870* (Paris: Hachette, 1981).

Gaston Bouniols, *Histoire de la Révolution de 1848* (Paris: Delagrave, 1918).

Éric Anceau, *Napoléon III* (Paris: Tallandier, 2008).

Michel Carmona, *Haussmann* (Paris: Fayard, 2000).

Hervé Maneglier, *Paris Impérial; La Vie Quotidienne sous le Second Empire* (Paris: Armand Colin, 2009).

Patrice de Moncan, *Le Paris d'Haussmann* (Paris: Éditions du Mécène, 2007).

Pierre Milza, *Napoléon III* (Paris: Perrin, 2004).

Patricia Mainardi, *Art and Politics of the Second Empire: The Universal Expositions of 1855 and 1867* (New Haven and London: Yale University Press, 1987).

T. J. Clark, *The Painting of Modern Life: Paris in the Art of Manet and his Followers* (London: Thames & Hudson, 1985).

From the Paris Commune to the Paris of Today (Chapters 11–15)

Eugene Schulkind, ed., *The Paris Commune of 1871: The View from the Left* (London: Jonathan Cape, 1972).

Jacques Rougerie, *Procès des Communards* (Paris: Julliard, 1964).

Robert Tombs, *The Paris Commune, 1871* (London: Longman, 1999).

Christophe Charle, *Paris Fin de Siècle; Culture et Politique* (Paris: Éditions du Seuil, 1998).

Roger Shattuck, *The Banquet Years: The Arts in France 1885–1918* (London: Faber and Faber, 1955).

Bernard Dorival, *Les Étapes de la Peinture Française contemporaine* (Paris: Gallimard, 1948).

Nigel Gosling, *Paris 1900–1914: The Miraculous Years* (London: Weidenfeld and Nicolson, 1978).

Brian Moynahan, *The French Century* (Paris: Flammarion, 2007).

Charles Rearick, *The French in Love and War: Popular Culture in the Era of the World Wars* (New Haven and London: Yale University Press, 1997).

Jean-Pierre Rioux and Jean-François Sirenelli (eds), *La Culture de Masse en France de la Belle Époque à aujourd'hui* (Paris: Fayard, 2002).

Jay Winter and Jean-Louis Roberts (eds), *Capital Cities War: Paris, London, Berlin, 1914–1919* (Cambridge: Cambridge University Press, 1997).

André Breton, *Les Manifestes du Surréalisme* (Paris: Sagittaire, 1946).

William Wiser, *The Crazy Years: Paris in the Twenties* (London: Thames & Hudson, 1983).

Ralph Schor, *Écrire en Exil; Les écrivains étrangers en France, 1910–1939* (Paris: CNRS Éditions, 2013).

Arianna Stassinopoulos Huffington, *Picasso, Creator and Destroyer* (London: Pan Books, 1989).

Eugen Weber, *The Hollow Years: France in the 1930s* (London: Sinclair-Stevenson, 1995).

Henri Dubief, *Le Déclin de la Troisième République, 1929–1938* (Paris: Éditions du Seuil, 1976).

Alfred Sauvy, *Histoire Économique de la France entre les deux Guerres* (Paris: Fayard, 1965).

Herman Lebovics, *True France: The Wars over Cultural Identity, 1900–1945* (Ithaca, London: Cornell University Press, 1992).

Gilles Perrault, *Paris Under the Occupation* (London: André Deutsch, 1989).

Henri Michel, *Paris Allemand* (Paris: Albin Michel, 1981).

Henri Michel, *Paris Résistant* (Paris: Albin Michel, 1982).

Frederic Spotts, *The Shameful Peace: How French Artists and Intellectuals Survived the Nazi Occupation* (New Haven, London: Yale University Press, 2008).

Stéphane Courtois, *Le PCF dans la Guerre* (Paris: Éditions Ramsay, 1980).

Jean Bastié, *La Croissance de la Banlieue Parisienne* (Paris: Presses Universitaires de France, 1964).

Simon Texier, *Paris Contemporain* (Paris: Parigramme, 2005).

Antony Beevor and Artemis Cooper, *Paris after the Liberation: 1944–1949* (London: Hamish Hamilton, 1994).

Jean-Baptiste Duroselle, *Deux Types de Grands Hommes; le Général de Gaulle et Jean Monnet* (Geneva: Institut Universitaire de Hautes Études Internationales, 1977).

Éric Roussel, *Pierre Mendès France* (Paris: Gallimard, 2007).

Éric Roussel, *Charles de Gaulle* (Paris: Gallimard, 2002).

Raphaëlle Branche, *La Torture et l'Armée pendant la guerre d'Algérie, 1954–6* (Paris: Gallimard, 2001).

Charles de Gaulle, *Mémoires d'Espoir, I, Le Renouveau, 1958–1962* (Paris: Plon, 1970).

Raymond Aron, *La Révolution introuvable* (Paris: Arthème Fayard, 1968).

Georges Pompidou, *Le Noeud gordien* (Paris: Plon, 1974).

Annette Fierro, *The Glass State: The Technology of the Spectacle, Paris 1981–1998* (Cambridge, MA: MIT Press).

Alain Duhamel, *La République giscardienne* (Paris: Grasset, 1980).

Solenn de Royet, *Le Dernier Secret* (Paris: Grasset, 1921).

Carter Wiseman, *I. M. Pei: A Profile in American Architecture* (New York: Abrams, 1990).

Philippe Lançon, *Disturbance: Surviving Charlie Hebdo* (New York: Europa, 2019).

Emmanuel Todd, *Les luttes de classes en France au XXIe siècle* (Paris: Éditions du Seuil, 2020), p. 359.

Sophie Corbillé, *Paris bourgeoise, Paris bohème: La ruée vers l'Est* (Paris: Presses Universitaires de France, 2013), p. 242.

SELECTED WEBSITES

paris.fr – official site of Ville de Paris
paris.fr/culture – wide range of topics
archéologie.culture.fr.paris – Gallic and Roman period
apur.org – current developments towards Greater Paris

Index